As of May 17, 2012, this guidance applies to federal savings associations in addition to national banks.*

EP-CBS

I0448249

Comptroller of the Currency
Administrator of National Banks

Community Bank Supervision

Comptroller's Handbook

January 2010

*References in this guidance to national banks or banks generally should be read
to include federal savings associations (FSA). If statutes, regulations,
or other OCC guidance is referenced herein, please consult those sources
to determine applicability to FSAs. If you have questions about how to apply
this guidance, please contact your OCC supervisory office.

Contents

Introduction

Background

This booklet explains the philosophy and methods of the Office of the Comptroller of the Currency (OCC) for supervising community banks. Community banks are generally defined as banks with less than $1 billion in total assets and may include limited-purpose chartered institutions, such as trust banks and community development banks. As banks grow in size and complexity, the supervisory process transitions to that outlined in the "Large Bank Supervision" booklet of the *Comptroller's Handbook*. The "Community Bank Supervision" booklet serves as the primary guide to the OCC's overall supervision of community banks and should be used in conjunction with other booklets of the *Comptroller's Handbook*, as well as the FFIEC *Information Technology Examination Handbook* and the FFIEC *Bank Secrecy Act/Anti-Money Laundering Examination Manual.*[1]

The OCC's community bank supervision process is designed to:

- Determine the condition of the bank, as well as the levels and trends of the risks associated with current and planned activities.
- Evaluate the overall integrity and effectiveness of risk management systems by conducting periodic validation.[2]
- Determine compliance with banking laws and regulations.
- Communicate findings, recommendations, and requirements to bank management and directors in a clear and timely manner, and obtain commitments to correct significant deficiencies.
- Verify the effectiveness of corrective actions or, if actions have not been undertaken or accomplished, pursue timely resolution through supervisory or enforcement actions.

The community bank supervision process also gives examiners flexibility when developing supervisory strategies and conducting supervisory activities. The process integrates all functional areas of the bank under one supervisory plan, which helps ensure consistency in the assessment of risks and the degree of supervisory attention warranted.

The OCC's supervisory framework for community banks consists of three components — core knowledge, core assessment, and expanded procedures:

- **Core Knowledge** — The OCC's database that contains core information about the bank (its profile, culture, risk tolerance, operations and environment) and key examination indicators and findings, including risk assessments. This database enables examiners to document and communicate critical data with greater consistency and efficiency.

---

[1] FFIEC is the Federal Financial Institutions Examination Council.
[2] Validation is accomplished by a combination of observation, inquiry, and testing.

- **Core Assessment** — Objectives and procedures that guide examiners in reaching conclusions regarding regulatory ratings under the Uniform Financial Institutions Rating System (UFIRS, more commonly referred to as CAMELS or capital, asset quality, management, earnings, liquidity, and sensitivity to market risk), the Uniform Rating System for Information Technology (URSIT), the Uniform Interagency Trust Rating System (UITRS), and the Uniform Interagency Consumer Compliance Rating System.[3]

  The core assessment assists examiners in assessing the bank's overall risk profile using risk assessments made under the OCC-developed community bank risk assessment system (RAS). The core assessment also defines the conclusions that examiners must reach each supervisory cycle to meet the requirements of a full-scope, on-site examination.[4] Supervisory activities, including periodic monitoring, are tailored specifically to the risk profile of each community bank. When examining low-risk banks or low-risk areas of banks, generally only the first (or minimum) objective under each section of the core assessment is completed. For all other community banks or areas of community banks, examiners tailor the scope of the supervisory activity by selecting objectives and procedures appropriate to the bank's complexity and risk profile. For details on flexibility of timing and scope of supervisory activities, see the "Examining" section of this booklet.

  For Bank Secrecy Act/anti-money laundering (BSA/AML) reviews performed during the supervisory cycle, examiners should refer to the Core Examination Overview and Procedures sections of the FFIEC *BSA/AML Examination Manual*. (Updated 09/28/2012)

- **Expanded Procedures** — Detailed guidance that explains how to examine specialized activities or specific products that warrant extra attention beyond the core assessment. These procedures are found in the other booklets of the *Comptroller's Handbook*, the FFIEC *IT Examination Handbook*, and the FFIEC *BSA/AML Examination Manual*. Examiners determine which expanded procedures to use, if any, during examination planning or after drawing preliminary conclusions during the core assessment. (Updated 09/28/2012)

The supervisory framework is designed to achieve the following operational and administrative objectives:

- Ensure that supervision by risk is applied consistently throughout the community bank supervision process by tailoring supervisory strategies that integrate all examining areas to the risk profile of each community bank.

---

[3] For more information on UFIRS, URSIT, and other regulatory ratings systems, refer to the "Bank Supervision Process" booklet of the *Comptroller's Handbook*. The group of regulatory ratings required for banks is sometimes referred to as CAMELS/ITCC, with ITCC referring to the information technology, trust, consumer compliance, and Community Reinvestment Act ratings.

[4] The frequency (12 or 18 months) of full-scope, on-site safety and soundness examinations is based on the bank's condition and complexity as prescribed by 12 USC 1820(d) and 12 CFR 4.6.

- Ensure that the assistant deputy comptroller (ADC) is responsible for the supervision of the bank and is accountable for the development and execution of appropriate integrated risk-based strategies.
- Define minimum conclusions that examiners must reach during the supervisory cycle, while providing the flexibility to vary the amount of supporting detail or volume of work.
- Ensure conformance with statutory requirements for full-scope examinations.
- Provide direction for less-experienced examiners through detailed procedural guidance to be used, as needed, to reach key conclusions and objectives.

The OCC also conducts targeted reviews and examinations of functions and areas not covered by the core assessment section of this booklet. For example, an examination of the bank's Community Reinvestment Act (CRA) performance is conducted every 36 to 78 months depending on the bank's asset size, and the previous composite CRA rating. The first CRA examination for de novo (or newly chartered) banks is between 24 and 36 months.

Supervision by Risk

The OCC recognizes that banking is a business of assuming risks in order to earn profits. Banking risks historically have been concentrated in traditional banking products and services, but community banks today offer a wide array of new and complex products and services. Whatever products and services they offer, community banks must have risk management systems that identify, measure, monitor, and control risks. Therefore, risk management systems in community banks vary depending on the complexity and volume of risks assumed by the bank.

OCC supervision of community banks focuses on the bank's ability to effectively manage risk.[5] Using the core assessment, OCC examiners draw conclusions about the adequacy of banks' risk management systems. When risks are high; when activities, products, and services are more complex; or when significant issues or problems are identified, examiners expand the scope of their supervisory activities to ensure that bank management has appropriately identified, measured, monitored, and controlled risk. However, the extent of the additional supervisory activities varies depending on the impact those activities, products, services, or significant issues may have on the overall risk profile or condition of the bank.

The community bank supervision process focuses on the individual national bank. Nevertheless, supervision by risk requires examiners to determine whether the risks at an individual bank are satisfactorily managed or increased by the activities and condition of the entire holding company. To perform a consolidated risk analysis, examiners may need to obtain information from banks and affiliates (as prescribed in the Gramm-Leach-Bliley Act of 1999 [GLBA]), review transactions flowing between banks and affiliates, and obtain information from other regulatory agencies as well as technology service providers. GLBA is important legislation that addresses a number of significant issues affecting both national banks and the supervision process. While GLBA reaffirms the OCC's responsibility for

---

[5] For more information on supervision by risk and risk management, refer to the "Bank Supervision Process" booklet of the *Comptroller's Handbook*.

evaluating the consolidated risk profile of the individual national bank, the act also establishes a functional regulatory framework for certain activities conducted within banks and through functionally regulated affiliates.

Banking Risks

From a supervisory perspective, risk is the potential that events, expected or unexpected, will have an adverse effect on a bank's earnings, capital, or franchise or enterprise value.[6] The OCC has defined eight categories of risk[7] for bank supervision purposes: (Updated 5/06/2013)

- Credit.
- Interest rate.
- Liquidity.
- Price.
- Operational.
- Compliance.
- Strategic.
- Reputation.

These categories are not mutually exclusive. Any product or service may expose a bank to multiple risks. Risks also may be interdependent and may be positively or negatively correlated. Examiners should be aware of this interdependence and assess the effect in a consistent and inclusive manner. Examiners also should be alert to concentrations that can significantly elevate risk. Concentrations can accumulate within and across products, business lines, geographic areas, countries, and legal entities. (Updated 5/06/2013)

The presence of risk is not necessarily reason for supervisory concern. Examiners determine whether the risks a bank assumes are warranted by assessing whether the risks are effectively managed, consistent with safe and sound banking practices. Generally, a risk is effectively managed when it is identified, understood, measured, monitored, and controlled as part of a deliberate risk/reward strategy, known as risk appetite. A bank should have the capacity to readily withstand the financial distress that such a risk, in isolation or in combination with other risks, could cause. (Updated 5/06/2013)

If examiners determine that a risk is unwarranted (i.e., not effectively managed or backed by adequate capital to support the activity), they must communicate to management and the board of directors the need to mitigate or eliminate the excessive risk. Appropriate actions may include reducing exposures, increasing capital, and strengthening risk management practices. (Updated 5/06/2013)

---

[6] Enterprise value is an assessment of a bank's overall worth based on market perception of its ability to effectively manage operations and mitigate risk.

[7] Risk definitions are in "Community Bank Risk Assessment System" in appendix A.

Risk Management

Because of the diversity in the risks community banks assume, no single risk management system works for all. Each bank should tailor its risk management system to its needs and circumstances.

Regardless of the risk management system's design, each system should

- Identify Risk — To properly identify risks, a bank must recognize and understand existing risks or risks that may arise from new business initiatives. Risk identification should be a continuing process, and risks should be understood at the transaction (or individual) level and the portfolio (or aggregate) level.
- Measure Risk — Accurate and timely measurement of risk is essential to effective risk management systems. A bank that does not have risk measurement tools has limited ability to control or monitor risk levels. Measurement tools in community banks vary greatly depending on the type and complexity of their products and services. For more complex products, risk measurement tools should be more sophisticated. All banks should periodically test their measurement tools to make sure they are accurate. Sound risk measurement tools assess the risks at the transaction and portfolio levels.
- Monitor Risk — Banks should monitor risk levels to ensure timely review of risk positions and exceptions. Monitoring reports should be timely, accurate, and informative and should be distributed to appropriate individuals to ensure action, when needed.
- Control Risk — Banks should establish and communicate risk limits through policies, standards, and procedures that define responsibility and authority. These limits should serve as a means to control exposures to the various risks associated with the bank's activities. The limits should be tools that management can adjust when conditions or risk tolerances change. Banks should also have a process to authorize and document exceptions or changes to risk limits when warranted.

Capable management and appropriate staffing are essential to effective risk management. Bank management is responsible for the implementation, integrity, and maintenance of risk management systems. Management also must keep the board of directors adequately informed about risk-taking activities and must do the following:

- Implement the bank's strategy.
- Develop policies that define the bank's risk tolerance and ensure that they are compatible with strategic goals.
- Ensure that strategic direction and risk tolerances are effectively communicated and adhered to throughout the organization.
- Oversee the development and maintenance of a management information system (MIS) to ensure that information is timely, accurate, and pertinent.

When examiners assess risk management systems, they consider the bank's policies, processes, personnel, and control systems. For small community banks engaged in limited or traditional activities, risk management systems may be less formal in scope and structure.

Examiners assess risk management systems consistent with the risk profile of each community bank.

- **Policies** are statements of actions adopted by a bank to pursue certain objectives. Policies often set standards (on risk tolerances, for example) and should be consistent with the bank's underlying mission, values, and principles. A policy review should always be triggered when the bank's objectives or standards change. (Updated 5/06/2013)
- **Processes** are the procedures, programs, and practices that impose order on a bank's pursuit of its objectives. Processes define how daily activities are carried out. Effective processes are consistent with the underlying policies and are governed by appropriate checks and balances (such as internal controls). (Updated 5/06/2013)
- **Personnel** are the bank staff and managers who execute or oversee processes. Personnel should be qualified and competent, and should perform appropriately. They should understand the bank's mission, values, principles, policies, and processes. Banks should design compensation programs to attract, develop, and retain qualified personnel. In addition, compensation programs should be structured in a manner that encourages strong risk management practices. (Updated 5/06/2013)
- **Control systems** are the functions (such as internal and external audits, risk review, and quality assurance) and information systems that bank managers use to measure performance, make decisions about risk, and assess the effectiveness of processes. Control functions should have clear reporting lines, adequate resources, and appropriate authority. Management information systems should provide timely, accurate, and relevant feedback. (Updated 5/06/2013)

Risk Assessment System

The community bank RAS is designed to prospectively identify and measure the risks in a bank and to aid examiners in determining the depth and type of supervisory activities that are appropriate for each community bank. For effective use of the system, examiners consider the current condition of the bank and other factors that indicate a potential change in risk. Examiners should watch for early warning signs that the level of risk may rise.

The RAS gives examiners a consistent means of measuring the eight banking risks as defined by the OCC and of determining when the core assessment should be expanded. In making their assessments, examiners use conclusions from the core assessment or expanded procedures and guidance on the RAS. For six of the risks — credit, interest rate, liquidity, price, operational, and compliance — the examiner assesses a bank's risk profile according to four dimensions. Any one of these four dimensions can influence the supervisory strategy, including the extent to which expanded procedures might be used:

- **Quantity of risk** is the level or volume of risk that the bank faces and is characterized as low, moderate, or high.
- **Quality of risk management** is how well risks are identified, measured, controlled, and monitored and is characterized as strong, satisfactory, or weak.
- **Aggregate risk** is a summary judgment about the level of supervisory concern. It incorporates judgments about the quantity of risk and the quality of risk management.

(Examiners weigh the relative importance of each.) Examiners characterize aggregate risk as low, moderate, or high.

- **Direction of risk** is a prospective assessment of the probable movement in aggregate risk over the next 12 months and is characterized as decreasing, stable, or increasing. The direction of risk often influences the supervisory strategy, including how much validation is needed. If risk is decreasing, the examiner expects, based on current information, aggregate risk to decline over the next 12 months. If risk is stable, the examiner expects aggregate risk to remain unchanged. If risk is increasing, the examiner expects aggregate risk to be higher in 12 months.

The quantity of risk and quality of risk management should be assessed independently. The assessment of the quantity of risk should not be affected by the quality of risk management, no matter how strong or weak. Also, strong capital support or strong financial performance should not mitigate an inadequate risk management system. The examiner should not conclude that high risk levels are bad and low risk levels are good. The quantity of risk simply reflects the level of risk the bank assumes in the course of doing business. Whether this quantity is good or bad depends on whether the bank's risk management systems are capable of identifying, measuring, monitoring, and controlling that amount of risk.

Because an examiner expects aggregate risk to increase or decrease does not necessarily mean that he or she expects the movement to be sufficient to change the aggregate risk level within 12 months. An examiner can expect movement *within* the risk level. For example, aggregate risk can be high and decreasing even though the decline is not anticipated to change the level of aggregate risk to moderate. In such circumstances, examiners should explain in narrative comments why a change in the risk level is not expected. Aggregate risk assessments of high and increasing or low and decreasing are possible.

When assessing direction of risk, examiners should consider current practices and activities in addition to other quantitative and qualitative factors. For example, the direction of credit risk may be increasing if a bank has relaxed underwriting standards during a strong economic cycle, even though the volume of troubled credits and credit losses remains low. Similarly, the direction of liquidity risk may be increasing if a bank has not implemented a well-developed contingency funding plan during a strong economic cycle, even though existing liquidity sources are sufficient for current conditions.

The two remaining risks — strategic and reputation — affect the bank's franchise or enterprise value, but they are difficult to measure precisely. Consequently, the OCC assesses only **aggregate risk** and **direction of risk**. The characterizations of aggregate and direction of risk are the same as for the other six risks.

The RAS is updated and recorded in Examiner View[8] whenever the examiner becomes aware of changes in the bank's risk profile. For example, examiners could identify changes in the bank's risk profile while performing periodic monitoring activities. Assessments are always formally communicated to the bank at the conclusion of the supervisory cycle by including a

---

[8] Examiner View is a software application designed by the OCC to assist examiners in preparing for, conducting, and maintaining work papers of supervisory activities completed at community banks.

page in the report of examination (ROE) containing a matrix with all of the risk categories and assessments. Examiners may also inform the bank of their assessments using other methods of communication. Changes in the aggregate risk assessments during the supervisory cycle must be formally communicated to the bank at the time they are identified.

Examiners should discuss RAS conclusions with management and the board. Bank management may provide information that may help the examiner clarify or modify those conclusions. After the discussions, the OCC and bank management should have a common understanding of the bank's risks, strengths and weaknesses of risk management systems, management's commitment and action plans to address weaknesses, and future OCC supervisory plans.

Supervisory Process

Community bank supervision is an ongoing process. Supervisory planning, examining through the use of the core assessment and expanded procedures, and communicating examination findings are integral parts of the supervision process.[9]

The OCC uses an integrated risk-based approach to supervision. The goal of this approach is to maximize the effectiveness of our supervision process by assessing all bank activities under one supervisory plan. With this integrated approach, the supervisory office ADC has responsibility for all supervisory activities, including safety and soundness, information technology, asset management, and compliance. Integrating all examining areas under one ADC ensures that the OCC assesses risks in all areas using the same criteria and that the most significant risks to the bank receive the most supervisory attention.

A significant benefit of integration is that the coordination of supervisory activities minimizes duplication of effort and leverages resources in the supervisory process. For example, audit and internal controls may be reviewed once for all bank areas, rather than at different times for separate safety and soundness, information technology, asset management, and compliance examinations.

On-Site Examination Frequency

The frequency of on-site examinations of depository institutions insured by the Federal Deposit Insurance Corporation (FDIC) is prescribed by 12 USC 1820(d). The OCC applies this statutory examination requirement to all types of national banks, regardless of FDIC-insured status.[10] National banks must receive a full-scope, on-site examination at least once during each 12-month period. This requirement may be extended to 18 months if all of the following criteria are met:

---

[9] Refer to the "Bank Supervision Process" booklet of the *Comptroller's Handbook* for more detailed information.

[10] Refer to 12 CFR 4.6 and 4.7. Note that the examination frequency for federal branches and agencies is prescribed by 12 USC 3105(c) and 12 CFR 4.7. Also, there are special considerations when applying the supervisory cycle to new charters and converted banks. Certain bank activities, such as those under the CRA, have separate statutory examination frequencies.

- Bank has total assets of less than $500 million.
- Bank is well capitalized as defined in 12 CFR 6.
- At the most recent examination, the OCC assigned the bank a rating of 1 or 2 for management as part of the bank's rating under UFIRS and assigned the bank a composite UFIRS rating of 1 or 2.
- Bank is not subject to a formal enforcement proceeding or order by the FDIC, OCC, or the Federal Reserve System.
- No person acquired control of the bank during the preceding 12-month period in which a full-scope, on-site examination would have been required but for this section.

The statutory requirement sets a maximum amount of time between full-scope, on-site examinations. OCC supervisory offices may schedule examinations more frequently under certain circumstances (e.g., when potential or actual deterioration requires prompt attention, when there is a change in control of the bank, or when there is a supervisory office scheduling conflict). However, supervisory offices should consider how OCC resources can be used most efficiently and the potential impact on the bank before increasing the frequency of examinations.

Planning

Supervisory strategies are dynamic documents that outline all supervisory activities and help ensure that sufficient resources are available to assess bank risks and fulfill statutory requirements. The strategy focuses examiners' efforts on monitoring the condition of the bank and seeking commitments from the bank's board of directors and management to correct previously identified deficiencies. All community bank strategies are maintained in Examiner View.

The portfolio manager assigned by the OCC is responsible for developing a supervisory strategy that integrates all examining areas and is specifically tailored to the bank's complexity and risk profile. The portfolio manager consults with specialty examiners as needed to ensure that significant issues have been appropriately addressed in the supervisory activities planned for the cycle. The portfolio manager schedules centralized reviews of matters that affect more than one examination area (e.g., audit and internal controls) within the bank. The portfolio manager must communicate results to all examiners completing supervisory activities on the bank to minimize duplication in the supervisory process.

At a minimum, the strategy for community banks includes completing the core assessment during the supervisory cycle. For areas of low risk, the scope of the planned supervisory activities generally consists of the minimum objectives. For areas of higher risk or supervisory concern, the strategy may direct examiners to complete other objectives beyond the minimum and may even expand the examination beyond the core assessment. When determining the appropriate depth of supervisory activities for a specific examination area, the portfolio manager takes into account both the level of risk of the area to be reviewed and the potential impact that area would have on the bank as a whole. For BSA/AML reviews, examiners should refer to the FFIEC *BSA/AML Examination Manual*.

The strategy includes an estimate of resources, including level of expertise and number of days, that the OCC needs to effectively supervise the bank. The strategy also includes a narrative supporting the specific strategy that has been developed for the supervisory cycle. The supporting narrative's level of detail varies based on risk profile and complexity of the planned supervisory activities.

Each supervisory strategy is based on several factors.

- **Core knowledge** of the bank including, but not limited to
  - Management.
  - Control environment.
  - Audit functions.
  - Compliance risk management system.
  - Market(s).
  - Information technology support and services.
  - Products and activities.

- Ratings.
- Risk profile.

- OCC supervisory guidance and other factors, including
  - Core assessment.
  - Supervisory history.
  - Applicable economic conditions.
  - Other examination guidelines, such as expanded procedures in the *Comptroller's Handbook*, the FFIEC *IT Examination Handbook*, and the FFIEC *BSA/AML Examination Manual* (which includes core and expanded procedures). (Updated 09/28/2012)
  - Supervisory priorities of the agency that may arise from time to time.

- Statutory examination requirements.

The portfolio manager is responsible for discussing with bank management the scope of the supervisory strategy, including specific types of supervisory activities planned for the cycle. Before scheduling activities that extend throughout a supervisory cycle, the portfolio manager should discuss proposed timing with bank management.

The planning process for a specific activity continues until that activity is initiated. A request for bank information that examiners must review is sent to bank management shortly before an activity is scheduled to begin. The portfolio manager or other assigned examiner then reviews all information that has been submitted to determine whether to adjust supervisory strategy for that activity. For example, the most recent loan review report submitted by the bank may prompt the portfolio manager to reduce or increase the scope of the asset quality review. This final step in the planning process allows the portfolio manager to effectively allocate supervisory resources based on the most current information available.

Examining

Examining is a continual process of integrated and tailored supervisory activities. Supervisory activities are designed to determine the condition and risk profile of a bank, identify areas in need of corrective action, and monitor ongoing bank activities. Because risk profiles of community banks are diverse, the OCC recognizes that effective and efficient supervision cannot be accomplished using a rigid set of examination procedures. Examiners use the core assessment (and expanded procedures when necessary) to tailor supervisory activities to ensure that risks within each community bank are appropriately identified and managed or to provide additional guidance to less-experienced examiners.

The OCC's approach to community bank supervision also stresses the importance of determining and validating the bank's condition during the supervisory cycle. However, the process itself is flexible and activities can be completed through different means. Although on-site activities are essential to supervision, parts of the core assessment may be effectively performed away from the bank.

There also is flexibility about when on-site activities should be completed. Supervisory activities can be completed at one time or at various times throughout the supervisory cycle. The scheduling of supervisory activities should maximize efficiency and effectiveness of the supervisory process and should be appropriate for the bank's size, risk profile, and condition. For example, if an accounting firm or vendor does internal audit work for a number of banks in an area, it may be more efficient to review the firm's work papers as part of a targeted supervisory activity than to review each bank's audit work papers during its on-site examination. Examiners may want to coordinate such reviews with other field offices whose banks employ the same vendor or firm for the same purpose. Targeted reviews in other examination areas also provide scheduling flexibility when a specific area of examination expertise is needed. In addition, horizontal reviews (conducting coordinated reviews of particular functional areas across multiple institutions) are being performed more frequently, and use of this approach is expected to continue as it is an effective tool in the supervisory process.

Examiners identify supervisory concerns and monitor their correction throughout the supervisory cycle. Generally, during on-site activities, examiners focus on identifying the root cause of deficiencies and ensuring that management is taking appropriate and timely steps to address and correct all deficiencies.

Periodic monitoring, which is a key element of the OCC's supervisory process, is designed to identify changes in the bank's condition and risk profile and to review the bank's corrective action on issues identified during previous supervisory activities. The depth and scope of monitoring activities vary based on the bank's size, risk profile, and condition, but in all cases examiners complete some level of activities quarterly. By monitoring community banks, examiners can modify supervisory strategies in response to changes in a bank's risk profile and respond knowledgeably to bank management's questions. Periodic monitoring makes supervision more effective and on-site activities more focused.

Completing the Core Assessment

To assist examiners in developing risk-based supervisory strategies for each community bank, the supervisory office ADC, with input from the portfolio manager, characterizes the overall risk profile of each community bank as low, moderate, or high.[11] In addition to the overall risk profile, specific areas of the bank are also characterized as low, moderate, or high risk. For example, a bank's overall risk profile could be moderate while specific areas or activities could be low or even high risk. The OCC's portfolio manager develops a supervisory strategy using this overall risk classification, his or her knowledge of specific risks in the areas of the bank, effectiveness of the bank's audit function, and strength of the bank's internal controls and compliance risk management systems. In general, minimum objectives are used in low-risk areas, with other objectives from the core assessment or expanded procedures used in areas of higher risk. Ultimately, the portfolio manager has the flexibility to select which combination of objectives and procedures should be used (in

---

[11] High-risk banks typically include community banks with composite ratings of 3, 4, or 5.

addition to minimum objectives and procedures) to effectively and efficiently supervise and meet statutory examination requirements for the bank(s) in his or her portfolio.

Minimum Objectives

Minimum objectives, which are the foundation for review in low-risk areas, determine whether significant changes have occurred in business activities, risk profile, performance of management, or condition of a low-risk area from the previous supervisory cycle. The OCC has determined that these objectives are sufficient to effectively complete the required supervisory activities in low-risk areas and assign appropriate CAMELS/ITC ratings. If no significant changes in the bank's risk profile are identified after completion of the minimum objectives, no further work is done. However, if findings identify supervisory concerns, the examiner-in-charge (EIC) of the activity, with approval from his or her ADC, has the flexibility to expand the scope of the supervisory activities by completing other objectives from the core assessment or expanded procedures. Guidance provided by additional objectives and expanded procedures may be useful as training tools for less-experienced examiners.

Supervision requires periodic testing and validating of every bank's risk monitoring functions — audit, loan review, and other control functions — to ensure that they are effective. Even when an area is consistently identified as low risk, examiners should periodically expand supervisory activities beyond the minimum objectives to determine whether supervisory concerns or issues are present and to ensure that all control systems continue to be effective. Expansion of supervisory activities or baseline testing does not mean that every area of the bank gets examined with expanded procedures. Expansion should be used to confirm level of risk present.

The ADC is responsible for ensuring when and to what extent periodic expansion is appropriate for each low-risk area. In addition, expanded reviews and procedures may be appropriate in larger community banks; when banks engage in more complex operations; when the OCC conducts training assignments; when assignments are being completed by less-experienced examiners; and in other situations that benefit from increased testing and validation, as determined by the EIC and ADC.

Other Objectives

For areas not identified as low risk, examiners complete other selected objectives from the core assessment or expanded procedures consistent with the bank's complexity and level of supervisory concern. The other objectives in the core assessment contain detailed procedures or clarifying steps, but examiners typically do not need to carry out every procedure listed. Instead, experienced examiners can simply summarize their conclusions under each objective, consistent with the bank's condition and risk profile. For less-experienced examiners, the clarifying steps provide additional guidance to help them achieve the objectives.

Expanded Procedures

When specific products or risks warrant a detailed review, examiners should widen the scope of supervisory activities by completing expanded procedures found in other booklets of the *Comptroller's Handbook*, the FFIEC *IT Examination Handbook*, and the FFIEC *BSA/AML Examination Manual*. For example, if a bank has a higher-than-average risk profile, the OCC expects the bank to have more sophisticated and formalized policies and procedures to identify, measure, monitor, and control risk. In these cases, the EIC, with the ADC's approval, typically expands the supervisory activities by using procedures from the appropriate booklet of the *Comptroller's Handbook* to more fully assess risk management processes. If significant issues or areas of increasing risk are identified during the completion of the core assessment, the EIC, with the ADC's approval, may also expand the supervisory activities to review areas of concern in more depth. Expanded procedures may include additional transaction testing or a more thorough assessment of the risk management process. (Updated 9/28/2012)

For example, an experienced EIC may decide to complete minimum objectives for all areas in a low-risk community bank except asset quality if the bank has been experiencing growth in its credit card portfolio. After completing other objectives from the core assessment for asset quality and finding that supervisory concerns remain, the EIC may then (with approval from the ADC) use selected expanded procedures from the "Credit Card Lending" booklet of the *Comptroller's Handbook*. By selecting all types of procedures available to tailor the scope of the examination, the EIC effectively focuses on areas of highest risk.

Examiners must use judgment in documenting the core assessment. The policy for work paper documentation requirements, outlined in PPM 5400-8 (rev), "Supervision Work Papers," states that examiners should retain only those files and documents (preferably in a digital format) necessary to support the scope of the supervisory activity, significant conclusions, ratings changes, or changes in a risk profile. In addition, work papers should clearly document which procedures were performed either fully or partially.

Summary

The core assessment directly links the risk evaluation process to the RAS and the assignment of regulatory ratings.

When using the core assessment, examiners should:

- Use reasoned judgment in determining when to expand the core assessment or to increase the level of detail needed to support the core assessment conclusions.
- Practice good communication and analytical skills.
- Consider the results of all supervisory activities conducted during the supervisory cycle.

The community bank core assessment does not address compliance with all applicable laws, rules, regulations, and policies. Nonetheless, examiners must understand the laws, rules, regulations, and policies that relate to the area under examination and must remain alert for noncompliance.[12] Examiners should note noncompliance and discuss corrective action with management. Detailed procedures that address compliance with legal and regulatory requirements can be found in other booklets of the *Comptroller's Handbook*. In addition, examiners should ensure that supervisory follow-up includes a review of corrective action for violations noted.

Audit and Internal Controls

The core assessment requires examiners to evaluate and validate the two fundamental components of any bank's risk management system — audit and internal controls. An accurate evaluation of audit and internal controls is crucial to the proper supervision of a bank. The examiner determines whether the overall audit program and internal control system are strong, satisfactory, or weak. Based on these assessments, the examiner determines the amount of reliance that areas of the examination can place on the audit program and internal control system. Effective audit functions and internal controls help:

- Leverage OCC resources.
- Establish the scope of current and planned supervisory activities.

Internal Controls

A system of strong internal controls is the backbone of a bank's risk management system. The community bank core assessment includes objectives for assessing a bank's control environment during each supervisory cycle. The objectives are consistent with industry-accepted criteria[13] for establishing and evaluating the effectiveness of sound internal controls. When examiners use expanded procedures, they should refer to appropriate booklets of the *Comptroller's Handbook* or to the FFIEC *IT Examination Handbook* and the FFIEC *BSA/AML Examination Manual* for more information on the types of internal controls commonly used in a specific banking function.

Audit

The EIC, with approval from the supervisory office, tailors the scope of the audit assessment to the bank's size, activities, and risk profile. The examiners assigned to review the audit function — through coordination and integration with examiners reviewing other functional and specialty areas — determine how much reliance can be placed on the audit program by

---

[12] The "References" section of this booklet lists some laws, regulations, and other guidance commonly used in community bank examinations. More extensive lists of reference materials are included in other booklets of the *Comptroller's Handbook*, the FFIEC *IT Handbook*, and the FFIEC *BSA/AML Examination Manual*.

[13] The Committee of Sponsoring Organizations of the Treadway Commission's (COSO) 1992 report, "Internal Control — Integrated Framework," discusses control system structures and components. COSO is a voluntary private sector organization, formed in 1985, dedicated to improving the quality of financial reporting through business ethics, effective internal control, and corporate governance. COSO is sponsored by the American Accounting Association, American Institute of Certified Public Accountants, Financial Executives International, Institute of Management Accountants, and Institute of Internal Auditors.

validating the adequacy of the audit's scope and effectiveness during each examination cycle.[14]

Validation, which encompasses observation, inquiry, and testing, generally consists of a combination of examiner discussions with bank and audit management or personnel and a review of audit work papers and processes (e.g., policy adherence, risk assessments, follow-up activities). Examiners use the following three successive steps, as needed, to validate the audit program:

- Review of internal audit work papers.
- Expanded procedures.
- Verification procedures.

The review of internal audit work papers, including those from outsourced internal audit and director's examinations, may not be waived during any supervisory cycle.[15] However, the EIC has flexibility in limiting the scope of work paper reviews (i.e., number of internal audit programs or work papers to review) based on his or her familiarity with the bank's audit function and findings from the previous review of internal audit. Examiners typically do not review external audit work papers[16] unless the review of the internal audit function discloses significant issues (e.g., insufficient audit coverage) or questions are raised about matters normally within the scope of an external audit program.[17]

Examiners may identify significant audit or control discrepancies or weaknesses or may raise questions about the audit function's effectiveness after completing the core assessment. In those situations, examiners should consider expanding the scope of the review by selecting expanded procedures in the "Internal and External Audits" or "Internal Control" booklets of the *Comptroller's Handbook*.

When reviewing the audit function, significant concerns may remain about the adequacy of an audit or internal controls or about the integrity of a bank's financial or risk management controls. If so, examiners should consider further expanding the audit review to include verification procedures. Even when the external auditor issues an unqualified opinion, verification procedures should be considered if discrepancies or weaknesses call into question the accuracy of the opinion. The extent to which examiners perform verification procedures is decided on a case-by-case basis after consultation with the ADC. Direct confirmation with the bank's customers must have prior approval of the ADC and district

---

[14] National banks that are subject to 12 CFR 363 or that file periodic reports under 12 CFR 11 and 12 CFR 16.20 may be subject to the provisions of the Sarbanes-Oxley Act. For more information, refer to the "Internal and External Audits" booklet of the *Comptroller's Handbook*.

[15] When the director's examination serves as the sole internal audit function for the bank, a sample of supporting work papers must be reviewed. For additional guidance, refer to SM 2005-2.

[16] Before reviewing external auditor work papers, examiners should meet with bank management and the external auditor, consult with the district accountant, and obtain approval from the supervisory office ADC.

[17] For a comprehensive set of audit procedures, refer to the "Internal and External Audits" booklet of the *Comptroller's Handbook*. For internal control procedures, refer to the "Internal Control" booklet of the *Comptroller's Handbook*. Additional guidance and procedures are available in other booklets of the *Comptroller's Handbook* that address specific banking product lines and activities.

deputy comptroller. The Enforcement and Compliance Division, district counsel, and district accountant should also be notified when direct confirmations are being considered.

The examiner communicates to the bank his or her overall assessments (strong, satisfactory, or weak) of the audit function and internal controls, along with significant concerns or weaknesses, in the ROE. If examiners identify significant audit weaknesses, the EIC recommends to the appropriate supervisory office what formal or informal action is needed to ensure timely corrective measures. Consideration should be given to whether the bank complies with the laws and regulations[18] that establish minimum requirements for internal and external audit programs. Further, if the bank does not meet the audit safety and soundness operational and managerial standards of 12 CFR 30, appendix A, possible options to consider are having bank management develop a compliance plan, consistent with 12 CFR 30, to address weaknesses, or making the bank subject to other types of enforcement actions. In making a decision, the supervisory office considers the significance of the weaknesses, overall audit rating, audit-related matter requiring attention (MRA), management's ability and commitment to effect corrective action, and risks posed to the bank.

Information Technology

Information technology (IT) is an integral part of banking. Without technology, banks would be unable to provide the volume, variety, and complexity of products and services offered. Because IT can have a considerable effect on all banking activities, the OCC has integrated the review of technology into the core assessment in three ways:

- Examiners assess the management of key IT functions, such as information security, business continuity planning, audit, vendor management, and compliance with 12 CFR 30, appendix B.
- Examiners consider the effect of technology on each area they review, focusing on the integrity, confidentiality, and availability of data used in that area.
- Examiners assess the potential impact of technology on each of the eight OCC-defined risks.

Technological risk is not a separate RAS category. But because technology affects all areas of the bank, a single weakness can increase risk in several RAS categories. For example, a weakness in Internet banking controls could lead to increased fraud (operational risk). If this fraud becomes public knowledge, reputation risk may also increase. The bank's tarnished reputation can increase the cost of funding or reduce funding availability (interest rate and liquidity risks). Examiners should consider the domino effect in their assessment of a bank's total risk profile.

In conducting IT examinations, examiners focus on the four major issues that are common to all IT activities:

---

[18] For more information on the laws, regulations, and policy guidance relating to internal and external audit programs, refer to the "Internal and External Audits" booklet of the *Comptroller's Handbook*.

- **Management of Technology** — Planning for and oversight of technological resources and services and ensuring that they support the bank's strategic goals and objectives.
- **Integrity of Data** — Accuracy, reliability, and timeliness of automated information and associated MIS.
- **Confidentiality of Information** — Protection of bank and customer information from inadvertent disclosure.
- **Availability of Information** — Effectiveness of business resumption and contingency planning and adherence to data retention requirements.

The community bank core assessment includes minimum standards for IT supervision in the form of examination conclusions and objectives. The core assessment objectives for IT directly correspond to the four major IT issues. Examiners are required to reach conclusions on each issue and communicate their conclusions in the ROE.

The OCC has adopted the FFIEC's URSIT. Examiners assign an IT composite rating to all national banks. Examiners discuss this rating with bank management and disclose it in the ROE.

Asset Management

Many community banks provide asset management-related services, including traditional trust and fiduciary services, fiduciary-related services, and retail brokerage services.

- **Traditional trust and fiduciary services** include personal trust and estate administration, retirement plan services, investment management, as well as advisory and corporate trust administration.
- **Fiduciary-related services** include custody and safekeeping, security-holder services and transfer agencies, financial planning, cash management, as well as tax advice and preparation.
- **Retail brokerage services** include the sale of equities, fixed-income products, mutual funds, annuities, cash management sweep accounts, and other types of investment instruments.

The "Asset Management" booklet of the *Comptroller's Handbook* provides a complete overview of asset management services provided by national banks.

While asset management is not a defined RAS category, examiners assess the overall risk arising from both the type of activities conducted and the quality of risk management using the risk matrix in appendix B as a guide. The portfolio manager uses this assessment of asset management risk, along with the potential impact that risk has to the bank as a whole, to develop the scope of future asset management supervisory activities.

The asset management section of the core assessment is structured to conduct supervisory activities along the asset management product lines typically found in community banks, including limited-purpose trust banks. The results of these reviews are then used to assign the composite and component ratings under the Uniform Interagency Trust Rating System

(UITRS). Under UITRS, fiduciary activities of national banks are assigned a composite rating based on an evaluation and rating of five essential components of an institution's fiduciary activities: management; operations, internal controls and auditing; earnings; compliance; and asset management. The composite rating is discussed with bank management and disclosed in the ROE. The component ratings can, but are not required to, be discussed with management and disclosed in the ROE, at the discretion of the EIC and with approval of the ADC.

Bank Secrecy Act/Anti-Money Laundering

In all banks, the board of directors and management are required to monitor compliance with BSA/AML and Office of Foreign Assets Control (OFAC) laws and regulations. The board is responsible for creating a strong compliance culture within the bank that includes management accountability. Management should create a BSA/AML compliance program based on an evaluation of the bank's organization and structure, size, resources, diversity and complexity of operations, and delivery channels for its various products and services, including Internet and electronic banking. The BSA/AML compliance program should cover all BSA/AML/OFAC laws and regulations and incorporate all areas of the bank that present risk. Risk management processes should be included in the BSA/AML compliance program to ensure that necessary systems and controls are in place. (Updated 9/28/2012)

Examiners focus on areas of highest BSA/AML compliance risk for community banks. Findings are considered in a safety and soundness context as a part of the management component of a bank's CAMELS ratings. Serious deficiencies in a bank's BSA/AML compliance create a presumption that the bank's management component rating will be adversely affected because risk management practices are less than satisfactory. Examiners should be alert to situations in which management weaknesses identified in other areas of the bank reveal potential deficiencies in BSA/AML program oversight. (Updated 9/28/2012)

While BSA/AML/OFAC compliance is not a defined RAS category, examiners assess the quantity of risk and quality of risk management using the matrix in appendix B as a guide. These assessments are then considered when determining the overall compliance risk (and other appropriate risks) of the bank and used by the portfolio manager, along with the potential impact of those risks on the bank as a whole, to develop the scope of BSA/AML/OFAC supervisory activities. Guidance and examination procedures for BSA/AML/OFAC compliance are in the FFIEC *BSA/AML Examination Manual*. (Updated 9/28/2012)

Consumer Compliance

In all banks, the board of directors and management are required to monitor compliance with all applicable consumer protection laws and regulations. The board is responsible for creating a strong compliance culture within the bank that includes management accountability. Management should create a compliance program based on an evaluation of the bank's organization and structure, size, resources, diversity and complexity of operations, and delivery channels for its various products and services, including Internet and electronic banking. The compliance program should cover all consumer laws and regulations and incorporate all areas of the bank that present risk. Risk management processes should be included in the compliance program to ensure that necessary systems and controls are in place. (Updated 9/28/2012)

The consumer compliance section of the core assessment is structured to conduct supervisory activities along four specific functional areas of consumer compliance: (Updated 9/28/2012)

- Fair lending.
- Lending regulations (including the Flood Disaster Protection Act).
- Deposit regulations.
- Other consumer regulations.

The review focuses on areas of highest compliance risk for community banks — those with potential to cause customer harm or elicit public scrutiny. Results of these activities are then used to assign the consumer compliance rating using the Uniform Interagency Consumer Compliance Rating System. This rating is discussed with bank management and disclosed in the ROE. (Updated 9/28/2012)

While the risks arising from the four specific functional areas of consumer compliance are not formally defined RAS categories, examiners do assess quantity of risk and quality of risk management for each area. Appendix B includes an indicator for each functional consumer compliance area for examiners to use as needed to assist in this assessment. These assessments are then considered when determining the overall compliance risk (and other appropriate risks) of the bank and used by the portfolio manager, along with the potential impact of those risks on the bank as a whole, to develop the scope of consumer compliance supervisory activities. (Updated 9/28/2012)

Communicating

The OCC is committed to continual, effective communication with the banks that it supervises. All communications — formal and informal conversations and meetings, examination reports, other written materials — should be professional, objective, clear, informative, and consistent. When examiners find significant weaknesses or excessive risks, these issues should be thoroughly discussed with bank management and the board of directors. Depending on the extent and severity of the issues, the bank is generally given a reasonable opportunity to resolve differences and correct weaknesses.

The OCC must provide the bank's board of directors an ROE once every supervisory cycle. The ROE communicates the overall condition and risk profile of the bank, and it summarizes the examiner's activities and related findings conducted throughout the supervisory cycle. Examiners should detail significant deficiencies and excessive risks, along with the corrective action to which the board or management has committed, in the ROE's MRA page or in other written communications.[19] See appendix D for more detail on requirements for the ROE.

Examiners may choose to formally communicate the results of activities conducted throughout the supervisory cycle as they occur. Those results are included in the ROE issued at the end of the cycle. Most importantly, whenever significant deficiencies and excessive risks are identified during the supervisory cycle, examiners must clearly and concisely communicate these findings to the bank either by sending a written communication to the board or by meeting with the board or management. Written communication is required if there is any change in an aggregate risk assessment or any CAMELS/ITCC rating.

Appeals Process

The OCC desires consistent and equitable supervision and seeks to resolve disputes that arise during the supervisory process fairly and expeditiously in an informal, professional manner. When disputes cannot be resolved informally, a national bank may ask its supervisory office to review the disputed matter or appeal the matter to the OCC's ombudsman.

The ombudsman is independent of the bank supervision function and reports directly to the Comptroller of the Currency. With the Comptroller's prior consent, the ombudsman may stay any appealable agency decision or action (e.g., final regulatory ratings) during the resolution of the appealable matter.[20] The ombudsman may also identify and report weaknesses in OCC policy to the Comptroller and may recommend changes in OCC policy.

---

[19] For specific guidance on MRAs, refer to the "Examination Conclusions and Closing" section of this booklet, as well as the "Bank Supervision Process" booklet of the *Comptrollers Handbook*.
[20] For additional guidance on the appeals process and the definition of an appealable decision or action, refer to OCC Bulletin 2002-9, "National Bank Appeals Process." Examiners may also refer to PPM 1000-9 (Revised), "Administering Appeals from National Banks."

Core Assessment

Examiners use the core assessment to monitor community banks and to conduct supervisory activities. The core assessment is risk based and contains the objectives and conclusions that must be reached to meet the full-scope examination requirement and when completing monitoring activities within a bank's 12- or 18-month supervisory cycle. Risk considerations and references to the community bank RAS are noted throughout the core assessment.

Generally, each section has a minimum objective that examiners must meet to complete the core assessment. After considering the bank's risk profile and outstanding supervisory issues, examiners should perform additional objectives and procedures necessary to ensure that the bank's risk is appropriately managed. For banks or specific areas identified as low risk, completing minimum objectives in the core assessment should be sufficient to assess the bank's condition and risks. The examiner has the flexibility to expand the scope of the supervisory activity beyond the minimum objectives if necessary.

The core assessment comprises the following sections:

- Examination Planning.
- Audit and Internal Controls.
- Capital.
- Asset Quality.
- Management.
- Earnings.
- Liquidity
- Investment Portfolio and Bank-Owned Life Insurance.
- Sensitivity to Market Risk.
- IT.
- Asset Management.
- Bank Secrecy Act/Anti-Money Laundering. (Updated 9/28/2012)
- Consumer Compliance.
- Examination Conclusions and Closing
- Community Bank Periodic Monitoring.

Examiners must use judgment in deciding how much work or supporting detail is necessary to complete the objectives under the core assessment. The policy for work paper documentation requirements, outlined in PPM 5400-8 (rev), "Supervision Work Papers," states that examiners should retain only those files and documents, typically in a digital format, necessary to support the scope of the supervisory activity, significant conclusions, ratings changes, or changes in a risk profile. In addition, work papers should clearly document which procedures were either fully or partially performed.

Examination Planning

Planning for supervisory activities is crucial to effective supervision by risk. The following objectives should be completed at least once during the supervisory cycle. However, if significant supervisory activities are conducted separately, some objectives may be completed more than once. The underlying procedures for each objective are optional. The timing of supervisory activities is flexible. The portfolio manager or EIC should consider OCC resources, discussions with bank management, and supervisory objectives when scheduling various activities. This section is used to broadly plan the supervisory activities conducted throughout the cycle. The objectives finalizing the scope for each area are included in other sections of the core assessment.

Objective 1: Review the bank's characteristics and the supervisory activity's preliminary scope and objectives.

1. Obtain and review the following:

   - Prior reports of examination, with particular emphasis on outstanding MRAs
   - Other applicable regulatory agency reports (e.g., holding company reviews, IT servicer examination reports, shared application software reviews [SASRs])
   - OCC files:
     - Examination conclusions.
     - Periodic monitoring comments.
     - RAS ratings.
     - Analytical tools, including Canary system information.[21]
     - Financial and statistical models and databases (e.g., Uniform Bank Performance Report, or UBPR).
     - OCC correspondence.
   - Prior examination work papers.
   - Other internal or external information deemed pertinent to the bank.

2. Discuss the bank and associated risks with portfolio manager and ADC.

3. Open supervisory activity in Examiner View.

Objective 2: Develop a plan to conduct the supervisory activity.

1. Assign examining personnel to review information obtained under objective 1. Consider levels of expertise and expand procedures in specific areas.

2. Contact bank management to discuss the following:

   - Preference for obtaining request letter information in digital form.

---

[21] For additional guidance in reviewing the Canary system information, refer to PPM 5000-34, "Canary Early Warning System."

- Activity's timing
- Activity's general scope and objectives.
- General information about examiners' schedules, staffing levels, and projected time during which examiners are at the bank.
- Availability of key bank personnel during the activity.
- Actual or planned changes in bank's financial condition, including significant injection of capital and bank's plans to deploy such capital.
- Actual or planned changes in bank products, services, or activities including areas of growth.
- Actual or planned changes in bank management, key personnel, or operations.
- Results of audit and internal control reviews, compliance reviews, follow-up required by management, and audit staffing.
- Material changes to internal or external audit's schedule or scope.
- Bank-performed risk assessments since the last supervisory review.
- Significant trends or changes in local economy or business conditions.
- Broad economic and systemic trends affecting the condition of the national banking system, including those identified by the OCC's national or district risk committees.
- Purchase, acquisition, or merger considerations.
- Issues or changes in technology, including operational systems, technology vendors and servicers, critical software, Internet banking, or plans for new products and activities that involve new technology.
- Issues or changes in asset management lines of business.
- Issues or changes regarding consumer compliance, CRA, or BSA/AML/OFAC systems.
- Effects of, or changes to, new regulatory guidance.
- Other issues that may affect risk profile.
- Management concerns about the bank or OCC's supervision, including any areas bank management would like the OCC to consider in the examination scope.

Objective 3: Determine whether changes to the supervisory strategy are needed.

Determine whether the bank has been identified as low risk or if specific areas have been identified as low or high risk. Review and assess appropriateness of the current supervisory strategy for the bank. With approval from the supervisory office ADC, modify the strategy. Consider:

- Information obtained from bank management.
- Findings from periodic monitoring activities.
- Discussions with supervisory office personnel.
- Supervisory cycle for CRA examinations.

Objective 4: Prepare for the supervisory activity.

1. Prepare a scope memorandum.

2. Coordinate the activity with other regulatory agencies, as necessary.

3. If appropriate, ask the OCC's IT technical support staff to install a dedicated analog telephone line at the bank. Make request at least 20 days before the start date of the activity.

4. Designate assignments for examining staff.

5. Send the bank a request letter that provides:

   - Supervisory activity start date.
   - Activity's scope and objectives.
   - Advance information the bank must provide to the examination team, including due dates for submission of requested items.
   - Information the bank must have available for examiners upon their arrival at the bank.
   - Name, address, and telephone number of the OCC contact.
   - Instructions for delivering digital files.

   Note: Appendix C is a standard request letter for community bank examinations (including IT, asset management, consumer compliance, and BSA/AML compliance). The letter should be customized to reflect the supervisory activity's scope and the bank's risk profile. For other expanded examinations of specialized areas, refer to appropriate booklets of the *Comptroller's Handbook*, the FFIEC *IT Examination Handbook*, and the FFIEC *BSA/AML Examination Manual*. (Updated 9/28/2012)

6. Prepare supplies and equipment to take to the bank for the supervisory activity.

7. Generally within one week of the start of the activity, review the items and finalize the scope of the activity.

Objective 5: Conduct on-site planning meetings.

1. At the beginning of the supervisory activity, meet with chief executive officer, appropriate members of senior management, board members, and board committees to:
   - Explain scope of the activity, role of each examiner, and how the team conducts the activity.
   - Confirm availability of bank personnel.
   - Identify communications contacts.
   - Answer questions.

2. At the beginning of the activity, meet with examination staff to confirm:
   - Scope and objectives.
   - Work days.
   - Assignments and due dates.
   - Administrative duties.
   - Guidelines for contact and communication among the examining team, bank management, and the OCC supervisory office.

Audit and Internal Controls

Conclusion: The quality of audit is (strong, satisfactory, or weak). System of internal controls is (strong, satisfactory, or weak).

Complete this section's objectives to assess quality of the bank's overall audit and system of internal controls. In completing these assessments, the examiner should consult the EIC and other personnel. Consider the following when assessing quality of audit and internal controls:

- Board and management oversight.
- Management and processes.
- Reporting.
- Staffing.

Core Assessment

Minimum Objective: Determine quality of audit and internal control systems, and consider potential impact of these findings on the bank's risk assessment.

During the supervisory cycle, discuss with management actual or planned changes in the audit or internal control systems.

Obtain and review the following information:

- Results from OCC supervisory activities, including memorandums issued as part of a centralized review of outsourced internal audit vendors.
- Board or audit committee minutes and related internal or external audit packages and information submitted to the board or audit committee.
- Small sample of internal audit work papers. Sample should focus on high-growth or high-risk areas and new products or services offered by the bank. Refer to the *Sampling Methodologies Handbook*.

Communicate significant weaknesses identified by audit to the examiners assigned to review other functional areas for follow-up.

If the bank's activities, risk profile, or risk controls have changed significantly, or if review of the above information raises substantive issues, the examiner should expand the activity's scope to include additional objectives or procedures. If this review does not result in significant changes or issues, conclude audit and internal controls review by completing objective 7.

Other Assessment Objectives: NOTE: Examiners should complete only those objectives necessary to assess the bank's condition and risks.

Objective 1: Finalize the scope of the audit review. The examination includes a sample of internal audit work papers, representing a cross section of the bank's functions, activities, and bank-assigned internal audit ratings. The sample should include a review of BSA audit work papers. Refer to the FFIEC *BSA/AML Examination Manual*. The sample should focus on high-growth, substantive, or high-risk areas and new products or services offered by the bank. If a director's examination serves as the bank's only audit program and consists of both internal and external audit work, a sample of internal audit activity work papers should be reviewed.

1. If not previously provided, obtain and review the following, as applicable:

   - Most recent external audit engagement letter and other written communications between the bank and the external auditor.
   - Internal and external audit reports issued since the last examination, including management letters, attestation reports, and any Statement of Auditing Standards 70 (SAS 70) reports on IT servicers, or similar reports.
   - Current year internal and external audit plan or schedule and status reports.
   - Management's responses to internal and external audit reports issued since the last examination.
   - Detailed listing of job duties and responsibilities of internal auditor.
   - Audit staff resumés, including educational and work background, industry certifications, and recent developmental training.
   - Audit committee minutes or excerpts of board minutes applicable to audits since the last examination and audit packages and information submitted to the audit committee or board.
   - Internal audit outsourcing contracts and agreements/reports, etc.
   - Memorandums issued as part of an OCC centralized outsourced internal audit vendor review.

2. Discuss with examiners responsible for completing other functional areas of the core assessment any significant audit findings that require follow-up.

3. Consult with the EIC and examiners assigned major functional and specialized[22] examination areas to identify and select an appropriate sample of internal audit work papers for validation purposes. Consider having examiners who are responsible for other bank activity and specialized areas review internal audit work papers associated with those activities.

   Note: In most situations, a work paper review of the procedures and testing performed by the internal auditor should be sufficient in scope to substantiate conclusions about quality and reliability of auditing work. Audit procedures should not be re-performed.

---

[22] Refer to the appropriate booklets of the *Comptroller's Handbook*, if needed, for additional guidance when reviewing internal audit work papers of specialized examination areas.

Objective 2: Determine quality of board or audit committee oversight of the bank's audit programs.

1. Obtain audit-related information from examiner assigned to review board minutes. Review and discuss with management audit committee minutes or summaries and audit information packages to determine whether:

   - Internal and external audit plans, policies, and programs, including changes, updates, selection, and termination of external auditors or outsourced internal audit vendors, are periodically reviewed and approved by board or audit committee.
   - Board or audit committee meets regularly with internal and external auditors and receives sufficient information and reports to effectively monitor the audit and ensure that internal and external auditors are independent and objective in their findings.
   - Board or audit committee monitors, tracks, and, when necessary, provides discipline to ensure that management properly addresses control weaknesses noted by internal or external auditors and examiners.
   - Audit findings and management's responses are reported directly to board or audit committee.
   - Board or audit committee retains auditors who are fully qualified to audit the kinds of activities in which the bank is engaged. They work with internal and external auditors to ensure that the bank has comprehensive audit coverage to meet risks and demands posed by its current and planned activities.
   - Board or audit committee periodically evaluates operations of the internal audit function, including outsourced internal audit activities, and has significant input into the performance evaluation of the internal auditor, as well as into the decision of whether to renew and revise the contract with the outsourced internal audit vendor.
   - At least a majority of audit committee's members are outside directors when practicable (for banks not subject to 12 CFR 363).
   - If the bank has fiduciary powers, a fiduciary audit committee that complies with 12 CFR 9.9, Audit of Fiduciary Activities, directs the fiduciary audit program.

2. If the bank has total assets of $500 million or more, determine compliance with 12 CFR 363, Annual Independent Audits and Reporting Requirements, and auditor independence requirements of the U.S. Securities and Exchange Commission (SEC).

Objective 3: Determine adequacy of the bank's internal audit function.

1. If the bank has no internal audit function, determine management's rationale and mitigating factors (e.g., strong external audit or director's examination and internal control systems, limited complexity of operations or low risk).

2. Assess quality of internal audit activities, including outsourced internal audit activities, by considering:

   - Bank's size, complexity, and risk profile.

- Quality and effectiveness of internal control assessments, including those for financial reporting.
- Whether audit is focused on appropriate areas, given the bank's risk profile.
- Quality of audit reports and findings.
- Quality and timeliness of management responses to audit findings and whether audit follows up on significant findings in a timely manner to assess effectiveness of management's responses.
- Reporting lines to the board or audit committee.
- Quality and depth of audit coverage and audit procedures, including regular testing of internal controls and MIS.
- Whether audit provides constructive business advice or consulting on evaluating safeguards and controls in the acquisition and implementation of new products, services, and delivery channels, and what its role is in merger, acquisition, and transition activities.
- Whether audit plans address goals, schedules, staffing, and reporting.
- Progress made toward completing annual audit plans or schedules.
- Whether audit scope is adjusted for significant changes in the bank's environment, structure, activities, risk exposures, systems, or new products or services.
- Use of audit software and other computer-assisted audit techniques.

3. Determine competence and independence of internal audit staff, whether in-house or outsourced. Consider:

- Auditor and staff experience and training.
- Auditor and staff tenure, turnover, and vacancies.
- Incompatible duties performed by auditor or staff.
- Lines of reporting, operational duties assigned to the auditor, or other restrictions or relationships.
- Staff's ability to meet audit schedule.

4. Review internal audit outsourcing arrangement contracts or engagement letters, and determine whether they adequately address the roles and responsibilities of the bank and the internal audit outsourcing vendor. (See OCC Bulletin 2003-12, "Interagency Policy Statement on Internal Audit and Internal Audit Outsourcing.") Determine whether:

- Arrangement maintains or enhances quality of internal audit and internal controls.
- Key bank employees and vendor clearly understand lines of communication and how the bank addresses internal controls or other problems noted by the vendor.
- Board and management perform sufficient due diligence to verify vendor's competence and objectivity before entering into the outsourcing arrangement.
- Bank has an adequate process for periodically reviewing vendor's performance and ensuring that the vendor maintains sufficient expertise to perform effectively throughout life of the arrangement.
- Arrangement does not compromise the role or independence of a vendor who also serves as the bank's external auditor.

5. If the bank has fiduciary powers, determine quality of the fiduciary audit function and whether it complies with audit standards in 12 CFR 9.9, Audit of Fiduciary Activities. Determine whether:

- Suitable audit of all fiduciary activities is completed at least once every calendar year or under a continuous audit program.
- Audit results, including significant actions taken as a result of the audit, are noted in board minutes.
- If bank uses a continuous audit, results of all discrete audits performed since the last audit reports, including all significant action, are noted in board minutes at least once during the calendar year.

6. Determine quality of the bank's anti-money laundering program audit function and whether it complies with 12 CFR 21.21, BSA compliance. Determine whether:

- Compliance testing is completed on an annual basis.
- If testing is not completed annually, risk analysis used by management to set testing schedule, and frequency of audits is reasonable.
- Audit covered all regulatory provisions and bank's policies and procedures for complying with BSA/AML/OFAC regulations as required by the FFIEC *BSA/AML Examination Manual.*

Objective 4: Determine whether the bank has implemented an appropriate external audit function.

1. If the bank has no external audit function, determine management's rationale and mitigating factors (e.g., strong internal audit and internal control systems, limited complexity of operations or low-risk). Consider:

- Bank's size.
- Nature, scope, and complexity of bank activities.
- Bank's risk profile.
- Actions (taken or planned) to minimize or eliminate identified weaknesses.
- Extent of the bank's internal auditing program.
- Compensating internal controls in place.

2. Determine which of the following types of external audit programs the bank has:

- Financial statement audit.
- Attestation report on management's assertion of financial reporting internal controls.
- Balance sheet audit.
- Agreed-upon procedures (e.g., directors' examination, specialized audits such as IT, fiduciary, consumer compliance, or BSA/AML/OFAC). (Updated 9/28/2012)

3. If a financial statement audit was performed, determine what type of opinion was issued (unqualified, qualified, adverse, or disclaimer).

4. Determine whether external audit program is performed by an independent public accountant or other independent external party and whether the program is appropriate given the bank's size, nature and extent of its activities and operations, and risk profile.

5. Review engagement letter and assess its adequacy. Consider:

   - Purpose and scope of the audit.
   - Period of time to be covered by the audit.
   - Reports expected to be rendered.
   - Limitations placed on the auditor's scope or work.

6. Arrange with bank management to meet with the external auditor to discuss:

   - External audit's scope, results or significant findings, and upcoming audit plans or activities.
   - Reports, management letters, and other communications (written or oral) with the board or audit committee.
   - Audit planning methodologies, risk assessments, sampling techniques, and (if applicable) 12 CFR 363 control attestations.
   - How much the external auditor relies on the work of internal auditors and the extent of external audit's assessment and testing of financial reporting controls.
   - Assigned audit staff experience and familiarity with banking and bank auditing, particularly in specialized areas.

7. Determine whether the board or audit committee and the external auditor have discussed and resolved financial, employment, business, or nonaudit service relationships that compromise or appear to compromise the external auditor's independence.

8. Examiners are not required to review external audit work papers. However, external audit work papers may be subject to OCC review if the review of internal audit discloses significant issues (i.e., insufficient internal audit coverage) or questions are otherwise raised about matters that are normally within the scope of an external audit program. Examiners should consider whether to review external audit work papers for areas where problems or questions exist. Examiners should consider reviewing external audit work papers when:

   - Unexpected or sudden change occurs with the bank's external auditor.
   - Significant change occurs in the bank's external audit program.
   - Issues are raised that affect the bank's safety and soundness.
   - Issues are raised about the independence, objectivity, or competence of the external auditor.

Review of External Audit Work Papers

Examiners should meet with bank management and the external auditor, consult with their district accountant, and obtain approval from the supervisory office ADC before reviewing external audit work papers. These discussions may make the work paper review unnecessary, or they may help examiners focus their review on the most relevant work papers. Examiners should not make blanket requests to review all external audit work papers. All requests should go through bank management, specify areas of greatest interest, and provide reasons for the request.

Examiners should consider requesting that the external auditor make available, for the specific areas to be reviewed, related planning documents and other information pertinent to the area's audit plan (including the sample selection process). Consider having examiners responsible for reviews of other bank activity areas review the external audit work papers associated with those activities. If bank management or the external auditor fails to provide access to work papers, the EIC should contact the supervisory office ADC, district accountant, and district counsel to discuss how the situation might be resolved.

Objective 5: Use the findings from the audit review and other areas under examination to assess the bank's internal control system.

1. Assess the bank's control environment. Consider:

    - Organizational structure (e.g., centralized or de-centralized, authorities and responsibilities, and reporting relationships).
    - Management's philosophy and operating style (e.g., formal or informal, conservative or aggressive, success of risk strategy).
    - External influences affecting operations and practices (e.g., independent external audits).
    - Goals, objectives, attention, and direction provided by the board of directors and its committees, especially the audit or risk management committees.

2. Evaluate the bank's internal RAS. Consider:

    - Effectiveness of the system to identify, measure, monitor, and control risks.
    - Responsiveness of the system to changing risk conditions.
    - Competency, knowledge, and skills of personnel.
    - Adequacy of blanket bond coverage in relation to the bank's risk profile.

3. Assess the bank's control activities. Consider:

    - Quality of policies, procedures, and audit.
    - Quality and timeliness of management and staff training.
    - Timeliness of risk analysis and control processes.
    - Approvals and authorization for transactions and activities.

- Supervision and oversight of payments against uncollected funds (potential for check fraud, such as kiting).
- Segregation or rotation of duties to ensure that the same employee does not originate a transaction, process it, and then reconcile the general ledger account.
- Vacation requirements or periodic unannounced rotation of duties for personnel in sensitive positions.
- Safeguards for access to and use of sensitive assets and records, including wire transfer activities.
- Internal review of employee accounts and expense reports.
- Dual control or joint custody over access to assets (e.g., cash, cash collateral, official checks, and consigned items).
- Independent checks or verifications on function (e.g., lending and wire transfer), performance, and reconciliation of balances.
- Timely account reconciliation and resolution or clearing of outstanding items.
- Accountability for actions taken by bank staff and the responsibilities and authorities given to the staff.

4. Assess the bank's accounting, information, and communication systems. Determine whether the systems:

- Identify and capture relevant internal and external information in a timely manner.
- Ensure accountability for assets and liabilities.
- Ensure effective communication of positions and activities.
- Adequately address business resumption and contingency planning for information systems.

5. Evaluate the bank's self-assessment and monitoring systems. Consider:

- Periodic evaluations, self-assessments, or independent audits of internal controls.
- Whether the systems ensure timely and accurate reporting of deficiencies.
- Processes to ensure timely modification of policies and procedures.
- Audit requirements established by the bank's blanket bond company as specified in the insurance application and policy.

Objective 6: Determine whether expanding the scope of the supervisory activity or developing a plan for corrective action is warranted.

1. If the review of audit or internal controls, including the work paper review, discloses significant audit or control discrepancies or weaknesses that are not mitigated by a satisfactory or strong risk management program, consider whether expanded examination procedures (including internal control questionnaires should be performed to identify the extent of problems and determine their effect on bank operations. Consider expanding procedures if the following issues are identified:

- Concerns about the competency or independence of internal or external audit.

- Unexplained or unexpected changes in internal or external auditors or significant changes in the audit program.
- Inadequate scope of the overall audit program or in key risk areas.
- Audit work papers in key risk areas that are deficient or do not support audit conclusions.
- High-growth areas without adequate audit or internal controls.
- Inappropriate actions by insiders to influence findings or scope of audits.

2. If, after completing step 1, significant concerns remain about the adequacy of audit, adequacy of internal controls or integrity of the bank's financial controls, consider selecting certain verification procedures to determine root causes of the concerns and effect on bank operations. Examiners should use verification procedures if the following issues are identified:

- Key account records are significantly out of balance.
- Management is uncooperative or poorly manages the bank.
- Management attempts to restrict access to bank records.
- Significant accounting, audit, and internal control deficiencies remain uncorrected from prior examinations or from one audit to the next.
- Bank auditors are unaware of, or are unable to sufficiently explain, significant deficiencies.
- Management engages in activities that raise questions about its integrity.
- Repeated violations of law affect audit, internal controls, or regulatory reports.

Note: Examiners may find other instances warranting further investigation. Examiners should consider the risk posed by noted weaknesses in audit or controls and use judgment in deciding whether to perform verification procedures.

The extent to which examiners perform verification procedures is decided on a case-by-case basis after consultation with the ADC. Direct confirmation with the bank's customers must have prior approval of the ADC and district deputy comptroller. The Enforcement and Compliance Division, district counsel, and the district accountant should also be notified when direct confirmations are being considered.

In lieu of having examiners perform the verification procedures, the EIC may consider having the bank expand its audit program to address weaknesses or deficiencies. This alternative should be used only if management has demonstrated a capacity and willingness to address regulatory problems, if there are no concerns about management's integrity, and if management has initiated timely corrective action in the past. The EIC may consider having the bank contract with an independent third party to perform the verification procedures, especially if management's capabilities and commitments are inadequate or there are substantive problems in having the bank or its internal audit function perform the procedures. If used, these alternatives must resolve each identified supervisory problem in a timely manner. Supervisory follow-up must include a review of audit work papers in the areas where the bank audit was expanded.

Objective 7: Conclude the audit and internal controls review.

1. Determine quality of audit (strong, satisfactory, weak) and internal controls (strong, satisfactory, weak).[23]

2. If warranted, develop action plans to address audit or control deficiencies before conducting the exit meeting. Consider management's ability to correct the bank's fundamental problems.

3. Use results of the foregoing procedures and other applicable examination findings to compose comments (e.g., separate comments, part of management/administration, MRAs) for inclusion in the ROE.

4. Incorporate assessments into assigned CAMELS/ITCC and risk assessment ratings.

5. Consult with the EIC and other examining personnel to identify and communicate to other examiners conclusions and findings from the audit and internal control review that are relevant to other areas being reviewed.

6. Communicate conclusions regarding the quality of audit and the system of internal controls to the EIC or examiner responsible for consolidating conclusions from the "Management" section.

7. Update, organize, and reference work papers in accordance with PPM 5400-8 (rev).

8. Update Examiner View (e.g., ratings, core knowledge, MRAs, violations).

9. In discussion with the EIC, provide preliminary strategy recommendations for the next supervisory cycle.

---

[23] Refer to appendix I of the "Internal and External Audits" booklet for audit rating guidance.

Capital

Conclusion: Capital is rated (1, 2, 3, 4, 5).

Complete the appropriate objectives in this section to assign the capital component rating. When assigning the rating, the examiner should consult with the EIC and other examining personnel. Consider the following UFIRS factors:

- Level and quality of capital and overall financial condition of the bank.
- Ability of management to address emerging needs for additional capital.
- Nature, trend, and volume of problem assets, and adequacy of the allowance for loan and lease losses (ALLL) and other valuation reserves.
- Balance sheet composition, including nature and amount of intangible assets, market risk, concentration risk, and risks associated with nontraditional activities.
- Risk exposure represented by off-balance-sheet activities.
- Quality and strength of earnings, and reasonableness of dividends.
- Prospects and plans for growth and past experience in managing growth.
- Access to capital markets and other sources of capital, including support provided by a parent holding company.

Note: A financial institution is expected to maintain capital commensurate with the nature and extent of risks to the institution and the ability of management to identify, measure, monitor, and control these risks. When evaluating the adequacy of capital to assign the capital component rating, examiners should consider the bank's risk profile.

Core Assessment

Minimum Objective: Determine capital component rating and potential impact on the bank's risk assessment.

At the beginning of the supervisory activity, discuss with management the following:

- Bank's present condition and future plans (e.g., dividends, growth, new products, and strategic initiatives, including plans to raise and deploy significant new injections of capital).
- Actual or planned changes in controlling ownership.

As requested, follow up on significant capital-related audit or IT issues that examiners identified while reviewing the bank's audit and IT programs.

Obtain and review the following information:

- Bank's current risk-based capital computation.
- Results from OCC supervisory activities.

- Results from other areas of this and other supervisory activities that may affect capital adequacy (e.g., earnings, asset quality).
- Canary system information.
- UBPR and other OCC models.

If the bank's activities, risk profile, or risk controls have changed significantly, or if review of the above information raises substantive issues, the examiner should expand the activity's scope to include additional objectives or procedures. If this review does not result in significant changes or issues, conclude the capital review by completing objective 7.

Other Assessment Objectives: Note: Examiners should select the objectives and procedures necessary to assess the bank's condition and risks.

Objective 1: Determine the scope of the capital review.

1. Review the supervisory information to identify previous problems that require follow up in this area.

2. Discuss with the examiner responsible for completing the "Audit and Internal Controls" section of the core assessment whether significant audit findings require follow-up or whether a review of audit work papers is required.

3. Discuss with the examiner responsible for completing the IT section of the core assessment whether significant deficiencies raise questions about the integrity, confidentiality, or availability of data and require follow-up.

4. If not previously provided, obtain and review the following:

   - Bank's current risk based capital computation.
   - Findings from monitoring activities.
   - List of shareholders who own 5 percent or more and their percentage of ownership.

5. Calculate and distribute capital limits and shareholder information to other examiners.

Objective 2: Determine adequacy of capital.

1. Review applicable information to identify trends. Consider:

   - Results from monitoring activities.
   - Reports used by bank management to monitor and project capital requirements.
   - Canary system information.
   - UBPR and other OCC model calculations to compare the bank's ratios with those of peer banks.
   - Bank's present condition and future plans.

2. Obtain capital-related information from the examiner assigned to review board minutes.

3. Consider impact of the following on current or future capital adequacy:

- Dividends.
- Earnings.
- Asset quality and allowance adequacy.
- Historical and planned growth.
- On- and off-balance-sheet activities.
- Strategic initiatives, including plans to raise and deploy significant new injections of capital.
- Financial plans and budgets, including replacement costs for fixed assets and technology.
- New products, services, or distribution channels.
- Related organizations.

4. Evaluate sources of capital. Consider:

- Earnings retention.
- Ownership capacity — condition of principal shareholders, parent, or subsidiaries.
- History of public or private offerings.

Objective 3: Determine risk to capital posed by the aggregate level or direction of applicable risks.

Consult with the EIC and other examining personnel to decide whether the aggregate level or direction of risk has an adverse impact on current or future capital adequacy. Refer to the "Risk Assessment System" section.

Objective 4: Determine quality of risk management systems through discussions with key risk managers and analysis of applicable information.

1. Assess the bank's system of internal controls over the capital accounts. Take into consideration relevant controls listed in objective 5 of the "Audit and Internal Controls" section of the core assessment. Also take into consideration other controls pertinent to capital.

2. Assess integrity, confidentiality, and availability of data used to record, analyze, and report information related to capital. Consider input, processing, storage, access, and disposal of data. Focus on measures taken to limit access to the data and procedures in place to monitor system activities. Determine if these controls have been independently validated. Coordinate this review with examiners responsible for all functional areas of the examination, including internal controls, to avoid duplication of effort. Share findings with the examiner reviewing IT.

Objective 5: Determine whether to expand the procedures or develop a plan for corrective action. Consider whether:

- Management can adequately manage the bank's risks.
- Management can correct fundamental problems.
- To propose a strategy to address identified weaknesses and to discuss strategy with the supervisory office.

Refer to booklets of the *Comptroller's Handbook* for expanded procedures.

Objective 6: After completing additional procedures, determine whether risks and concerns indicate the need to perform additional verification procedures.

The extent to which examiners perform verification procedures is decided on a case-by-case basis after consultation with the ADC. Direct confirmation with the bank's customers must have prior approval of the ADC and district deputy comptroller. The Enforcement and Compliance Division, the district counsel, and the district accountant should also be notified when direct confirmations are being considered.

Objective 7: Conclude the capital review.

1. Adjust the bank's reported capital ratios to reflect the results of the examination and distribute them to examining personnel. Consider:

   - Asset charge-offs.
   - Examiner-directed additions to ALLL.
   - Errors in financial reporting.
   - Other capital adjustments.

2. Consult with the EIC and other examining personnel to identify and communicate to other examiners conclusions and findings from the capital review that are relevant to other areas being reviewed.

3. Use results of the foregoing procedures and other applicable examination findings to compose comments (e.g., capital adequacy, MRAs) for the ROE.

4. Update, organize, and reference work papers in accordance with PPM 5400-8 (rev).

5. Update Examiner View (e.g., ratings, core knowledge, MRAs, violations).

6. In discussion with the EIC, provide preliminary strategy recommendations for the next supervisory cycle.

Asset Quality

Conclusion: Asset quality is rated (1, 2, 3, 4, 5)

Complete this section's objectives to assign the asset quality component rating. When assigning the rating, the examiner should consult with the EIC and other examining personnel. Consider the following UFIRS factors:

- Quality of risk selection and underwriting standards, soundness of credit administration practices, and effectiveness of risk identification practices.
- Risk rating profile of the loan portfolio, including trend of multiple pass grades (if applicable) and the level, distribution, severity, and trend of problem, classified, nonaccrual, restructured, delinquent, and nonperforming assets for both on- and off-balance-sheet transactions.
- Adequacy of ALLL and other asset valuation reserves.
- Credit risk arising from or reduced by off-balance-sheet transactions, such as unfunded commitments, derivatives, commercial and standby letters of credit, and lines of credit.
- Diversification and quality of loan and investment portfolios.
- Extent of securities underwriting activities and exposure to counterparties in trading activities.
- Existence of asset concentrations.
- Adequacy of loan and investment policies, procedures, and practices.
- Ability of management to properly administer its assets, including the timely identification and collection of problem assets.
- Adequacy of internal controls and MIS.
- Volume and nature of policy exceptions including exceptions to underwriting and risk selection standards.
- Volume and nature of credit documentation and collateral exceptions.

Note: The examiner should consider ability of management to identify, measure, monitor, and control both the current and planned level of credit risk when assigning the component rating.

Core Assessment

Minimum Objective: Determine the asset quality component rating, adequacy of the ALLL, quantity of credit risk, and quality of credit risk management.

At the beginning of the supervisory activity, discuss with management actual or planned changes in:

- Administration of the loan portfolio.
- Lending area's management or staff.

- Loan products, marketing, loan acquisition channels (including third-party relationships), lending policies or practices, or loan growth.
- Number of loan policy, credit, and collateral exceptions.
- Loan review process or loan grading system.
- Other external or internal factors that could affect loan quality.
- ALLL balance or methodology.

As requested, follow up on significant asset quality-related audit or IT issues identified by examiners reviewing the bank's audit and IT programs.

Obtain and review the following information:

- Results from OCC supervisory activities.
- Canary system information.
- UBPR and other OCC models.
- Past-due and nonaccrual reports.
- Risk-rating distribution reports.
- Problem and "watch" loan lists.
- Insider loan list.
- Concentration of credit reports.
- ALLL analysis.
- List of participations (in whole or part) purchased and sold since the last examination.
- All loan review reports and responses since the last examination.
- Details from "other asset" accounts that are material to financial statements.

Review a sample of loans. Sample should generally include:

- At least five newly advanced credits, including loan commitments.
- Large insider loans.
- Past-due and nonaccrual loans.
- Previously criticized loans and loans from the bank's problem and "watch" loan lists.

The size of the sample should be based on the trends and overall risk posed by those segments of the loan portfolio. The purpose of the review is to determine whether the loans evidence any changes in the bank's risk selection, the bank's underwriting practices, credit administration, risk-rating criteria, or other aspect of its credit risk management, including compliance with credit-related laws and regulations. This may be accomplished by reviewing credit files, approval documents, and loan committee minutes. Documentation of credit file reviews can normally be limited to summary comments detailing the loan classification and the facts supporting it. Loan review discussions and meetings to discuss findings are to be held on site.

If the bank's activities, risk profile, or risk controls have changed significantly, or if review of the above information raises substantive issues, the examiner should expand the activity's scope to include additional objectives or procedures. If this review does not result in significant changes or issues, conclude the asset quality review by completing objective 9.

Other Assessment Objectives: Note: Examiners should select the objectives and procedures necessary to assess the bank's condition and risks.

Objective 1: Determine the scope of the asset quality review.

These procedures apply to both commercial and retail credit portfolios, unless specifically stated otherwise. Refer to the "Loan Portfolio Management" booklet of the *Comptroller's Handbook* on assessing the quality of risk management and setting the scope of asset quality reviews.

1. Review supervisory information to identify previous problems in this area that require follow-up.

2. Discuss with the examiner responsible for completing the "Audit and Internal Controls" section of the core assessment whether significant audit findings require follow-up or whether a review of audit work papers is required.

3. Discuss with the examiner responsible for completing the IT section of the core assessment whether significant deficiencies raise questions about integrity, confidentiality, or availability of data and require follow-up.

4. If not previously provided, obtain and review reports management uses to supervise the loan portfolio, including but not limited to:

   - Loan trial balances.
   - Risk rating reports.
   - Past-due and nonaccrual reports.
   - Problem and "watch" loan lists, including retail workout programs.
   - Concentration of credit reports.
   - Insider loan lists.
   - List of participations (in whole or in part) purchased and sold since the last examination.
   - Overdraft list.
   - Most recent ALLL analysis.
   - Loan policy, loan underwriting, credit, and collateral exception reports.
   - Findings from monitoring activities.
   - Latest loan review report, including responses from bank officers.

5. Review UBPR, Canary system information, and other OCC models, and request information to assess size, composition, and trends in the loan portfolio and off-balance-sheet exposures. Consider:

- Current and planned loan growth in relation to bank capital and risk limits.
- Segments of high growth.
- Concentrations of credit.
- Internal portfolio management reports (loan policy exceptions, credit exceptions, collateral exceptions, concentrations of credit, etc.).
- Unfunded loan commitments.
- Deteriorating trends in asset quality indicators.
- Other information related to risk characteristics of the loan portfolio, including:
- Local and national economic indicators.
    - Trends at other local financial institutions.
    - New products planned or already initiated.

6. In discussions with management, determine:

- How the bank manages the loan portfolio and monitors loan quality.
- Whether loan products, lending practices (underwriting and risk selection standards, out-of-area lending, etc.), or service distribution channels have changed significantly.
- Whether external or internal factors could affect loan quality (e.g., local industry reduction or expansion, management and lending staff changes, changes in credit concentrations, changes in product lines).

7. Obtain asset quality-related information from the examiner assigned to review board minutes. Review minutes of loan committee meetings to ascertain the bank's lending practices.

8. Obtain the bank's current loan policies and review changes since the last examination.

   Note: Policies should be used mainly as reference tools when completing the loan sample and determining exception levels.

9. Use bank reports to select a sample of loans from the bank's loan portfolio (commercial, retail, etc.) Consult with the EIC when selecting the sample. Consider:

- Large-dollar commercial loans.
- Loan participations (in whole or part) purchased and sold.
- Loans sourced or originated through brokers and other third parties.
- Significant loan concentrations.
- New loans in new loan products and in seasoned products or portfolios experiencing rapid growth.
- Loans securitized and sold that the bank services for investors.
- Insider loans and loans to affiliates.
- Lower-rated "pass" and "watch" loans.
- Loans previously identified as structurally weak and loans that are exceptions to lending policies, risk selection, and underwriting standards.

- Higher-risk lending products, such as leveraged finance, high loan-to-value real estate loans, and subprime loans.
- Loans or lending concentrations to businesses or industries exhibiting signs of weakness or higher risk.
- Loans on the problem loan list and loans previously classified, significant past-dues, nonaccruals, troubled debt, and restructured loans.
- Loans made under the lending limits pilot program (OCC Bulletin 2007-22).

Note: Loans not reviewed in detail should be discussed without preparing line sheets.

Because credit risk typically poses the largest single risk to a bank's earnings and capital, and loans are the largest asset concentration in most banks, the OCC usually samples a significant percentage of loan portfolios. Examiners should use a statistically valid sampling technique or take a judgmental sample.

Size and composition of the loan sample should be commensurate with the quantity of credit risk, adequacy of risk management, bank's condition, and objectives of the asset quality review. Examiners should use judgment when determining the focus and extent of testing.

Types of loans in the sample are as important as how much of the portfolio is reviewed. The sample should be skewed toward the predominant risks in the portfolio. The higher the risk posed to the bank, the more comprehensive the coverage and testing.

In a stable, well-managed bank exhibiting few signs of change, examiners should sample a smaller number of new and pass-rated credits for the purpose of determining the continued adequacy of loan quality and credit risk management.

If the number of exceptions to sound underwriting practices or risk selection practices is significant, or if a bank's risk identification or credit administration is suspect or deficient, the examiner should expand the sample to determine the problems' causes, their seriousness, and their effect on credit quality. Additional samples may also be required, for example, when banks have significant growth, loan or product mix changes, credit or economic conditions deteriorate, strategic direction or key personnel change, or loan portfolio management is suspect or deficient. The additional sample should target lending areas that prompted the expanded loan coverage.

10. Use reports or information obtained directly from external sources to verify balances of assets serviced by third parties. Examiners should reconcile balances indicated on the bank's financial records to information provided by the third party. Material differences should be investigated thoroughly.

Objective 2: Determine, by testing loans independently, quantity of credit risk inherent in the loan portfolio.

1. Analyze credits and discuss loans sufficiently to determine a risk rating for each loan reviewed. Analysis should include a review of related debt.

2. Document and support the reasons for each loan rating. Refer to PPM 5400-8 (rev), "Supervision Work Papers," for documentation and work paper requirements.

3. Maintain list of commercial loans identified as having structural weaknesses during the examiner's analysis of individual credits.

4. Maintain list of loans for which the examiner's or management's ability to rate the loan was impaired because of lack of sufficient information on credit or collateral. Consider:

   • Patterns or root causes of exceptions.
   • Relation of exceptions to credit processes.
   • Impact on credit risk.

5. For retail loans, perform a portfolio analysis. Consider:

   • Size of portfolio and rate of growth.
   • Changes in products, marketing channels, underwriting standards, operations, and technology.
   • Level and trends in delinquencies and losses by product.
   • Impact on credit risk.
   • Levels and trends in re-agings, extensions, deferrals, renewals, and rewrites.
   • Dependence on third-party vendors and adequacy of controls regarding the relationship.
   • Compliance with applicable OCC and interagency guidance.

6. Based on the results of the portfolio analysis of retail loans, select a sample of loans to determine the bank's underwriting and account management practices. While conducting reviews of lending activities, examiners should be alert to, and discuss with the EIC, policies, practices, or product terms that could indicate discriminatory, unfair, deceptive, abusive, or predatory lending issues.

7. Determine conformity with OCC 2000-20, "Uniform Retail Credit Classification and Account Management Policy":

   • Review past-due retail loans (residential real estate, consumer loans, check credit, etc.) and discuss with management. (Unless warranted, detailed line sheets should not be prepared.)
   • Review policies and controls, and determine practices for re-aging open-end accounts and extensions, deferrals, renewals, and rewrites of closed-end loans.

8. Determine credit risk inherent in the loan portfolio as a whole, considering the risk-rating profile, underwriting and risk selection practices, concentrations, loan policy exceptions, credit and collateral exceptions, pricing, collateral coverage, adequacy of analysis and credit administration practices, economic indicators, etc.

Objective 3: Determine quantity of credit risk associated with other assets.

1. Obtain and review a list of the following items:

    - Other real estate (ORE).
    - Repossessed assets.
    - Cash items.
    - Other asset accounts with material balances.

2. If level of credit risk associated with ORE appears significant, review a sample of ORE to determine whether management applies proper accounting treatment. Consider:

    - Timing and recognition of losses.
    - Accounting for expenses.
    - Risk to capital or adequacy of ORE reserves.

3. Obtain list of classified investments and other findings regarding quality and composition of investments from the examiner evaluating the investment portfolio.

4. In discussion with bank management and based on the review of other assets listed above, determine which items should be classified or charged off.

Objective 4: Determine adequacy of ALLL.

1. Evaluate method used to determine ALLL balance. Consider:

    - Reasonableness of management's process.
    - Quality and adequacy of the supporting documentation.
    - Findings from the asset quality review.
    - Applicable OCC and interagency guidance.

2. If ALLL methodology is considered flawed, consult with the EIC to independently determine adequacy of the ALLL balance. If ALLL is determined to be inadequate:

    - Calculate necessary provision to restore ALLL to an adequate level.
    - Direct bank management to make necessary adjustments to the call report.
    - Share findings with examining personnel.

Objective 5: Determine quality of credit risk management systems through discussions with key risk managers, analyses of applicable information, including loan review reports.

1. Determine whether the number and nature of credit, collateral, and policy exceptions; risk rating changes; or other loan review findings raise concerns about quality of the credit administration function.

2. Determine whether loan management and personnel are adequate to effectively oversee quantity of credit risk inherent in the loan portfolio. Consider:

   - Staffing size.
   - Staffing expertise.
   - Compensation systems.

3. Assess integrity, confidentiality, and availability of data used to record, analyze, and report information related to asset quality. Consider input, processing, storage, access, and disposal of data. Focus on measures taken to limit access to data and procedures in place to monitor system activities. Determine if controls have been independently validated. Coordinate review with examiners responsible for all functional areas of the examination, including internal controls, to avoid duplication of effort. Share findings with the examiner reviewing IT.

4. Using findings from achieving the previous objectives, consult with the EIC and other examining personnel to make preliminary judgments on adequacy of portfolio risk management systems. Consider whether:

   - Management recognizes and understands existing and emerging risks.
   - Management measures risk in an accurate and timely manner.
   - Board establishes, communicates, and controls risk limits.
   - Management accurately and appropriately monitors established risk levels.

5. Assess the bank's system of internal controls over the credit function. Examiners should take into consideration the relevant controls listed in objective 5 of the "Audit and Internal Controls" section of the core assessment. Examiners should also take into consideration other controls pertinent to the credit function.

Objective 6: Using findings from meeting the previous objectives, determine whether the bank's risk exposure from asset quality is significant.

Develop preliminary assessments of quantity of credit risk, quality of credit risk management, aggregate credit risk, and direction of credit risk. Refer to the "Risk Assessment System" section. Comment as necessary.

Consult with the EIC and other examining personnel to identify significant risks that should be considered in risk assessment conclusions.

Objective 7: Determine whether to expand procedures or develop a plan for corrective action. Consider whether:

   - Management can adequately manage the bank's risks.
   - Management can correct fundamental problems.
   - To propose a strategy to address identified weaknesses and discuss strategy with the supervisory office.

Refer to appropriate booklets of the *Comptroller's Handbook* for expanded procedures.

Objective 8: After completing expanded procedures, determine whether to perform additional verification procedures.

The extent to which examiners perform verification procedures is decided on a case-by-case basis after consultation with the ADC. Direct confirmation with the bank's customers must have prior approval of the ADC and district deputy comptroller. The Enforcement and Compliance Division, the district counsel, and the district accountant should also be notified when direct confirmations are being considered.

Objective 9: Conclude the asset quality review.

1. Provide and discuss with management a list of credit and collateral exceptions, policy exceptions, loans with structural weaknesses, classified assets, assets listed as special mention, and loan write-ups.

2. Consult with the EIC and other examining personnel to identify and communicate to other examiners conclusions and findings from the asset quality review relevant to other areas being reviewed.

3. Use results of the foregoing procedures and other applicable examination findings to compose comments (e.g., asset quality, concentrations, MRAs) for the ROE.

4. Update, organize, and reference work papers in accordance with PPM 5400-8 (rev).

5. Update Examiner View (e.g., ratings, core knowledge, MRAs, violations, concentrations).

6. In discussions with the EIC, provide preliminary conclusions about:

    *   Quantity of credit risk.
    *   Quality of credit risk management.
    *   Aggregate level and direction of credit risk or other applicable risk. Complete summary conclusions in the "Risk Assessment System" section.
    *   Supervisory strategy recommendations.

Management

Conclusion: Management is rated (1, 2, 3, 4, 5).

Complete this section's objectives to assign the management component rating. When assigning the rating, the examiner should consult the EIC and other examining personnel. Consider the following UFIRS factors:

- Conclusions from all areas.
- Level and quality of board and management oversight and support of all the bank's activities.
- Ability of the board of directors and management, in their respective roles, to plan for and respond to risks that may arise from changing business conditions or new activities or products.
- Adequacy of, and conformance with, internal policies and controls addressing the operations and risks of significant activities.
- Accuracy, timeliness, and effectiveness of management information and risk-monitoring systems appropriate to the bank's size, complexity, and risk profile.
- Adequacy of audit and internal control systems to promote effective operations and reliable financial and regulatory reporting, safeguard assets, and ensure compliance with laws, regulations, and internal policies.
- Adequacy of the compliance risk management process to ensure compliance with laws and regulations, including BSA/AML/OFAC. (Updated 9/28/2012)
- Responsiveness to recommendations from auditors and supervisory authorities.
- Management depth and succession.
- Extent to which the board of directors and management are affected by, or susceptible to, a dominant influence or concentration of authority.
- Reasonableness of compensation policies and avoidance of self-dealing.
- Demonstrated willingness to serve the legitimate banking needs of the community.
- Overall performance of the bank and its risk profile.

Note: To determine the component rating for management, examiners assess the capability of the board of directors and management to identify, measure, monitor, and control the risks of a bank's existing and planned activities.

Core Assessment

Minimum Objective: Determine the management component rating and the aggregate level of reputation and strategic risk, and consider potential impact of these findings on the bank's risk assessment.

At the beginning of the supervisory activity, discuss with management actual or planned changes in:

- Senior management or the board.
- Strategic plan or planning function.

Follow up on significant management-related issues identified by the examiners reviewing the bank's audit and IT programs.

Obtain and review the following information:

- Results from OCC supervisory activities.
- Board minutes and reports since the last examination.

If the bank's activities, risk profile, or risk controls have changed significantly, or if review of the above information raises substantive issues, the examiner should expand the activity's scope to include additional objectives or procedures. Serious deficiencies in a bank's BSA/AML compliance create a presumption that the bank's management component rating will be adversely affected because risk management practices are less than satisfactory. If this review does not disclose significant changes or issues, conclude the management review by completing objective 4.

Other Assessment Objectives: Note: Examiners should select the objectives and procedures necessary to assess the bank's condition and risks.

Objective 1: Determine scope of the management review.

1. Review supervisory information to identify previous problems that require follow-up in this area.

2. Discuss with the examiner responsible for completing the "Audit and Internal Controls" section of the core assessment whether significant audit findings require follow-up or whether review of audit work papers is required.

3. Discuss with the examiner responsible for completing the IT section of the core assessment whether significant deficiencies raise questions about integrity, confidentiality, or availability of data and require follow-up.

4. Obtain and review the following:

   - Board and significant committee minutes since the last examination.
   - Current organizational chart.
   - Findings from OCC monitoring activities.
   - List of directors and their backgrounds.
   - Recent representative packet of board meeting materials.
   - List of significant pending litigation, including description of the circumstances.
   - Details about the bank's blanket bond insurance.
   - List of related organizations (e.g., parent holding company, affiliates, operating subsidiaries, chain and parallel-owned banking organizations).

- Summary of payments to bank affiliates.

5. Update list of directors and executive officers in work papers and Examiner View.

Objective 2: Determine adequacy of management and board oversight.

1. At the beginning of the supervisory activity, discuss with senior management and other members of management:

   - Major risks (current or planned) and management's strategies to control them.
   - Board involvement in ensuring adequate risk management system is in effect.
   - Changes, or planned changes, in senior management or the board since the last examination.
   - Board or board committee structure.
   - Plans for growth or acquisition. Consider:
     - Board-approved strategic plan.
     - Financial and operational plans.
     - Changes in products, services, delivery channels, service providers, etc.
     - Resources and staffing necessary to accomplish strategic goals.
   - Potential impact of management succession plans.

2. Review minutes of board and significant committee meetings held since the last examination. Identify:

   - Areas of significant risk in the bank that are not being reported appropriately to the board.
   - Potential or actual violations of law or regulations. Report violations of insider laws, regulations, and policies to the EIC.
   - Actual or planned changes in bank operations or strategy and whether these were approved as part of the bank's strategic planning process.
   - Individuals or factions exercising control over the bank.
   - Directors involved in the management of the bank, and the degree of their involvement.
   - Designated BSA officer.
   - Changes in bylaws or articles of association.
   - Directors who do not regularly attend board or committee meetings. Determine:
     - Why they do not attend.
     - Whether these individuals are fulfilling their fiduciary responsibilities.

3. After reviewing board minutes, provide examiners of other functional areas with significant information acquired about those areas. Consider having the examiner responsible for a functional area review minutes of committees that oversee that area.

4. Review how the board and management select and retain competent staff. Consider:

- Requirements for annual performance reviews of senior management.
- Length of vacancies in key positions.
- Reasonableness of employment contracts.
- Compensation programs.
- Recruitment methods.

5. Review the bank's vulnerability to self-dealing and level of compliance with established laws, regulations, and policies regarding insider transactions and activities.

6. Review pending or threatened litigation with management to determine whether litigation has a potentially significant impact on the financial condition of the bank.

7. Review insurance policies (blanket bond, liability, fixed assets and equipment, operating activities, etc.) to determine whether they are current and provide adequate coverage. Consider:

- Blanket bond coverage in relation to the bank's risk profile and control systems.
- Compliance with requirements established by the blanket bond company.
- Board involvement in the insurance process.

8. Review the relationship — financial or operational — between the bank and the bank's related organizations. Determine whether the transactions between the bank and its related organizations are legal and conform to proper accounting standards and guidance. Consider impact on:

- Earnings.
- Capital.
- Funds management practices.
- Management.

9. Review how management plans for new products and services. Consider:

- Due diligence or feasibility process.
- Financial projections.
- Risk analysis.
- Legal opinions.
- Compliance implications.

Objective 3: Determine quality of risk management systems.

After completing the previous objectives, consult with other examining personnel to make preliminary judgments on adequacy of risk management systems. Consider whether:

- Management recognizes weaknesses and understands existing or emerging risks.
- Management measures risk in an accurate and timely manner.

- Board establishes, communicates, and controls risk limits.
- Management accurately and appropriately monitors established risk levels.

Consult with other examining personnel to determine whether findings from other areas (e.g., quantity of risk, quality of risk management practices, direction of risk, or aggregate risk) affect the management conclusion. Refer to the "Risk Assessment System" section. Comment as necessary.

Objective 4: Conclude the management review.

1. Consult with the EIC and supervisory office to develop action plans for addressing deficiencies before conducting the exit meeting. Consider management's ability to correct the bank's fundamental problems.

2. Consult with the EIC and other examining personnel to identify and communicate to examiners conclusions and findings from the management review that are relevant to other areas being reviewed.

3. Use results of the foregoing procedures, conclusions on quality of audit and system of internal controls, BSA/AML examination findings, and other applicable examination findings to compose comments (e.g., management/administration, MRAs) for the ROE. (Updated 9/28/2012)

4. Update, organize, and reference work papers in accordance with PPM 5400-8 (rev).

5. Update Examiner View (e.g., ratings, core knowledge, MRAs, violations).

6. In discussion with all examining personnel, draw preliminary conclusions about:

   - Quantity of risk.
   - Quality of risk management.
   - Aggregate level and direction of operational, reputation, compliance, strategic, or other applicable risk. Complete the summary conclusions in the "Risk Assessment System" section.
   - Supervisory strategy recommendations.

Earnings

Conclusion: Earnings are rated (1, 2, 3, 4, 5)

Complete this section's objectives to assign the earnings component rating. When assigning the rating, the examiner should consult the EIC and other examining personnel. Consider the following UFIRS factors:

- Level of earnings, including trends and stability.
- Ability to provide for adequate capital through retained earnings.
- Quality and sources of earnings.
- Level of expenses in relation to operations.
- Adequacy of the budgeting systems, forecasting processes, and MIS in general.
- Adequacy of provisions to maintain the ALLL and other valuation allowance accounts.
- Earnings exposure to market risks such as interest rate, foreign currency translation, and price risks.

Note: In rating earnings, the examiner should also assess the sustainability of earnings and potential impact on earnings of quantity of risk and quality of risk management.

Core Assessment

Minimum Objective: Determine earnings component rating and potential impact on the bank's risk assessment.

At the beginning of the supervisory activity, discuss with management the following:

- Actual or planned changes in the bank's budget or budgeting process.
- Bank's present condition and future plans.
- Earnings trends or variances.
- Changes in the bank's call report preparation processes and whether re-filings have occurred.

As requested, follow up on significant earnings-related audit or IT issues identified by the examiners reviewing the bank's audit and IT programs.

Obtain and review the following information:

- Results from OCC supervisory activities.
- Canary system information.
- UBPR and other OCC models.
- Budget and variance reports.

If the bank's activities, risk profile, or risk controls have changed significantly, or if review of the above information raises substantive issues, the examiner should expand the activity's scope to include additional objectives or procedures. If this review does not result in significant changes or issues, conclude the earnings review by completing objective 9.

Other Assessment Objectives: Note: Examiners should select the objectives and procedures necessary to assess the bank's condition and risks.

Objective 1: Determine scope of the earnings review.

1. Review supervisory information to identify previous problems that require follow-up in this area.

2. Discuss with the examiner responsible for completing the "Audit and Internal Controls" section of the core assessment whether significant audit findings require follow-up or whether a review of audit work papers is required.

3. Discuss with the examiner responsible for completing the IT section of the core assessment whether significant deficiencies raise questions about integrity, confidentiality, or availability of data and require follow-up.

4. If not previously provided, obtain and review the following:

   - Most current balance sheet and income statement.
   - Most recent budget, variance reports, and related items.
   - Most recent annual and quarterly reports.
   - Findings from OCC monitoring activities.

Objective 2: Determine quality and composition of earnings.

1. Review applicable information to identify trends. Consider:

   - Results from OCC monitoring activities.
   - Management reports used to monitor and project earnings.
   - UBPR and other OCC model calculations to compare the bank's ratios with those of peer banks.
   - Canary system information for potential impact on future earnings.
   - Bank's present condition and future plans.

2. Obtain earnings-related information from the examiner assigned to review board minutes.

3. Discuss earnings trends and variances with management. Coordinate discussions with those examining other functional areas.

4. Analyze earnings composition. Focus on:

- Core earnings.
- Net interest margins.
- Noninterest income and expenses.
- Loan loss provisions.
- Off-balance-sheet items.
- Changes in balance sheet composition.
- Impact of fair value adjustments (FAS 115).
- Loan and deposit pricing.
- Earnings from affiliate transactions.
- Earnings from high-risk lines of business.

5. If the bank has fiduciary powers, obtain fiduciary-related earnings information and evaluate the quantity and quality of fiduciary earnings. Refer to factors listed in UITRS, including:

- Level and consistency of profitability in relation to business volume and characteristics.
- Methods used to allocate direct and indirect expenses.
- Effects of fiduciary settlements, surcharges, and other losses.

6. Determine root causes of significant trends and impact of nonrecurring items. Consider:

- Whether earning trends are improving, stable, or declining.
- Bank earnings compared with:
  - Budget.
  - Peer group.
- Adequacy of bank earnings in relation to:
  - Debt service requirements of the bank's owner.
  - Dividend-paying capacity. (If appropriate — and in conjunction with the examiner reviewing capital — review and discuss with management the bank's dividend plans.)

7. Adjust the bank's reported earnings to reflect results of the examination and project current year's net income. Distribute adjustments to examining personnel.

Objective 3: Determine adequacy of the bank's budgeting process.

Review and determine reasonableness of the bank's budget. Consider:

- Economic, market, and other assumptions.
- Historical performance of the budgeting process.
- Examination results.
- Changes in bank management or strategies.
- Variance reports and other supplemental budgeting reports.

Objective 4: Determine adequacy of management processes to prepare call reports and validity of call report data.

1. If not previously provided, obtain and review the following:

   - Most recent call report.
   - Bank's work papers for that call report.

2. Review and determine the adequacy of the bank's process for preparing call reports. Determine whether the process is periodically and independently verified.

3. Verify call report data. Consider:

   - Asking other examiners whether their findings agree with call report information.
   - Determining whether follow-up is needed.
   - Testing call report accuracy by randomly checking selected call report line items against the bank's work papers and source documents. Consider having examiners assigned to review other functional areas verify the appropriate schedule in the call report.

Objective 5: Determine risk to bank earnings posed by aggregate level or direction of applicable risks.

Consult with the EIC and other examining personnel to decide whether aggregate level or direction of risk has adverse impact on the bank's current or future earnings. Refer to the "Risk Assessment System" section.

Objective 6: Determine quality of risk management systems through discussions with key risk managers and analysis of applicable internal or external audit reports.

1. Assess the bank's system of internal controls over income and expense accounts. Examiners should take into consideration relevant controls listed in objective 5 of the "Audit Functions and Internal Control" section of the core assessment. Examiners should also take into consideration other controls pertinent to earnings.

2. Assess integrity, confidentiality, and availability of data used to record, analyze, and report information related to earnings. Consider input, processing, storage, access, and disposal of data. Focus on measures taken to limit access to data and procedures in place to monitor system activities. Determine if controls have been independently validated. Coordinate this review with examiners responsible for all functional areas of the examination, including internal controls, to avoid duplication of effort. Share findings with the examiner reviewing IT.

Objective 7: Determine whether to expand procedures or develop a plan for corrective action. Consider whether:

- Management can adequately manage the bank's risks.
- Management can correct fundamental problems.
- To propose a strategy to address identified weaknesses and discuss strategy with the supervisory office.

Refer to appropriate booklets of the *Comptroller's Handbook* for expanded procedures.

Objective 8: After completing expanded procedures, determine whether additional verification procedures should be performed.

The extent to which examiners perform verification procedures is decided on a case-by-case basis after consultation with the ADC. Direct confirmation with the bank's customers must have prior approval of the ADC and district deputy comptroller. The Enforcement and Compliance Division, the district counsel, and the district accountant should also be notified when direct confirmations are being considered.

Objective 9: Conclude the earnings review.

1. Use results of the foregoing procedures and other applicable examination findings to compose comments (e.g., earnings, MRAs) for the ROE.

2. Consult with the EIC and other examining personnel to identify and communicate to other examiners conclusions and findings from the earnings review relevant to other areas being reviewed.

3. Update, organize, and reference work papers in accordance with PPM 5400-8 (rev).

4. Update Examiner View (e.g., ratings, core knowledge, MRAs, violations).

5. In discussion with the EIC, provide preliminary strategy recommendations for the next supervisory cycle.

Liquidity

Conclusion: Liquidity is rated (1, 2, 3, 4, 5)

Complete this section's objectives to assign the liquidity component rating. When assigning the rating, the examiner should consult the EIC and other examining personnel. Consider the following UFIRS factors:

- Adequacy of liquidity sources to meet present and future needs and ability of the bank to meet liquidity needs without adversely affecting operations or condition.
- Availability of assets readily convertible to cash without undue loss.
- Access to money markets and other sources of funding.
- Level of diversification of funding sources, both on- and off- balance-sheet.
- How much the bank relies on short-term, volatile sources of funds, including borrowings and brokered deposits, to fund longer-term assets.
- Trend and stability of deposits.
- Ability to securitize and sell certain pools of assets.
- Capability of management to properly identify, measure, monitor, and control the bank's liquidity position, including effectiveness of funds management strategies, liquidity policies, MIS, and contingency funding plans (CFP).

Core Assessment

Minimum Objective: Determine liquidity component rating, quantity of liquidity risk, and quality of liquidity risk management.

At the beginning of the supervisory activity, discuss with management actual or planned changes in:

- Liquidity risk management.
- Liquidity planning or funding sources and needs.
- Investment strategy.
- Liquidity policy or CFP.

As requested, follow up on significant liquidity-related audit or IT issues identified by the examiners reviewing the bank's audit and IT programs.

Obtain and review the following information:

- Results from OCC supervisory activities.
- Canary system information.
- UBPR and other OCC models.
- Liquidity reports.

60

- Investment trial balance.
- Asset-liability committee (ALCO) minutes and reports since the last supervisory activity.

If the bank's activities, risk profile, or risk controls have changed significantly, or if review of the above information raises substantive issues, the examiner should expand the activity's scope to include additional objectives or procedures. If this review does not result in significant changes or issues, conclude the liquidity review by completing objective 15.

Other Assessment Objectives: Note: Examiners should select the objectives and procedures necessary to assess the bank's condition and risks.

Objective 1: Determine the scope of the liquidity review.

1. Review supervisory information to identify previous problems that require follow-up in this area.

2. Discuss with the examiner responsible for completing the "Audit and Internal Controls" section of the core assessment whether significant audit findings require follow-up or whether a review of audit work papers is required.

3. Discuss with the examiner responsible for completing the IT section of the core assessment whether significant deficiencies raise questions about integrity, confidentiality, or availability of data and require follow-up.

4. Obtain and review the following items:

   - Most recent liquidity reports.
   - CFP.
   - Investment trial balance.
   - List of investments purchased and sold (within a reasonable time frame).
   - List of securities acquired using the bank's lending authority.
   - Findings from monitoring activities.
   - Other information or reports management uses (asset and liability committee packages and minutes, etc.).
   - Canary system information.
   - Other OCC-generated filters that pertain to liquidity (e.g., Federal Home Loan Bank or FHLB borrowings).

5. Discuss current investment, liquidity, and funds management strategies with management.

Objective 2: Determine whether available liquidity sources are adequate to meet current and potential needs.

1. Evaluate volume and trends of sources of liquidity available to meet liquidity needs.

From assets:

- Compare level of money market assets and other liquid assets (easily convertible into cash) with current and potential short-term liquidity needs.
- Determine amount of free (unencumbered) marketable investment securities available for cash conversion or collateral for available borrowing lines.
- Determine level and impact of asset depreciation.
- Determine impact of fair value accounting on asset liquidity and distribution of securities designated "held-to-maturity" and "available-for-sale."
- Determine adequacy of cash flows (payments, prepayments, maturities) from such assets as loans, investments, and off-balance-sheet contracts.
- Review other potential sources of asset liquidity (securitization, loan sales) and determine trends in pricing and spreads (e.g. market acceptance).

From liabilities:

- Compare estimated cash flows and capacity to borrow under established lines to short-term liquidity needs, including required collateral availability.
- Consider the bank's capacity to increase deposits through pricing and direct-marketing campaigns to meet medium- and long-term liquidity needs.
- Consider the bank's capacity to borrow under the FHLB collateralized loan program or other similar collateralized borrowing facilities.
- Consider the capacity to issue longer-term liabilities and capital to meet medium- and long-term liquidity needs. Options may include:
  - Deposit-note programs.
  - Medium-term note programs.
  - Subordinated debt.
  - Trust preferred securities.
- Consider the capacity and collateral available to borrow from the Federal Reserve discount window and whether the bank qualifies for the primary or secondary borrowing program.

2. Identify volume and trends of liquidity needs by reviewing

- Historical and prospective behavioral cash flow reports, sources and uses analyses, and behavioral gap reports used by management to identify expected liquidity requirements over short-, medium-, and long-term horizons. This review should include an assessment of
  - Management's support for significant assumptions and projections in prospective cash flow and behavioral gap reports.
  - Reasonableness and consistency of assumptions and projections with historical performance and management's budgets and operating forecasts.
- Static and prospective policy limits including compliance with those limits.
- Projected liability reductions, including
  - Managed balance-sheet restructuring, and

      − Potential erosion due to credit-sensitive funds providers.
- Potential unanticipated asset growth due to impairment in the bank's ability to sell or securitize assets.
- Potential off-balance-sheet requirements.

Objective 3: Determine impact of the cost of liquidity on the bank's ability to generate reasonable profits.

Review level and trend in funding costs and impact on the net interest margin and overall earnings. Determine

- Bank's margin performance and causes for changes since the last examination.
- Level and trend in the spread between liability costs and assets they fund.
- Comparison of retail and wholesale deposit rates against local and national competitors.
- Changes in deposit funding costs in comparison with peer banks, market interest rates, and asset yields.
- Reasons for change in the rate or spread of other wholesale deposit sources (generally deposits of more than $100,000 and professionally managed).
- Whether anxiety for income has hampered prudent liquidity actions.

Objective 4: Determine stability, credit and rate sensitivity, and character of the bank's deposit structure.

1. Analyze reports generated from the bank's internal MIS, Canary system information, and UBPR data on insured deposits to determine

   - Changes and trends in deposit volume and product mix.
   - Material shifts between deposit types and reasons for these shifts.
   - Offering rates and costs for all major deposit types, including those gathered through the Internet and deposit-splitting arrangements, compared with peer banks and market interest rates.
   - Ability and likelihood of renewal or retention of these funds at maturity.
   - Management's deposit pricing policies and the success of recent pricing decisions.
   - Success of recent branch expansion and marketing efforts to attract and retain deposit relationships.

2. Review list of deposits greater than $100,000 (i.e., uninsured deposits). To determine stability of these accounts, discuss with management

   - Aggregate number and volume of these accounts and degree of the bank's reliance on this funding source.
   - Nature of account holders' relationship with the bank (insider, multiple product or service relationships, location of account holder and proximity to the bank's branch network).
   - Rate paid on these accounts relative to local and national market competitors.

- Whether the aggregate dollar amount of these accounts originated through an intermediary (brokered deposits).
- Concentrations.
- Ability to retain and replace these funds.
- Recent success of marketing efforts related to these accounts.
- Pledging requirements and management's controls over collateral availability.
- Policies of large wholesale funds depositors and whether the policies require them to reduce or remove funds on deposit because of a decline in the bank's credit rating or deterioration in the bank's financial condition.
- Competitive pressures, economic conditions, or other factors that may affect retention of these deposits.

Objective 5: Evaluate level of risk in wholesale and other non-deposit funding activities.

1. Determine the bank's level of reliance on wholesale funding and other borrowings.

2. Through discussion with management and analysis of relevant bank data, determine:

- Purpose of the bank's wholesale funding activities and strategy for the current or future use of these funds. (Are they temporary or permanent?)
- Assets or activities being funded. If funds are part of an effort to leverage capital, consult with the examiner reviewing sensitivity to market risk and determine if risks associated with this strategy are properly understood by management and are measured, monitored, and controlled.
- Profitability or spread between these sources and their uses. Determine reasonableness of these profits and compare with management's objectives and risks assumed. This step should be coordinated with the examiner(s) evaluating bank earnings and sensitivity to market risk.
- Types of maturity mismatches that exist between wholesale sources and the assets they fund.
- Structural characteristics of wholesale funding sources (call or put options, complex interest rate rules or calculations, complex prepayment schedules, etc.), liquidity risks they present, and management's understanding and ability to control those risks.
- Whether there has been deterioration in the bank's ability to raise or renew wholesale funds by reviewing such items as
  - Interest rates paid by the bank for these funds that exceed prevailing market rates.
  - Impact of costs associated with these funds on bank profitability;
  - Bank's credit rating.
  - Frequent or recent changes in wholesale lenders.
  - Changes in sensitivity to credit risk of the bank's wholesale funding providers.
  - Changes in amount and availability of collateral.
  - Requests for, increases in, or changes to collateral requirements of wholesale funding providers.
  - Significant concentrations in these funding sources.

    – Changes in the bank's Federal Reserve discount window status (primary or secondary lending program).

Objective 6: Determine whether adequate contingent funds are available to meet the needs required in liquidity stress or crisis scenarios.

1. Review the bank's CFP. Determine whether management is properly planning for contingent liquidity in identified crisis scenarios. Review:

   - Management's short- and long-term contingency funding scenarios and adequacy of cash flows and other sources to meet liquidity needs. (This review should consider assessment of the reasonableness of all material assumptions used in the planning process.)
   - Identified market disruptions (nationally and within the bank's trade area) and adequacy of bank-contingent liquidity to meet short- and long-term funding needs.

2. Determine impact of current or potential deterioration in the bank's credit or reputation on liquidity and ability of identified contingent sources to support related outflows of funds.

3. Assess impact of aggressive short- or longer-term growth patterns or strategies.

4. Determine impact of a disruption to the bank's asset sales or securitization activities. Consider:

   - Level of reliance on these funding sources.
   - Availability of contingent funding sources and capital if the bank has to refund or repurchase a portion or all of these assets.

5. Consider potential effects of destabilization in the market or trade area caused by:

   - Competitor or peer bank failure.
   - General market trends (e.g., net emigration from the bank's market area).
   - Disintermediation (i.e., loss of deposits).
   - Changes in investor preference (e.g., to mutual funds).
   - Stock or real estate market declines resulting in reduced customer wealth.
   - Systemic technology failure.

Objective 7: Assess appropriateness and integrity of corporate governance over liquidity risk management.

1. Review policies, procedures, and reports to the board and senior management to determine effectiveness of board and senior management oversight. Consider:

   - Clearly defined lines of authority and responsibility.

- Articulation of general strategies and approach to liquidity management.
- Understanding of contingency plans for liquidity.
- Periodic review of the bank's liquidity risk profile.

2. Review senior management structures to determine adequacy in overseeing and managing the bank's liquidity. Consider:

- Designation of a representative ALCO or other management decision-making body.
- Whether ALCO composition includes managerial and departmental leadership necessary to communicate issues integral to assessing liquidity and to carry out tactical and strategic initiatives relevant to liquidity management.
- Frequency and documentation of ALCO meetings and adequacy, accuracy, and timeliness of the reports presented.
- Decisions made by ALCO and validation of follow-up, including policy compliance assessments and ongoing review of open issues.
- Technical and managerial expertise and responsibilities of management and personnel involved in liquidity management.
- Clear delineation of centralized and decentralized liquidity management responsibilities.

Objective 8: Determine that liquidity policies, procedures, and limits are appropriate for size, complexity, and sophistication of the bank.

Review and discuss with management liquidity policies, procedures, and risk limits, and determine their appropriateness and comprehensiveness with respect to:

- Identification of objectives and strategies of the bank's liquidity management and its expected and preferred reliance on various sources of funds to meet liquidity needs under alternative scenarios.
- Clear delineation of responsibility and accountability over liquidity risk management and management decision making.
- Specification of and rationale for quantitative limits and guidelines that define acceptable level of risk for the bank. Examples include use of maximum and targeted amounts of projected cash flow mismatches, liquidity reserves, volatile liabilities, collateral usage, maximum usage of borrowing capacity, and funding concentrations.
- Specification of methods used to measure and monitor liquidity risk and their frequency.
- Definition of specific procedures and approvals necessary for exceptions to policies, limits, and authorizations.

Objective 9: Assess adequacy of the bank's liquidity risk measurement systems.

1. Review liquidity risk measurement policies, procedures, methodologies, models, and assumptions. Discuss with management:

- Adequacy and comprehensiveness of cash flow analyses and sources and uses of funds projections used to manage liquidity.
- Appropriateness and comprehensiveness of the scenarios analyzed and reported for cash flow and sources and uses projections. Consider impact of the following on the bank's projections:
    - Volatility or unpredictability of the bank's cash flows.
    - Changes to business strategies.
    - Current interest rate environment.
    - Local and national economic conditions.
- Appropriateness of summary measures and ratios to reflect adequately the bank's liquidity risk profile.
- Appropriateness of the identification of stable and volatile sources of funding.
- Validity of assumptions used to construct liquidity risk measures and frequency of management's review.
- Comprehensiveness and breadth of alternative contingent liquidity scenarios incorporated in the ongoing estimation of liquidity needs.
- Frequency, independence, and scope of procedures to validate models used to quantify liquidity risk.

2. Assess integrity, confidentiality, and availability of data used to record, analyze, and report information about liquidity. Consider input, processing, storage, access, and disposal of data. Focus on measures taken to limit access to data and procedures in place to monitor system activities. Determine if these controls have been independently validated. Coordinate this review with examiners responsible for all functional areas of the examination, including internal controls, to avoid duplication of effort. Communicate findings to the examiner reviewing IT. Consider whether MIS monitors:

- Compliance with risk limits.
- Sources and uses.
- Funding concentrations.
- Funding costs.
- Availability under wholesale funding lines.
- Projected funding needs.

Objective 10: Determine whether policies and practices regarding wholesale funding are adequate.

Review formal and informal wholesale funding policies and determine whether they:

- Designate lines of authority and responsibility for decisions.
- Outline objectives of bank wholesale funding activities.
- Describe the bank's wholesale funding philosophy relative to risk considerations (e.g., leverage/growth, liquidity/income).
- Control concentration exposure by diversifying sources and staggering maturities. Determine whether funding decisions are based largely on cost.

- Limit wholesale funds by amount outstanding, specific type, individual source, market source, or total interest expense.
- Provide a system of reporting requirements to monitor wholesale funding activity.
- Provide controls over wholesale funding cash flow uncertainty by limiting amount and type of embedded options.
- Require material strategies and transactions be reviewed and approved by the board, senior management, or a committee thereof (ALCO).
- Review and revise established policy at least annually.

Objective 11: Assess adequacy of liquidity CFPs.

Review liquidity CFP and minutes from ALCO meetings and board meetings and discuss with management adequacy of the bank's contingent planning processes for liquidity. Consider:

- Customization of CFP to fit the bank's liquidity risk profile.
- Identification of potential sources of liquidity under stress events.
- Breadth of potential stress triggers and events and analyses of various levels of stress to liquidity that can occur under defined scenarios.
- Quantitative assessment of short- and intermediate-term funding needs in stress events.
- Reasonableness of assumptions used in forecasting potential contingent liquidity needs and frequency of management's review of these assumptions to ensure they remain valid.
- Comprehensiveness in forecasting cash flows under stress conditions including incorporation of off-balance-sheet cash flows.
- Use of contingent liquidity risk triggers to monitor, on an ongoing basis, the potential for contingent liquidity events.
- Consideration of the limitations of payment systems and their operational implications to the bank's ability to access contingent funding.
- Operating policies and procedures to be implemented in stress events, including assignment of responsibilities for communicating with various stakeholders.
- Prioritization of actions for responding to stress situations.

Objective 12: Determine significance of liquidity risk by using findings from meeting the foregoing objectives.

Consult with the EIC and other examining personnel to decide whether aggregate level or direction of risk identified during the liquidity review has had, or is expected to have, an adverse impact on the bank's capital or earnings. Refer to the "Risk Assessment System" section. Comment as necessary.

Objective 13: Determine whether to expand the procedures or develop a plan for corrective action. Consider whether:

- Management can adequately manage the bank's risk.
- Management can correct fundamental problems.

- A strategy should be proposed to address identified weaknesses and discussed with the supervisory office.

Refer to booklets of the *Comptroller's Handbook* for expanded procedures.

Objective 14: After completing expanded procedures, determine whether additional verification procedures should be performed.

The extent to which examiners perform verification procedures is decided on a case-by-case basis after consultation with the ADC. Direct confirmation with the bank's customers must have prior approval of the ADC and district deputy comptroller. The Enforcement and Compliance Division, the district counsel, and the district accountant should also be notified when direct confirmations are being considered.

Objective 15: Conclude the liquidity review.

1. Provide the examiner evaluating asset quality with a list of classified investments, and communicate findings to other examining personnel.

2. Consult with the EIC and other examining personnel to identify and communicate to other examiners conclusions and findings from the liquidity review that are relevant to other areas being reviewed.

3. Use results of the foregoing procedures and other applicable examination findings to compose comments (e.g., liquidity adequacy, liquidity management processes, or MRAs) for the ROE.

4. Update, organize, and reference work papers in accordance with PPM 5400-8 (rev).

5. Update Examiner View (e.g., ratings, core knowledge, MRAs, violations).

6. In discussion with the EIC, provide preliminary conclusions about:

   - Quantity of liquidity risk.
   - Quality of liquidity risk management.
   - Aggregate level and direction of liquidity risk or other applicable risk. Complete summary conclusions in the "Risk Assessment System" section.
   - Supervisory strategy recommendations.

Investment Portfolio and Bank Owned Life Insurance

Conclusion: The assessment of the investment portfolio and bank-owned life insurance should be included in the asset quality rating.

Complete this section's objectives to assess relevant risks in the bank's investment portfolio and bank-owned life insurance (BOLI) and quality of management and board oversight of investment portfolio activities. The examiner should consult the EIC and other personnel when completing these assessments. Consider the following factors when assessing the investment portfolio:

- Nature, level, and complexity of relevant investment portfolio risks.
- Investment portfolio strategies and future plans.
- Ability of management to adequately understand and monitor relevant risks.
- Board and management oversight policies, practices, and procedures.

Core Assessment

Minimum Objective: Determine quality of oversight of the investment portfolio, including BOLI. Evaluate how and to what degree investments contribute to relevant risk areas.

At the beginning of the supervisory activity, discuss with management actual or planned changes in:

- Investment portfolio strategies.
- Investment risk appetite or types of securities purchased.
- Policies or procedures governing investments.

As requested, follow up on significant investment and BOLI-related audit or IT issues identified by the examiners reviewing the bank's audit and IT programs.

Obtain and review the following information:

- Results from OCC supervisory activities.
- Canary system information.
- UBPR and other OCC models.
- Investment portfolio trial balance.
- Investment portfolio analytics.

If the bank's activities, risk profile, or risk controls have changed significantly, or if the review of the above information raises substantive issues, the examiner should expand the

---

activity's scope to include additional objectives or procedures. If this review does not result in significant changes or issues, conclude the review by completing objective 10.

Other Assessment Objectives: Note: Examiners should select the objectives and procedures necessary to assess the bank's condition and risks.

Objective 1: Determine the scope of the investments review.

1. Review supervisory information to identify previous problems that require follow-up in this area.

2. Discuss with the examiner responsible for completing the "Audit and Internal Controls" section of the core assessment whether significant audit findings require follow-up or whether a review of audit work papers is required.

3. Discuss with the examiner responsible for completing the IT section of the core assessment whether significant deficiencies raise questions about integrity, confidentiality, or availability of data and require follow-up.

4. Obtain and review the following items:

   - Internal audit reports and management responses.
   - Portfolio price sensitivity.
   - Portfolio yields.
   - Portfolio appreciation/depreciation.
   - Whether a large portion of the portfolio was acquired during a short time period or whether it has a concentration in assets with embedded options or maturity dates.
   - Potentially higher risk holdings, such as:
     - Zero coupon bonds.
     - Securities denominated in a foreign currency.
     - Securities with low credit ratings.
     - Non-rated securities.
     - Long maturities.
     - Variable principal redemption bonds.
     - Floating rate assets with low interest rate caps or long periods between rate resets.

5. Contact and discuss the following with the bank's investment portfolio officer and money market personnel:

   - Significant risk issues and management strategies.
   - Significant changes in policies, strategies, procedures, controls or personnel.
   - Whether the bank emphasizes yield or total return in its investment activities.
   - How management supervises risks (e.g., types of reports reviewed, frequency of committee meetings, etc.).
   - Degree of price sensitivity of the investment account, and how the bank measures it.

- Volume of securities with options.
- Whether the bank owns variable principal redemption bonds (i.e., securities for which the maturity amount may be less than par because of a formula that determines the redemption amount).
- Practices for documenting pre-purchase analyses.
- Whether and extent to which the bank uses its lending authority to acquire securities.
- Whether the bank owns securities denominated in a foreign currency.
- Issues identified by internal or external auditors.
- Bank's philosophy for taking credit risk in the portfolio.
- Distribution of credit ratings and existence of defaulted securities.
- Whether the bank uses outside consultants to manage the portfolio or execute purchase and sale transactions.
- Level of unrealized appreciation or depreciation.
- Bank's tax position and plans to acquire tax-advantaged assets (including BOLI).
- Credit or accounting concerns related to the portfolio, including FAS 159 implications.

6. Develop a preliminary risk assessment and discuss it with the EIC for perspective and examination planning coordination. Consider:

- Purchases and sales between examinations.
- Policy or strategy changes.
- Bank's reliance on the investment portfolio for income.
- Price sensitivity or credit concerns raised from preliminary discussions with management.

Objective 2: Determine appropriateness and effectiveness of the risk management practices of the investment portfolio.

1. Evaluate board and senior management oversight. Consider:

- Procedures for approving major policies.
- Annual review of investment strategies and policies.
- Establishment of risk limits and procedures to ensure compliance.
- How well board members and management not involved directly or daily in investment activities understand those activities.

2. Review pre-purchase analyses of recent investments, and determine whether analyses provide adequate information to understand the price sensitivity of the security. Determine whether pre-purchase analyses conform to guidance prescribed in OCC Bulletin 98-20, "Investment Securities – Policy Statement."

3. Determine whether limits (pre-purchase and portfolio sensitivity) established by management are reasonable and serve as an appropriate subset of bank-wide interest rate risk (IRR) limits, given the bank's capital, earnings and management's expertise.

4. Evaluate credit risk management of the portfolio. Assess whether the process establishes an appropriate framework for pre-acquisition credit due diligence that analyzes the repayment capacity of the issuer. Confirm whether the management process regularly monitors holdings so risk ratings are reviewed and updated when significant new information is received.

5. Determine how well management monitors the investment portfolio. Consider:

- Whether significant risks in the bank's investment activities are understood and properly reported.
- Completion and documentation of stress testing on the types of securities as required in the bank's investment policy or procedures.
- Periodic evaluations of aggregate risk exposure and the overall performance of the investment portfolio.

Objective 3: Evaluate the quality of the investment portfolio as a potential source of liquidity. Consider:

- Percentage and quality of investment portfolio that is unpledged.
- Level and impact of portfolio depreciation.
- Maturity distribution and average life sensitivity of the investment portfolio.
- Distribution of securities designated hold-to-maturity and available-for-sale.
- Marketability of available-for-sale securities.
- Trends in monthly cash flow from the investment portfolio.
- Potential impact of embedded options on cash-flow patterns.
- Volume and quality of securities not priced or securities that show a constant price of par.

Objective 4: Assess the level of credit risk in the investment portfolio.

1. Review the UBPR and the bank's MIS to evaluate:

- Investment yields and market values.
- Investment portfolio ratings distribution.
- Holdings of structured products.
- Significant holdings of nonrated securities, BOLI, below-investment-grade securities, zero or low coupons, and long maturities.

2. Evaluate credit analysis performed on investment securities and determine whether the level of due diligence is appropriate.

3. Review credit analysis on nonrated securities and assess whether securities are the credit equivalent of investment grade.

4. Evaluate holdings of structured products to determine whether risks in these securities are understood and consistent with policy. Determine whether bank management analyzed

cash-flow modeling assumptions including default and recovery rates, collateral risk, structural risk, and call risk.

5. Determine whether securities acquired using the bank's lending authority conforms to lending policies for credit analysis, underwriting, and approval.

6. Assess trend in credit quality of the investment portfolio between examinations. Determine whether there has been a significant change in the credit risk profile and whether that change has been appropriately managed.

7. Determine whether there are issues in the portfolio that are ineligible, in default, or below investment grade. Classify defaulted or below-investment-grade securities based on OCC Bulletin 2004-25 and distribute findings to examiners reviewing asset quality, earnings, and capital adequacy.

8. If a security is rated below investment grade, assess the security structure and determine if that security is providing credit enhancement to other tranches. If so, consult with 12 CFR 3 appendix A, section 4, to determine whether the bank is appropriately applying capital requirements for that security. Distribute those findings to the examiner assessing capital adequacy.

9. Review credit information for securities purchased under the "reliable estimates" authority (12 CFR 1.3(i)), nonrated securities, and below-investment-grade securities.

10. Review the bank's process for setting and monitoring settlement limits with securities dealers.

Objective 5: Determine IRR level in the investment portfolio. Consider:

- Price sensitivity of the investment portfolio.
- Level and nature of optionality in the investment portfolio.
- Impact of changing interest rates on average life, effective duration, and cash-flow projections.
- Impact of depreciation or amortization on earnings performance and capital adequacy.

Objective 6: Determine compliance risk, operational risk, and strategic risk posed by the investment portfolio. Consider:

- Levels of type I, type II, type III, type IV, and type V securities and whether those levels exceed regulatory limits.
- Documentation maintained to ensure ongoing monitoring of portfolio and individual security quality, purchase documentation, and reconciliation.
- Purchase and sales records, with particular attention to the timing and products being purchased and sold.
- Significance of changes to portfolio strategy, including board awareness and resulting impact on operations and performance.

Objective 7: Develop an overview of BOLI activities via a review of bank policies and procedures that address BOLI and pertinent BOLI information. Refer to OCC Bulletin 2004-56, "Bank Owned Life Insurance: Interagency Statement on the Purchase and Risk Management of Life Insurance." Compile a brief description of the bank's BOLI program(s), including the following elements:

- Dates policies were purchased.
- Purpose(s) for the bank's BOLI program(s) (e.g. key man, employee benefit cost recovery, funding deferred compensation plans, insurance on borrowers, etc).
- How policies were acquired (purchased, acquired via merger, DPC)
- List of employees covered and amount of insurance.
- Temporary (term) or permanent insurance.
- Original premium paid along with ongoing premium requirements.
- History of credit rates on policies.
- Whether CSV of the policy is invested in a general account of the carrier or in a separate account; if a separate account:
  - Obtain recent list of investments and provide a holdings summary.
  - Determine whether the bank purchased stable value protection (SVP). If so, obtain SVP and the parameters on which the SVP provider can limit its liability.
  - Obtain list of authorized investments and most current investment manager reports.
  - Determine if policies are leveraged.
- Obtain a list of changes in investments made in the prior year.
- Determine if policies are a modified endowment contract.

Objective 8: Using findings from the previous objectives and discussions with management and the bank EIC, determine whether to expand the procedures or develop a plan for corrective action. Consider whether:

- Management can adequately manage the bank's risk.
- Management can correct fundamental problems.
- To propose a strategy to address identified weaknesses and discuss strategy with the supervisory office.

Objective 9: After completing expanded procedures, determine whether additional verification procedures should be performed.

The extent to which examiners perform verification procedures is decided on a case-by-case basis after consultation with the ADC. Direct confirmation with the bank's customers must have prior approval of the ADC and district deputy comptroller. The Enforcement and Compliance Division, the district counsel, and the district accountant should also be notified when direct confirmations are being considered.

Objective 10: Conclude the review of the bank's investment activities.

1. Use the results of the foregoing procedures and other applicable examination findings to compose comments for the ROE.

2. Consult with the EIC and other examining personnel to identify and communicate to other examiners conclusions and findings from the investment review.

3. Update, organize, and reference work papers in accordance with PPM 5400-8 (rev).

4. Update Examiner View (e.g. ratings, core knowledge, MRAs, violations).

5. In discussion with the EIC, provide preliminary strategy recommendations for the next supervisory cycle.

Sensitivity to Market Risk

Conclusion: Sensitivity to market risk is rated (1, 2, 3, 4, 5).

Complete this section's objectives to assign the sensitivity to market risk component rating. When assigning the rating, the examiner should consult the EIC and other examining personnel. (**Note:** Market risk includes interest rate and price risk.) Consider the following UFIRS factors:

- Sensitivity of the bank's earnings or the economic value of its equity to adverse changes in interest rates, foreign exchange rates, commodity prices, or equity prices.
- Ability of management to identify, measure, monitor, and control exposure to market risk given the bank's size, complexity, and risk profile.
- Nature and complexity of IRR exposure arising from non-trading positions.
- Nature and complexity of market risk exposure arising from trading and foreign operations.

Core Assessment

Minimum Objective: Determine the sensitivity to market risk component rating, quantity of risk, and quality of risk management for IRR and price risk.

At the beginning of the supervisory activity, discuss with management actual or planned:

- Changes to IRR policy (e.g., limit structures, risk measurement).
- Changes in IRR management process.
- Material changes in the bank's asset and liability structure.
- Changes in the investment portfolio's impact on IRR.
- Changes in mortgage banking activities.
- Changes in the total volume of assets and liabilities accounted for at fair value through earnings, such as mortgage servicing rights and other real estate (ORE).
- Changes in the size of held-for-sale loan portfolios.

As requested, follow up on significant market risk-related audit or IT issues that examiners identified while reviewing the bank's audit and IT programs.

Obtain and review the following information:

- Results from OCC supervisory activities.
- Canary system information.
- UBPR and other OCC models.
- IRR reports.

If the bank's activities, risk profile, or risk controls have changed significantly, or if review of the above information raises substantive issues, the examiner should expand the activity's scope to include additional objectives or procedures. If this review does not result in significant changes or issues, conclude the sensitivity to market risk review by completing objective 11.

Other Assessment Objectives: Note: Examiners should select the objectives and procedures necessary to assess the bank's condition and risks.

Objective 1: Determine the scope of the sensitivity to market risk review.

1. Review supervisory information to identify previous problems that require follow-up in this area.

2. Discuss with the examiner responsible for completing the "Audit and Internal Controls" section of the core assessment whether significant audit findings require follow-up, or whether a review of audit work papers is required.

3. Discuss with the examiner responsible for completing the IT section of the core assessment whether significant deficiencies raise questions about the integrity, confidentiality, or availability of data and require follow-up.

4. Obtain and review the UBPR, Canary system information, other OCC-generated information, and the most recent bank-prepared reports used to monitor and manage IRR.

Objective 2: Evaluate balance sheet composition for types and levels of market risk.

Note: The examiner should refer to the "Interest Rate Risk" booklet of the *Comptroller's Handbook* on the considerations listed below.

1. Review and analyze the bank's balance sheet structure, off-balance-sheet activities, and trends in its balance sheet composition to identify major sources of IRR exposures. Consider:

   - Composition, risk characteristics, and re-pricing structures of the bank's loans, investments, liabilities, and off-balance-sheet items.
   - Whether the bank has substantial holdings of products with explicit or embedded options — prepayment options, caps, or floors — or products whose rates considerably lag market interest rates.
   - Various indices used by the bank to price its variable rate products (e.g., prime, Libor, Treasury) and the level or mix of products tied to these indices.
   - Use and nature of derivative products.
   - Other off-balance-sheet items (e.g., letters of credit, loan commitments).

2. Assess and discuss with management the bank's vulnerability to various movements in market interest rates including:

- Timing of interest rate changes and cash flows because of maturity or re-pricing mismatches.
- Changes in key spread or basis relationships.
- Changes in yield curve relationships.
- Nature and level of embedded options exposures.

3. Evaluate quantity of IRR posed by the loan portfolio. Consider the following:

   - If the bank has substantial volumes of loans with unspecified maturities, such as credit card loans, ascertain the effective maturities or re-pricing dates for those loans and assess the potential exposure for the bank.
   - If the bank has substantial volumes of medium- or longer-term fixed rate loans, assess how appreciation or depreciation of these loans could affect the bank's capital.
   - If the bank has substantial volumes of adjustable-rate mortgage products and other loans with explicit caps, evaluate the effect of those caps on the bank's future earnings and at what level of interest rates those caps would come into effect.
   - Assess how a substantial increase in interest rates would affect credit performance of the bank's loan portfolio.
   - If the bank incorporates and enforces prepayment penalties on medium- or longer-term fixed-rate loans, assess the effect of penalties on optionality of these loans.

4. In discussions with the examiner performing the investment review, determine IRR exposure posed by the investment portfolio.

5. If the bank has other sources of interest rate risk, such as mortgage servicing, credit card servicing, or other loan servicing assets, determine the sensitivity of these other sources to changes in interest rates and the potential impact on earnings and capital.

Objective 3: Evaluate derivatives and hedging activities

1. Review the use of derivative products. If the bank's exposure to derivative products is new or is of significant volume, expand the review and refer to the "Risk Management of Financial Derivatives" booklet of the *Comptroller's Handbook*.

2. Determine whether management uses off-balance-sheet derivative interest rate contracts to manage IRR exposure. Distinguish between the following activities:

   - Risk reduction activities that use derivatives to reduce volatility of earnings or to stabilize the economic value in a particular asset, liability, or business.
   - Positioning activities that use derivatives as investment substitutes or specifically to alter the bank's overall IRR profile.

3. Evaluate ongoing performance and effectiveness of hedging strategies.

Objective 4: Determine the type and adequacy of systems and MIS used to measure and monitor market risk.

1. Review level and trend of earnings-at-risk as indicated by the bank's risk measurement system. Risk to earnings should be measured under a minimum change in interest rates of plus or minus 200 basis points within a 12-month horizon.

2. Determine whether the risk management system used to measure earnings-at-risk is appropriate for the level and complexity of the bank's exposure. Determine whether major assumptions used to measure earnings-at-risk are reasonable.

3. Review exposure to the bank's economic value of equity. If the bank has a significant volume of medium-term to longer term re-pricing risk or options-related positions, review level and trend of exposure to economic value of equity. Risk to economic value of equity should be measured under a minimum change in interest rates of plus or minus 200 basis points within a 12-month horizon.

   Note: Calculating economic value of equity in base-case and rising and falling interest rate environments is the most effective risk measurement method for banks with significant longer term or options-related risk positions.

4. Determine whether the risk management system used to measure economic value-at-risk is appropriate for the level and complexity of the bank's exposure. Determine whether the major assumptions used to measure the economic value-at-risk are reasonable.

5. Identify the interest rate scenarios the bank uses to measure its potential IRR exposures. Assess adequacy of such rate scenarios. Do they:

   - Cover a reasonable range of potential interest rate movements in light of historical rate movements?
   - Allow the bank to consider the impact of at least a 200 basis point interest rate change over a one-year time horizon?
   - Reasonably anticipate holding periods or the time it may take to implement risk-mitigating actions given the bank's strategies, activities, market access, and management abilities?
   - Sufficiently capture potential risks arising from option-related positions?

6. Determine whether the bank's method of aggregating data is sufficient for analysis purposes given the nature and scope of the bank's IRR exposure(s). Consider the following:

   - If a bank has significant holdings of fixed-rate residential mortgage-related products, determine if coupon data are captured in sufficient detail to allow the bank to reasonably assess its prepayment and extension risks.
   - If a bank has significant holdings of adjustable-rate residential mortgage-related products, determine whether:

- Data on periodic and lifetime caps is captured in sufficient detail to permit adequate analysis.
- Effect of teaser rates as well as the type of rate indices used (current versus lagging) has been factored into the bank's risk measurement system.
- Data permits the bank to monitor the prepayment, default, and extension risks of the products.

7. Discuss with management the key assumptions underlying the bank's risk measurement models. Determine if:

- Assumptions are periodically reviewed for reasonableness.
- Major assumptions are documented and their sensitivity tested, and results communicated to senior management and the board at least annually.
- Assumptions are reasonable in light of the bank's product mix, business strategy, historical experience, and competitive market.
- Cash flow assumptions for products with option features are reasonable and consistent with the interest rate scenario that is being evaluated.

8. Determine whether assumptions used in the risk measurement system are documented with sufficient detail so as to allow verification of their reasonableness and accuracy.

9. Determine whether the bank's MIS provide sufficient historical, trend, and customer information to help bank personnel formulate and evaluate assumptions regarding customer behavior. Consider, where material, if information is available to analyze:

- Loan or mortgage-backed security prepayments.
- Early deposit withdrawals.
- Spreads between administered rate products, such as prime-based loans and non-maturity deposit accounts, and market rates of interest.

10. Determine whether the bank's MIS provides adequate and timely information for assessing the IRR exposure in the bank's current on- and off-balance-sheet positions. Determine whether information is available for all the bank's material portfolios, lines of business, and operating units. Consider:

- Current outstanding balances, rates/coupons, and re-pricing indices.
- Contractual maturities or re-pricing dates.
- Contractual caps or floors on interest rates.
- Scheduled amortizations and repayments.
- Introductory "teaser" rates.

11. Assess integrity, confidentiality, and availability of data used to recording, analyze, and report information related to IRR. Consider the input, processing, storage, access, and disposal of data. Focus on measures taken to limit access to the data and procedures in place to monitor system activities. Determine if these controls have been independently validated. Coordinate this review with examiners responsible for all functional areas of

the examination, including internal controls, to avoid duplication of effort. Share findings with the examiner reviewing IT.

Objective 5: Determine the characteristics, nature, and methods of management oversight of deposit accounts.

1. Analyze trends in deposit accounts. Consider:

   - Stability of offering rates.
   - Increasing or declining balances.
   - Large depositor concentrations.
   - Seasonal and cyclical variations in deposit balances.

2. Assess how the bank's deposits might react in different rate environments. Consider management's assumptions for:

   - Implicit or explicit floors or ceilings on deposit rates.
   - Rate sensitivity of the bank's depositor base and deposit products.
   - Determine the reasonableness of the bank's assumptions about the effective maturity of the bank's deposits and evaluate to what extent the bank's deposit base could offset interest rate risk.

3. Determine whether management performs a sensitivity analysis on deposit assumptions. In particular, determine whether management analyzes how its interest rate exposure may change if those assumptions change or prove to be incorrect and what action, if any, would be taken.

Objective 6: Determine the nature and adequacy of policies, processes, procedures and controls over market risk.

1. Obtain interest rate risk-related information from the examiner assigned to review board minutes. Review minutes of committees responsible for overseeing IRR.

2. Determine whether the board has approved policies that:

   - Establish a risk management process for identifying, measuring, monitoring, and controlling risk.
   - Establish risk tolerances, risk limits, and responsibility for managing risk.
   - Is appropriate for the nature and complexity of the bank's IRR exposure.
   - Is periodically reassessed in light of changes in market conditions and bank activities.

3. Assess effectiveness of management and the board in overseeing IRR. Consider:

   - Existence and reasonableness of board-approved limits for earnings or economic value-at-risk.

- Compliance with established risk limits.
- Adequacy of controls over the IRR management process.
- Management's understanding of IRR and ability to anticipate and respond appropriately to changes in interest rates or economic conditions.

4. Evaluate management's ability and effectiveness in managing IRR. Consider:

- Level of understanding of the dynamics of IRR.
- Ability to respond to competitive pressures in financial and local markets.
- Whether a balanced presentation of risk and return are appropriately considered in asset/liability strategies.
- Ability to anticipate and respond to adverse or changing economic conditions and interest rates.
- Whether staff skills are appropriate for the level of complexity and risk.

5. Determine whether a competent, independent review process periodically evaluates the effectiveness of the IRR management system. In reviewing measurement tools, evaluators should determine whether the assumptions used are reasonable and whether the range of interest rate scenarios considered are appropriate. Refer to the "Interest Rate Risk" booklet of the *Comptrollers Handbook* and OCC Bulletin 2000-16, "Risk Modeling — Model Validation."

6. Determine whether the internal controls are appropriate for the type and level of IRR of the bank. Consider the following:

- Do risk limits address a range of possible interest rate changes?
- Do risk limits address the potential impact of interest changes on both earnings and economic value of equity?
- Does the bank operate within established limits and risk tolerances?
- How are limit exceptions monitored, reported to management, and approved?
- Are separation of duties and lines of responsibility enforced?

Examiners should take into consideration the relevant controls listed in objective 5 of the "Audit and Internal Control" section of the core assessment. Examiners should also take into consideration other controls pertinent to IRR.

7. Assess integrity, confidentiality, and availability of data used to record, analyze, and report information related to IRR. Consider input, processing, storage, access, and disposal of data. Focus on measures taken to limit access to the data and procedures in place to monitor system activities. Determine if these controls have been independently validated. Coordinate this review with the examiners responsible for all functional areas of the examination, including internal control, to avoid duplication of effort. Share findings with the examiner reviewing IT.

8. Using the findings under this objective, determine whether the risk management system to identify, measure, monitor, and control IRR is effective.

Objective 7: Determine the level of price risk.

1. If the bank engages in trading activities, has investments denominated in foreign currencies, or engages in banking activities whose value changes are reflected in the income statement, consider:

    - Quantity of risks in relation to bank capital and earnings.
    - Quality of risk management systems including:
        - Ability or expertise of bank management.
        - Adequacy of risk management systems.

2. Determine whether appropriate accounting treatment is used (i.e., fair value accounting).

    For additional guidance, refer to the "Large Bank Supervision" booklet of the *Comptroller's Handbook* and other OCC guidance on trading activities, investments, ORE, and mortgage banking.

Objective 8: Using the findings from meeting the foregoing objectives, determine the significance of market risk (IRR, price risk) to the bank's capital and earnings.

Consult with the EIC and other examining personnel to decide whether the aggregate level or direction of risk noted during the review of sensitivity to market risk has had, or is expected to have, an adverse impact on the bank's capital or earnings. Refer to the "Risk Assessment System" section. Comment as necessary.

Objective 9: Determine whether to expand the procedures or develop a plan for corrective action. Consider whether:

- Management can adequately manage the bank's risks.
- Management can correct fundamental problems.
- To propose a strategy to address identified weaknesses and discuss strategy with the supervisory office.

Refer to booklets of the *Comptroller's Handbook* for expanded procedures.

Objective 10: After completing expanded procedures, determine whether additional verification procedures should be performed.

The extent to which examiners perform verification procedures is decided on a case-by-case basis after consultation with the ADC. Direct confirmation with the bank's customers must have prior approval of the ADC and district deputy comptroller. The Enforcement and Compliance Division, the district counsel, and the district accountant should also be notified when direct confirmations are being considered.

Objective 11: Conclude the review of the bank's sensitivity to market risk.

1. Use results of the foregoing procedures and other applicable examination findings to compose comments (e.g., sensitivity to market risk, MRAs) for the ROE.

2. Consult with the EIC and other examining personnel to identify and communicate to other examiners conclusions and findings from the sensitivity to market risk review that are relevant to other areas being reviewed.

3. Update, organize, and reference work papers in accordance with PPM 5400-8 (rev).

4. Update Examiner View (e.g., ratings, core knowledge, MRAs, violations).

5. In discussion with the EIC, provide preliminary conclusions about:

   - Quantity of risk.
   - Quality of risk management.
   - Aggregate level and direction of interest rate, price, foreign currency translation, or other applicable risk. Complete the summary conclusions in the "Risk Assessment System" section.
   - Supervisory strategy recommendations.

Information Technology

Conclusion: URSIT composite rating is (1, 2, 3, 4, 5).

Complete this section's objectives to assign the IT composite rating using as a guide OCC Bulletin 99-3, "Uniform Rating System for Information Technology (URSIT)," and OCC Memorandum 2001-2, "Composite Rating for IT." The composite URSIT rating should reflect:

- Adequacy of the bank's risk management practices.
- Management of IT resources.
- Integrity, confidentiality, and availability of automated information.
- Degree of supervisory concern posed by the bank.

To assign the rating, the examiner should consult the EIC, examiners assigned to review management and audit, and other examining personnel to avoid duplication of effort. Although the OCC does not assign URSIT component ratings to the financial banks it supervises, risks arising from the areas covered by the component ratings are considered when assigning the URSIT composite rating.

Core Assessment

Minimum Objective: Determine the IT composite rating, quantity of operational risk, and quality of operational risk management.

At the beginning of the supervisory activity, discuss with management the following:

- Actual security events or service interruptions during the supervisory cycle.
- Changes in the financial condition of, or quality of service provided by, IT vendors and servicers.
- Actual or planned changes in vendors, systems, applications, distribution channels, or personnel.
- Changes in the audit plan or risk assessment relating to IT areas.
- Changes in the information security or contingency planning processes.
- Changes in the processes or reports management uses to monitor IT activity.
- Impact of the changes noted above on the bank's written information security program.

Follow up on significant IT-related audit issues identified by the examiner reviewing the bank's audit program.

Obtain and review the following information:

- Results from OCC supervisory activities.
- Results of tests of the bank's information security program and management's response.

- Results of tests of the bank's contingency plan and management's response.
- IT audit risk assessment.
- Annual report to the board required by 12 CFR 30, appendix B.
- IT-related MIS reports, including recent fraud and processing losses.
- Documentation for major IT initiatives.

If the bank's activities, risk profile, or risk controls have changed significantly, or if review of the above information raises substantive issues, the examiner should expand the activity's scope to include additional objectives or procedures. If this review does not result in significant changes or issues, conclude the IT review by completing objective 11.

Other Assessment Objectives: Note: Examiners should select the objectives and procedures necessary to assess the bank's condition and risks.

Objective 1: Determine the scope of the IT review.

1. Review the supervisory information to identify previous problems that require follow-up in this area.

2. Discuss with the examiner responsible for completing the "Audit and Internal Controls" section of the core assessment whether significant IT audit findings require follow-up or whether a review of audit work papers is required. Ensure that the scope of the IT audit includes testing of the bank's information security program and contingency plan, as well as the annual report to the board required by 12 CFR 30, appendix B. If a more detailed review of the IT audit is necessary, refer to the "Audit" booklet of the FFIEC *IT Examination Handbook.*

3. Discuss with examiners assigned to other areas their assessments of integrity, confidentiality, and availability of data used record, analyze, and report information.

4. If not previously provided, obtain and review lists describing the complexity of the bank's processing environment and reports management uses to supervise the IT area, including but not limited to:

   - List of technology vendors and servicers, description of products or services provided, and bank's analysis of vendors' and servicers' financial condition.
   - A report or diagram that illustrates computer systems and networks, application and software deployment, vendor and external connectivity, and data flows, including primary data repositories.
   - Reports used to monitor computer activity, network performance, system capacity, security violations, and network intrusion attempts.

5. Determine in discussions with management:

   - How management administers and controls IT activities throughout the organization.

- Significant changes or planned changes in systems, applications, distribution channels, or personnel since the last examination.
- How management monitors quality and reliability of outsourced services and support functions.

6. Review and consider other factors:

- New regulatory guidance.
- Actual or planned organizational changes.
- Significance of the system or application in supporting bank products and services.
- Volume or average dollar size of transactions processed.
- Overall complexity of the bank's IT environment.
- Management reliance on the application or its output.
- Recent audit coverage provided internally or externally.
- Scope of the most recent OCC supervisory activity and changes since that review.

7. Using information obtained above, determine which IT processes represent the most significant risks to the bank. The following table lists some areas that examiners should consider:

IT Processes	Systems	Applications
<ul><li>Board and management oversight</li><li>Vendor management</li><li>System controls and data integrity</li><li>Information security and compliance with 12 CFR 30 appendix B</li><li>Business continuity</li><li>Providing services to other financial institutions</li><li>Project management</li><li>System development with in-house programming</li></ul>	<ul><li>Mainframe or midrange system</li><li>In-house networks</li><li>Departmental LANs</li><li>Wireless networks</li><li>Imaging systems</li><li>Item processing systems</li></ul>	<ul><li>Core applications (e.g., general ledger, loans, deposits)</li><li>Electronic banking</li><li>Wire transfer</li><li>Trust processing</li><li>Mortgage processing</li><li>Credit cards</li></ul>

8. If an area of higher risk is identified (e.g., in-house programming, account aggregator, certificate authority, cross border Internet banking, online account origination, Internet service provider, or providing automated services to other financial institutions), expand the review to assess additional risks inherent in such activities using procedures from the FFIEC *IT Examination Handbook*.

Objective 2: Assess the adequacy of IT management including oversight of technological resources and strategic planning

1. Obtain technology-related information from the examiner assigned to review board minutes. Review minutes of committees responsible for overseeing and coordinating IT resources and activities to determine user involvement and organizational priorities.

2. Review organizational charts, job descriptions, compensation, turnover, and training programs to ensure that the bank has a sufficient number of technology personnel with the expertise the bank requires (consider the bank's outsourcing arrangements).

3. Review the bank's strategic planning as it relates to IT and determine if the goals and objectives are consistent with the bank's overall business strategy. Consider whether:

   - IT audit risk assessment and the Business Continuity Planning Impact Analysis are included in the planning process.
   - IT has the ability to meet business needs.
   - Strategic plan defines the IT environment.

4. Review documentation supporting major projects or initiatives to determine effectiveness of technology planning, implementation, and follow-up activities. Consider:

   - Decision process, including options considered and basis for final selection.
   - Reasonableness of implementation plans, including periodic milestones.
   - Effectiveness of monitoring of implementation activities.
   - Whether validation testing of new programs or systems is conducted before putting the programs into production.

5. Discuss pending litigation and insurance coverage pertaining to IT activities with the examiner responsible for evaluating bank management. Ensure adequacy of insurance coverage for employee fidelity, IT equipment and facilities, e-banking activities, loss resulting from business interruptions, and items in transit.

6. Review MIS reports for significant IT systems and activities to ensure that risk identification, measurement, control, and monitoring are commensurate with the complexity of the bank's technology and operating environment. Consider:

   - Systems capacity, including peak processing volumes.
   - Up-time performance and processing interruptions.
   - Network monitoring, including penetration attempts and intruder detection.
   - Activity logs and security reports for operations, program and parameter changes, terminals use, etc.
   - Volume and trends of losses from errors, fraud, or un-reconciled items.

7. Assess timeliness, completeness, accuracy, and relevance of MIS for IT systems and operational risk. Consider source of reports, controls over report preparation, and independent validation of report accuracy.

Objective 3: Assess the effectiveness of the bank's management and monitoring of vendor or servicer activities. Consider the guidance in the "Outsourcing Technology Services" booklet of the FFIEC *IT Examination Handbook*.

1. Obtain the bank's vendor management policy and procedures to determine how the bank assesses risks associated with technology service provider relationships. Review the policy and practices for adequacy. Determine if the policy has board or IT committee level approval. Use procedures below to determine if the bank is in compliance with policy.

2. Evaluate the vendor or servicer selection process, particularly if a change in vendors or new products or services have been implemented since the last examination or anticipated during this supervisory cycle. Consider whether:

   - References were checked.
   - Financial condition was evaluated.
   - Insurance and disaster recovery plans were evaluated.
   - Information security practices are sufficient and meet regulatory guidelines.

3. Review contract guidelines, including customer privacy protections. Consider whether:

   - Contract contains adequate measurable service level agreements.
   - Allowed pricing methods adversely affect the bank's safety and soundness.
   - Required contract clauses address financial reporting, right to audit, ownership of data and programs, and data confidentiality.
   - Application source code and documentation for software developed or maintained by the vendor or server are available (generally applies to turnkey software).

4. Assess whether the bank monitors the vendor's or servicer's performance under the contract. Consider whether:

   - Servicer's financial information is available and analyzed.
   - Bank reviews servicer's operations and security audits.
   - Bank is meeting key level-of-service agreements.
   - Service provider's disaster recovery program and testing are effective.
   - Information security practices are sound.
   - Bank participates in user groups and other mechanisms to communicate and influence the service provider.

Objective 4: Assess the adequacy of controls to ensure integrity of data and resulting MIS.

1. Determine that system and network administrator access is appropriately monitored and adequately controlled. Determine whether segregation of duties exists between the responsibility for networks and the responsibility for computer operations. Evaluate

overall separation of duties and responsibilities in the bank operations and data processing areas.

2. Review controls and audit trails over file change requests (e.g., address changes, due dates, loan payment extensions or renewals, loan or deposit interest rates, and service charge indicator). Consider:

   - Individuals authorized to make changes and potential conflicting job responsibilities.
   - Documentation and audit trail of authorized changes.
   - Procedures used to verify accuracy of file changes.

3. Assess adequacy of controls over changes to systems, programs, data files, and personal-computer-based applications. Consider:

   - Procedures for implementing program updates, releases, and changes.
   - Controls to restrict and monitor use of data-altering utilities.
   - Process that management uses to select system and program security settings (i.e., whether settings were made based on sound technical advice or were default settings).
   - Controls to prevent unauthorized changes to system and programs security settings.
   - Process and authorizations to change application parameters.

4. Determine whether employees' levels of online access (blocked, read-only, update, override, etc.) match current job responsibilities.

5. Evaluate effectiveness of password administration for employee and customer passwords considering the complexity of the processing environment and type of information accessed. Consider:

   - Whether passwords are confidential (known only to the employee or customer).
   - Whether procedures to reset passwords ensure confidentiality.
   - Frequency of required changes in passwords.
   - Password design (number and type of characters).
   - Security of passwords while stored in computer files, during transmission, and on printed activity logs and reports.

6. Determine whether the bank has removed or reset default profiles and passwords from new systems and equipment, and determine whether access to the system administrator level is adequately controlled.

Objective 5: Evaluate the effectiveness of controls to protect data confidentiality (i.e., to prevent inadvertent disclosure of confidential information). Determine compliance with 12 CFR 30, appendix B, "Guidelines Establishing Information Security Standards."

1. Obtain the bank's annual information security risk assessment. Review risk assessment to determine whether the bank has:

- Identified and ranked information assets (customer information that the bank houses, maintains, utilizes, and uses to conduct transactions).
- Identified all reasonable threats to the bank.
- Analyzed technical and organizational vulnerabilities.
- Considered potential effect of a security breach on customers and the bank.
- Update risk assessment to reflect changes in new products or services or changes in external conditions.

2. Determine if risk assessment provides adequate support for security strategy, controls, and testing plan implemented by the bank.

3. Review information security policy to ensure that it sufficiently addresses the following:

- Authentication and authorization.
- Network access controls.
- Physical controls over access to hardware, software, media storage, data disposal, and paper records.
- System configuration.
- Operating system access.
- Intrusion detection and response.
- Service provider oversight.
- Encryption controls.
- Employee training.

4. Evaluate systems used to monitor access and detect unauthorized internal or external attempts to access the bank's systems (e.g., intruder detection, review of activity logs). Determine whether the bank has an intrusion response and customer notification program that meets requirements of OCC Bulletin 2005-13, "Response Programs for Unauthorized Access to Customer Information and Customer Notice: Final Guidance." Evaluate need for or adequacy of testing (i.e., vulnerability assessments or penetration testing) the more complex aspects of the bank's security program. If the bank has had a breach in security, determine why and what was done to correct the issue and improve security.

5. Evaluate control and security for data transmitted to or from remote locations. Consider:

- Type of data transmitted.
- Use of encryption or other security techniques (e.g., firewalls).
- Access to network components (e.g., servers, routers, phone lines) that support data transmission.

6. Evaluate controls over remote access (by modem or Internet link) to ensure use and access by authorized users only.

7. If the bank offers e-banking services (e.g., transaction Internet banking, online cash management, e-bill payment, or telephone banking), determine whether the bank is in

conformance with OCC Bulletin 2005-35 "Authentication in an Internet Banking Environment."

8. Determine whether the bank's information security program conforms with 12 CFR 30, appendix B, "Guidelines Establishing Information Security Standards." The program must:

- Be approved and overseen by the board.
- Be adjusted for changes in the bank's (or servicer's) processing environment or systems.
- Be tested and validated.
- Provide employee training.
- Include an annual report to the board (or committee) describing overall status of the program and the bank's conformance with guidelines.

9. Determine whether the bank's risk assessment process for customer information and its test of key controls, systems, and procedures in the bank's information security program are commensurate with sensitivity of the information and complexity and scope of the bank's activities.

Objective 6: Assess the adequacy of the bank's policies and procedures to ensure the availability of automated information and ongoing support for technology-based products and services.

1. Review business impact analysis. Determine whether mission-critical activities are identified and prioritized and maximum allowable downtimes are considered.

2. Review business resumption contingency plan to ensure that the plan is consistent with requirements of interagency guidelines. Consider whether:

- Plan complies with corporate-wide focus of interagency guidelines and is appropriate for the organization's size and complexity.
- Plan takes into account personnel, facilities, technology, telecommunications, vendors, utilities, geographical diversity, and data records.
- Plan considers reasonable scenarios, significant threats, and vulnerabilities.
- Board of directors or a board committee annually reviews the plan.

3. Review annual validation of the contingency plan, including backup and alternate site test findings. Determine whether the board and senior management were apprised of the scope and results of the backup test, whether they have confidence that the plan operates as expected, and whether the plan meets requirements of the business impact analysis. Consider whether:

- Test has realistic conditions.
- Test utilizes actual backup systems and data files, and establishes network connectivity.
- Post-test analysis is conducted with recommendations and plans for corrective action.

- Test is adequate for the bank's size and complexity.
- Test validates recovery time frames.

4. If third-party servicers provide mission-critical activities or systems, ensure that the bank's recovery plan is compatible with business recovery plans of the servicers. Determine whether the bank has reviewed primary vendor testing results.

5. Evaluate planning for event management activities. Consider:

- Emergency procedures and evacuation plans.
- Response to network attack or penetration.
- Reporting to appropriate regulatory or law enforcement agencies.

6. Assess processes and procedures to prevent destruction of electronic files and other storage media. Consider:

- Frequency of file backup.
- Access to backup files and storage media (e.g., disks, tapes).
- Location of off-site file storage.
- Virus protection for networks and personal computers.

7. Determine whether only authorized personnel have access to the computer area, electronic media, supplies of negotiable items. Determine whether equipment and networks supporting mission-critical services are appropriately secured. Consider physical security and environmental controls.

8. Determine how management ensures that record retention practices are in compliance with legal, regulatory, and operational requirements. Consider records at the bank, at service provider locations, and in off-site or long-term storage.

Objective 7: Assess the bank's processes for managing information security risk and operational risk using the findings from meeting the foregoing objectives, by discussing the processes with key managers, and by analyzing applicable internal or external audit reports.

1. Determine whether the volume and nature of fraud and processing losses, network and processing interruptions, customer-reported processing errors, or audit criticisms lower quality of automated activities and services.

2. Determine whether the bank's risk assessment process for customer information and its test of key controls, systems, and procedures in the bank's information security program are commensurate with the sensitivity of the information and complexity and scope of the bank's activities.

3. Assess timeliness, completeness, accuracy, and relevance of MIS for operational risk. Consider the source of reports, controls over report preparation, and independent

validation of report accuracy. Risk management reports should cover major sources of operational risk identified above.

4. Using the findings from meeting the previous objectives, combined with the information from the EIC and other examining personnel, make preliminary judgments on the quality of operational risk management systems. Consider whether:

- Management recognizes and understands existing and emerging risks.
- Management measures risk in an accurate and timely manner.
- Board establishes, communicates, and controls risk limits.
- Management accurately and appropriately monitors established risk limits.

Objective 8: Using the findings from meeting the foregoing objectives, identify significant risk exposures from the IT review.

Develop preliminary assessments of quantity of operational risk, quality of operational risk management, aggregate operational risk, and direction of operational risk. Refer to the "Risk Assessment System" section. Comment as necessary.

Consult with the EIC and other examining personnel to identify findings from the IT review that have significance for other risk rating categories.

Objective 9: Determine whether to expand the procedures or develop a plan for corrective action. Consider whether:

- Management can adequately manage the bank's risks.
- Management can correct fundamental problems.
- To propose a strategy to address identified weaknesses and discuss strategy with the supervisory office.

Refer to booklets of the *Comptroller's Handbook* or FFIEC *IT Examination Handbook* for expanded procedures.

Objective 10: After completing expanded procedures, determine whether additional verification procedures should be performed.

The extent to which examiners perform verification procedures is decided on a case-by-case basis after consultation with the ADC. Direct confirmation with the bank's customers must have prior approval of the ADC and district deputy comptroller. The Enforcement and Compliance Division, the district counsel, and the district accountant should also be notified when direct confirmations are being considered.

Objective 11: Conclude the review of the bank's IT activities.

1. Provide management with a list of deficiencies for consideration.

2. Consult with the EIC and other examining personnel to identify and communicate to other examiners conclusions and findings from the IT review that are relevant to other areas being reviewed.

3. Use results of the foregoing procedures and other applicable examination findings to compose comments (e.g., IT, MRAs) for the ROE.

4. Update, organize, and reference work papers in accordance with PPM 5400-8 (rev).

5. Update Examiner View (e.g., ratings, core knowledge, MRAs, violations).

6. In discussion with the EIC, provide preliminary conclusions about:

   - Quantity of risk.
   - Quality of risk management.
   - Aggregate level and direction of operational risk or other applicable risk. Complete the summary conclusions in the "Risk Assessment System" section.
   - Supervisory strategy recommendations.

Asset Management

Conclusions:
Aggregate Asset management risk is (low, moderate, high)
UITRS ratings: Composite (1, 2, 3, 4, 5)
Management (1, 2, 3, 4, 5)
Operations, Internal Controls, and Auditing (1, 2, 3, 4, 5)
Earnings (1, 2, 3, 4, 5)
Compliance (1, 2, 3, 4, 5)
Asset Management (1, 2, 3, 4, 5).

The examiner completes appropriate objectives from this section to assign the asset management aggregate risk rating. This rating is derived from an assessment of the quantity of risk and the quality of risk management for those activities.

In accordance with the "Bank Supervision Process" booklet of the *Comptroller's Handbook*, the examiner assigns the UITRS composite and component ratings. In UITRS, fiduciary activities are assigned a composite rating based on an evaluation and rating of five essential components of a bank's fiduciary activities. These components address management; operations, internal controls, and auditing; earnings; compliance; and asset management.

When assigning the aggregate risk rating and UITRS rating, the examiner consults the EIC; examiners assigned to review management, audit and internal controls, IT, and earnings; and other examining personnel.

Core Assessment

Minimum Objective: Determine the quantity of risk and the quality of risk management for asset management and assign UITRS composite and component ratings.

At the beginning of the supervisory activity, discuss with management:

- Actual or planned changes in:
  - Management, key and operational staff including portfolio managers and advisors.
  - Board and fiduciary committee structure and oversight.
  - Facilities and operating systems, processes, and controls.
  - Audit plan or risk assessment relating to asset management areas.
  - Policies, procedures, and controls.
- New products and services.
- New or expanded third-party vendor relationships, including investment advisors.
- Strategic plans for asset management activities.
- Asset management business plan, budget, or budgeting process.

- Asset management earnings performance.
- Significant transactions with related parties including businesses of directors, officers, or employees of the bank and bank affiliates.

Obtain and review the following information:

- Results from OCC supervisory activities.
- Most recent committee minutes and information packages.
- Asset management organizational chart.
- Most recent financial reports, including budget and variance reports.
- Appropriate UBPR pages.
- Policies and procedures if significant changes or additions have been made.
- Asset management risk assessment.
- Audit and compliance reports and follow-up.
- Call report Schedule RC-T Fiduciary and Related Services for significant changes in account types and volumes.

Follow up on significant asset management-related audit or IT issues identified by the examiners reviewing the bank's audit and IT programs:

- Discuss outstanding asset management audit or IT issues with management.
- If warranted based on the above discussions or if requested by the examiners reviewing audit and IT, obtain and review a risk-based sample of internal asset management audit or IT reports and management follow-up.
- Discuss with management changes in scope, personnel, or frequency of the asset management audit function that could increase or decrease the function's reliability.
- Discuss with management changes in asset management IT processes or MIS that could increase or decrease their reliability.

Select a risk-based sample of fiduciary accounts opened since the last examination. The sample should be representative of the type and size of accounts opened during the time period of the review and should focus on accounts with higher risk potential such as personal trusts with complex family relationships or unique asset types, insider accounts, complex retirement accounts, and successor and co-trustee accounts. Determine whether:

- Accounts were opened in compliance with policy and applicable law.
- Risks associated with new accounts are consistent with the bank's business plan and risk tolerance.

If the bank's activities, risk profile, or risk controls have changed significantly or if review of the above information raises substantive issues, the examiner should expand the activity's scope to include additional objectives or procedures. If this review does not result in significant changes or issues, conclude the review of asset management activities by completing objective 10.

Other Assessment Objectives: Note: Examiners should select objectives and procedures necessary to assess the bank's condition and risks.

Objective 1: Determine the scope of the asset management review.

1. Review the supervisory information to identify previous problems that require follow-up in this area.

2. As necessary, obtain and review the following information:

   - Asset management organizational chart and manager job descriptions.
   - Policies and operating procedures.
   - Strategic and business plans.
   - Committee minutes and information reports.
   - Asset management reports provided to the board of directors.
   - Compliance reviews and management responses.
   - Descriptions of data processing and accounting systems including third-party vendor arrangements.
   - Management reports including those used to monitor new and closed accounts, account investment reviews, overdrafts, financial results, exceptions and compliance/risk information related to asset management.
   - Information on investment activities, including investment performance and approved securities lists.
   - Operational reports, such as transaction volumes and reconcilement reports.
   - Fee schedules.
   - A report on significant losses and settlements sustained since last fiduciary supervisory activity.
   - Regulatory reports.

3. Discuss with the examiner responsible for completing the "Audit and Internal Controls" section of the core assessment whether significant audit findings require follow-up or whether a review of audit work papers is required.

4. Discuss with the examiner responsible for completing the IT section of the core assessment whether significant deficiencies raise questions about integrity, confidentiality, or availability of data and require follow-up.

5. Discuss pending litigation and insurance coverage pertaining to asset management activities with the examiner responsible for evaluating bank management.

Objective 2: Determine the quality and effectiveness of board and management supervision of asset management lines of business.

1. Evaluate board supervision by considering the following:

- Committee structures, responsibilities, and reporting standards.
- Management selection and appraisal processes.
- Strategic planning and monitoring processes.
- Information reports received from committees and management.
- Policy review and approval processes.
- Oversight of audit and compliance functions.
- Use of legal counsel and the monitoring of litigation.
- Insurance coverage reviews.

2. Evaluate management by reviewing quality of the following:

- Management and support staff, including competence, turnover, and succession planning.
- Policies and procedures, including compliance.
- Department reports provided to management committees on a monthly, quarterly, or annual basis.
- Internal controls, including system access and segregation of duties.
- Audit and compliance functions, including responses to deficiencies and recommendations.
- Supervision of third-party service providers.
- Insurance coverage and review processes.
- Litigation management.
- Complaint resolution processes.

3. Evaluate the earnings of asset management activities. Identify non-recurring income or expense items and assess trends.

4. For national trust banks, determine the adequacy of capital and liquidity monitoring in accordance with OCC Bulletin 2007-21, "Supervision of National Trust Banks – Revised Guidance on Capital and Liquidity".

5. Consider the findings from the other examination sections and incorporate them into the board and management evaluation.

Objective 3: Determine the quantity of risk and quality of risk management relating to the administration of fiduciary accounts.

1. Determine types and level of risk associated with the administration of fiduciary and related accounts. Discuss the following with management:

- Volume and types of fiduciary accounts under administration.
- Types and level of policy exceptions, audit and internal control deficiencies, and law violations internally identified and reported.
- Amount and status of significant litigation and client complaints.

2. Review account acceptance processes. For fiduciary accounts, evaluate compliance with 12 CFR 9.6(a), Pre-acceptance Reviews. Determine whether the process:

- Is formalized and adequately documented.
- Includes Enhanced Due Diligence and Customer Identification Program procedures.
- Ensures appropriate information is obtained and effectively used.
- Includes appropriate approval process for policy exceptions.

3. Review policies and procedures for fiduciary account administration. Policies and procedures should address:

- Compliance with applicable fiduciary law.
- Account administration guidelines.
- Policy exceptions including monitoring and reporting processes.
- Customer complaint resolution procedures.

4. Evaluate cash management processes:

- Identify and review large, un-invested or undistributed funds and discuss them with management. Determine whether administration is appropriate and complies with 12 CFR 9.10, Fiduciary Funds Awaiting Investment or Distribution.
- Review account overdrafts, giving attention to large and long-standing items. Determine why they exist and discuss management's plans to resolve them.

5. Select a risk-based sample of recently accepted fiduciary and related accounts. The sample should focus on accounts with higher-risk potential, such as personal trusts with complex family relationships or unique asset types, insider accounts, complex retirement accounts, and successor and co-trustee accounts. Consider requirements of objectives 4 and 5 when selecting the sample. For each account, determine compliance with internal policy and applicable law and whether the account acceptance process was adequate and effective. For fiduciary accounts, include the pre-acceptance and initial post acceptance review required by 12 CFR 9.6 (a) and (b).

6. Select a risk-based sample of established fiduciary and related accounts, including personal, retirement, and corporate trust accounts and Individual Retirement Accounts. Review each account and determine whether administrative processes and controls are adequate and effective. Consider whether account administration:

- Complies with terms of the governing instrument, applicable law, court orders, and directions and is consistent with needs and circumstances of account beneficiaries.
- Includes account reviews in accordance with 12 CFR 9.6(c) and other applicable law.
- Avoids unauthorized conflicts of interest and self-dealing.
- Charges and reports accurate account fees and complies with compensation provisions of 12 CFR 9.15, document provisions, and Uniform Principal and Income Act.

7. For personal fiduciary accounts, evaluate the discretionary distribution processes:

- Is the decision-making authority for discretionary distributions expressly defined and communicated to all personnel?
- Are decisions fully documented and authorized by designated personnel or committees?
- Are distributions consistent with the guidelines established in the governing instrument?

8. For Individual Retirement Accounts, determine whether the bank is fulfilling its duties and responsibilities in compliance with Internal Revenue Code section 408 and the prohibited transaction provisions of Internal Revenue Code section 4975.

9. For retirement accounts, determine compliance with the applicable sections of the Employee Retirement Income Security Act (ERISA), including prudence requirements of section 404, asset diversification, compliance with plan provisions and section 406, prohibited transactions.

10. If potential violations of ERISA were identified during the retirement account review, consult with the EIC and ADC and report to the OCC Asset Management Group for possible referral to the Department of Labor. Refer to OCC Bulletin 2006-24 "Interagency Agreement on ERISA Referrals."

For corporate trust accounts, determine whether the bank is fulfilling all its duties and responsibilities, which may include serving as paying agent, disbursing agent, registrar, and trustee.

Objective 4: Determine the quantity of risk and the quality of risk management relating to conflicts of interest and self-dealing.

1. Determine whether conflicts of interests have been reported internally. Discuss the following with management:

- Processes used to identify, assess, and resolve conflicts of interest.
- Significant changes in policies, processes, personnel, or controls.
- Internal or external factors that could affect conflicts of interests.

2. Review policies and procedures developed to control the risks associated with conflicts of interest and self-dealing. Consider the requirements of:

- 12 CFR 9.5, Policies and Procedures.
- 12 CFR 9.12, Self-dealing and Conflicts of Interest.
- 12 CFR 12.7(a), Securities Trading Policies and Procedures.
- ERISA.
- Other federal and state law and court rulings.
- Industry practices relating to employee ethics and acceptable behaviors.

3. Determine whether conflicts of interest or self-dealing were identified during the fiduciary account administration review and whether policies, processes, and controls are effective.

4. Review processes and controls for discretionary funds awaiting investment or distribution and determine compliance with the provisions of 12 CFR 9.10. Determine whether the bank:

   - Does not allow discretionary funds to remain un-invested or undistributed any longer than is reasonable for proper management of the account.
   - Obtains rate of return for the funds that is consistent with applicable law.
   - Sets aside adequate collateral for the portion of the funds deposited with the bank that exceed the FDIC insurance limit. Note: The deposit of discretionary funds with the bank may be prohibited by applicable law.

5. Review processes and controls governing fiduciary compensation and compliance with 12 CFR 9.15, fiduciary compensation, as well as the Uniform Principal and Income Act. Consider whether:

   - Fiduciary-related compensation complies with applicable law. If not set or governed by applicable law, fees must be reasonable for services provided.
   - Bank officers or employees act as co-fiduciary with the bank in the administration of fiduciary accounts and receive compensation for such services. Payment of compensation to a bank officer or employee serving as a co-fiduciary with the bank is prohibited unless specifically approved by the bank's board of directors.
   - Revisions or changes in fees charged to fiduciary accounts with set or fixed-fee schedules are appropriate and properly authorized.
   - Fee concessions for officers, directors, and other employees are granted under a general policy that is uniformly applied and approved.
   - Management obtains proper authorization for charging cash sweep and termination fees.
   - Policies and procedures address the receipt and acceptance of 12 b-1 fees.

6. Review process used by the bank to administer own bank and bank holding company stock. This includes decisions and documentation to retain stock and procedures for voting proxies. Determine whether:

   - Bank has a policy that prevents purchase of own bank and bank holding company stock in discretionary accounts.
   - Bank complies with 12 USC 61 and does not vote shares of own bank stock in the election of directors.
   - Bank considers the best interest of beneficiaries and applicable law when voting shares of its own bank holding company stock.

- Bank considers the best interest of beneficiaries when deciding to vote proxies for companies in which directors, officers, employees, or related organizations have an interest that might interfere with the bank's judgment.

7. If mutual funds (or proprietary mutual funds) advised by an affiliate are used in discretionary accounts, evaluate the bank's procedures for ensuring that proprietary funds are appropriate fiduciary investments. Consider whether:

- Such investment is authorized under applicable law.
- Proprietary mutual funds are monitored in much the same way as unaffiliated funds.
- Fee practices comply with 12 CFR 9.12 and applicable law.
- Disclosures are made or the investment prospectus is delivered to appropriate parties in accordance with applicable law.

8. Review brokerage placement practices. Determine whether:

- Brokerage allocation decisions and brokerage fees are monitored to ensure that fees are reasonable relative to the services provided.
- Soft-dollar arrangements fall within safe harbor provisions of section 28(e) of the Securities and Exchange Act of 1934.
- Brokerage fees are not subject to arrangements that impair the bank's judgment or prevent the best execution of trades.
- Trades are fair and equitably allocated to all accounts, subject to applicable law.

9. If the bank uses an affiliated broker to effect securities transactions for fiduciary accounts, determine whether:

- Applicable law does not prohibit use of an affiliated broker.
- Bank does not profit from securities transactions executed through an affiliated broker. (Payment by bank to the affiliated broker can cover only the cost of executing the transaction).
- Bank provides adequate disclosure of such relationships to affected clients or obtains consent from parties with capacity to give consent.

Objective 5: Determine the quantity of risk and the quality of risk management relating to investment management services.

1. Review investment management policies and procedures. Policies should address:

- Compliance with applicable law including 12 CFR 9.11 and state laws' prudent investor requirements.
- Business goals and objectives, investment philosophy, fiduciary responsibilities, ethical culture, risk tolerance standards, and risk management framework.
- Descriptions of investment products and services.
- Use of investment policy statements.

- Periodic investment portfolio reviews.
- Investment research, including economic and capital market analyses and reporting.
- Securities trading policies and procedures (12 CFR 12.7) and brokerage placement processes.
- Selecting and monitoring third-party service providers.
- Portfolio MIS and technology applications.
- Proxy voting for discretionary accounts.

2. Evaluate processes used to develop, approve, implement, and monitor fiduciary account investment policies.

   Note: Refer to the "Investment Management Services" booklet of the *Comptroller's Handbook* and OCC Bulletin 96-25, "Fiduciary Risk Management of Derivatives and Mortgage-backed Securities."

3. Evaluate investment selection and acquisition processes. Consider:

   - Processes used to research, value, and estimate rates of return and correlations for potential investments.
   - Processes used to value portfolio assets and account for portfolio transactions.
   - Portfolio trading systems and controls.

4. Evaluate adequacy and effectiveness of risk reporting and exception tracking processes. Does the division maintain appropriate management reports relating to investment performance, risk levels, and policy exception identification and follow-up?

5. If the bank delegates investment management authority, review process used to select and monitor third-party investment managers or advisors. Refer to OCC Bulletin 2001-47, "Third-party Relationships: Risk Management Principles."

6. Select a sample of fiduciary accounts for which the bank has investment discretion or provides investment advice for a fee. If possible, select from the sample of accounts used in the fiduciary account administration review under objective 3. In reviewing these accounts:

   - Determine compliance with investment objectives and guidelines in the governing instrument, applicable law, as well as bank policies and procedures.
   - Determine that the investment objective is current and trust assets are invested consistently with the current asset allocation.
   - Investigate holdings of securities not on approved lists and review asset concentrations exceeding 10 percent of the market value of the account. Determine if retention is prudent.
   - Determine whether asset holdings (e.g., investments in own bank, affiliate stock or deposit products) could present a conflict of interest and whether proprietary mutual funds are properly supported.
   - Verify that client or co-trustee approvals are obtained where necessary.

- Determine whether unique assets are managed appropriately.
- Evaluate effectiveness of investment review processes in identifying and addressing investment-related issues (12 CFR 9.6).

7. For marketable securities, review the following:

- Quality of investment research and documentation, including use of third-party vendors.
- Use of approved securities lists. Evaluate process for maintaining such lists, including follow-up on sale or other disposition of assets from the list.
- Approval authorities and policy exception tracking systems.
- Monitoring processes to ensure compliance with applicable law and internal policies and procedures.

8. For investment company securities (mutual funds):

- Review quality of the investment analysis, selection, and approval processes.
- Review quality of information reports and ongoing monitoring. (Monitoring should consider such factors as investment performance, risks, and fees.)
- If the bank maintains an approved mutual fund list, determine the bank's policy on purchase or retention of unapproved mutual funds. If the bank invests in unapproved funds, determine whether these investments:
  - Are appropriately approved and adequately documented.
  - Comply with applicable law.
  - Are included on exception reports and adequately monitored.

9. For closely held businesses, determine whether:
- Closely held ownership interests are managed in accordance with terms of the governing instrument and other applicable laws. Consider:
  - Role of the bank and its fiduciary duties and responsibilities.
  - Quality and timeliness of decisions to acquire, retain, or dispose of such assets.
  - Quality of business valuation processes. Ensure adherence to Internal Revenue Services (IRS) Revenue Ruling 59-60 is part of the process.
  - Receipt and use of financial information on the business and its industry.
  - Management succession planning for closely held companies.
  - Quality of relationships with account beneficiaries, family members, and other investors.

- Bank employees serve on the board of directors, or in a similar capacity, of a closely held company. If so, does the bank:
  - Maintain adequate insurance coverage?
  - Reimburse the account for the payment of benefits or fees to the bank or its employees for representing the interests of beneficiaries, unless the governing document specifically authorizes the bank to receive such compensation?

10. For discretionary real estate investment, determine whether:

- Decisions to acquire, retain or dispose of the investment were appropriate and supported.
- Real estate valuation and inspection processes are adequate.
- Appropriate financial information on real estate and its market is periodically obtained and evaluated.
- Title to property is properly perfected.
- Environmental review was performed and completed before acceptance or acquisition.
- Adequate insurance coverage is maintained with the bank as loss payee.
- Real estate taxes are paid on time.
- Farm management accounts are properly administered and documented. Consider whether:
  - Bank has signed a contract with the owner that clearly details the bank's responsibilities.
  - Bank has signed leases with tenants that detail each party's responsibilities.
  - Farm manager keeps adequate records, including financial statements, tax returns, and periodic reports on the operation.

11. For real estate loans, evaluate the quality of:

- Loan underwriting standards.
- Collection processes and past-due trends.
- Collateral valuation and inspections processes.
- Tax payment processes.
- Insurance coverage.
- Management of environmental liability issues.

12. For mineral interests, determine whether:

- Receipt of lease, royalty, and delay rental payments is timely.
- Bank takes appropriate action if payments are not received.
- Working interests are reviewed for profitability and potential environmental hazards.
- Expenditures are analyzed and approved before they are paid.

13. Review a sample of the bank's collective investment funds and determine whether such funds are managed in compliance with 12 CFR 9.18. Evaluate effectiveness of the bank's processes for limiting participation in funds to eligible accounts.

    Note: Refer to the "Collective Investment Funds" booklet of the *Comptroller's Handbook.*

Objective 6: Determine the quantity of risk and the quality of risk management for fiduciary operations.

Note: Coordinate this review with examiners responsible for the major CAMELS/ITCC areas and the "Audit and Internal Controls" portion of the examination to avoid duplication of effort.

1. For asset management operations, consider audit and compliance reports of operational areas. Follow up on significant deficiencies and determine whether effective corrective action has been taken.

2. Discuss the following with the examiner reviewing IT and follow up with management:

   - Existing IT systems and planned changes to IT systems.
   - Whether IT systems are sufficient to support current and planned fiduciary activities.
   - Quality of the bank's information security and business resumption and contingency planning processes.
   - Quality of the bank's process for selecting and monitoring third-party vendors.
   - Logical access controls on computer systems to adequately segregate duties.

   Assess integrity, confidentiality, and availability of data used to record, analyze, and report information related to fiduciary operations. Consider input, processing, storage, access, and disposal of data. Focus on measures taken to limit access to data and procedures in place to monitor system activities. Determine if these controls have been independently validated. Coordinate this review with examiners responsible for all functional areas of the examination, including internal controls, to avoid duplication of effort. Share findings with the examiner reviewing IT.

3. Evaluate quality of written policies and procedures. Consider:

   - Approval authorities and accountability standards.
   - Separation of duties among transaction initiation, posting, settlement, asset control, and reconciling functions.
   - Cross training or rotation of duties.
   - Dual control or joint custody standards for financial records, money movement, and assets.
   - Third-party vendor administration.
   - Information security, business resumption, and contingency planning systems.

4. If the bank has outsourced data processing or other operational functions, evaluate the bank's process for selecting and monitoring third-party vendors. Discuss the process with management and document significant weaknesses. Consider the following in reaching conclusions:

   - Quality of due diligence review process.
   - Contract negotiation and approval process.
   - Risk assessment processes.
   - Compliance and audit division participation.

- Monitoring processes, such as the assignment of responsibility, frequency of reviews, and quality of information reports.
- Problem resolution processes.

For more information, refer to OCC Advisory Letter 2000-9, "Third Party Risk," and OCC Bulletin 2001-47, "Third Party Relationships: Risk Management Principles."

5. Review record keeping for compliance with 12 CFR 9.8, 12 CFR 12, and other applicable law. Determine whether the bank:

- Adequately documents establishment and termination of each fiduciary account and maintains adequate records.
- Retains fiduciary account records for three years from the termination of the account or the termination of litigation relating to the account, whichever comes later.
- Maintains fiduciary account records separate and distinct from other records of the bank.
- Maintains minimum trading records (12 CFR 12.3).
- Provides customer notifications consistent with 12 CFR 12.4 and 12 CFR 12.5.

6. Review controls over asset set-up and maintenance, including pricing, administration of corporate actions, including proxy voting, and income collection. Consider:

- Use of independent sources for information on assets.
- Use of asset models and secondary review over asset set-ups.
- Controls over changes to the security master file.
- Periodic asset pricing.
- Timely and accurate processing of corporate actions, such as stock dividends, stock splits, and proxy voting. Determine whether controls are in place to ensure timely action is taken on voluntary corporate actions, including obtaining approval from outside parties.
- Review distribution of proxy materials and disclosure of information about shareholders whose securities are registered in a bank nominee name for compliance with SEC Rules 17 CFR 240.14-17. Determine whether the bank:
  - Obtains a clear consent or denial for disclosure of beneficial owner information for each account.
  - Appropriately passes information received from issuers, such as proxies and annual reports, to beneficial owners.
  - Responds to issuers' requests for information in a timely manner.
- Review controls over income collection, including dividends and interest.

7. Review transaction processing controls. Consider:

- Timeliness and accuracy of transaction documentation and posting.
- Management of routine and non-routine manual instructions.
- Transaction and account balancing processes and controls.

- Controls over the release or disbursement of assets or funds.

8. Review balancing and reconcilement controls. Consider:

   - Transaction and account balancing processes and controls.
   - Reconcilement functions and exception reporting standards.
   - Controls for suspense (house) accounts.

9. Evaluate security trade settlement processes. Determine whether:

   - Proper trade instructions are received and documented.
   - Trade tickets are properly controlled and contain required information.
   - Broker confirmations are reconciled to trade tickets.
   - Failed trades are promptly identified and effectively addressed.
   - Confirmations are sent as required and contain required information.
   - Depository position changes are matched to changes on the bank's accounting system.
   - Policies and procedures have been established to prevent free riding (refer to Banking Circular 275, "Free Riding in Custody Accounts").

10. Evaluate asset custody and safekeeping processes and controls (12 CFR 9.13). Determine whether:

    - Fiduciary assets are placed in joint custody or control of not fewer than two fiduciary officers or employees.
    - Fiduciary account assets are kept separate from bank assets and other fiduciary account assets.
    - Third-party custodian or depository holds fiduciary assets. If so, determine whether such action is consistent with applicable law and supported by adequate safeguards and controls (e.g., dual control over free deliveries).
    - Fiduciary assets physically held by the bank are kept in a controlled vault or securities cage with access controls such as dual controls, vault entry records, asset tickets, physical security measures (12 CFR 21), and periodic vault counts.
    - Bank has adequate controls over unissued checks and securities.

    Refer to the "Custody Services" booklet of the *Comptroller's Handbook*.

11. Review processes and controls for the escheatment of unclaimed items. Consider whether the bank ages outstanding checks and suspense (house) account entries and files escheatment reports with the proper jurisdiction.

12. Review processes and controls for managing collateral set aside for self-deposits of fiduciary assets and compliance with 12 CFR 9.10(b) and state requirements, if applicable.

13. If the bank serves as transfer agent for a "qualifying security" under section 12 of the Securities Exchange Act of 1934, determine whether the bank has registered as a transfer agent by filing Form TA-1 with the OCC (17 CFR 240.17A).

If the bank is a registered transfer agent, open the Registered Transfer Agent Examination in Examiner View. Also, refer to OCC 2007-6, "Registered Transfer Agents: Transfer Agent Registration, Annual Reporting, and Withdrawal from Registration." If the bank is a transfer agent but is not required to register, ensure that appropriate controls are in place.

Objective 7: Assess the bank's retail brokerage program and determine the level of risk it poses to the bank and the effectiveness of program risk management.

Note: Most retail non-deposit investment products sales programs involve arrangements with affiliated or unaffiliated securities brokers that are regulated by the SEC. GLBA's functional regulation requirements apply.

1. If not previously provided, obtain and analyze bank-level information applicable to the retail brokerage program:

   - Board and oversight committee minutes and reports.
   - Policies and procedures.
   - Risk management, compliance, and internal audit reports.
   - Financial information.
   - Written agreement between the bank and the retail broker.
   - Complaints, litigation, and settlement information.

2. Determine level of risk to the bank from the program. Consider:

   - Nature and complexity of activities.
   - Financial significance to the bank's earnings and capital.
   - Identified deficiencies.

3. Assess effectiveness of the bank's oversight and risk management systems:

   - Evaluate appropriateness of the board and senior management reports for overseeing the bank's retail brokerage program.
   - Evaluate effectiveness of the initial and ongoing due diligence process in selecting and monitoring the securities broker.
   - Determine effectiveness of the bank's controls systems (compliance, internal audit, independent risk management).
   - Determine the bank's compliance with applicable legal requirements, including provisions covering transactions between affiliates and the bank (12 USC 371c and c-1), consumer protection requirements (12 CFR 14), and privacy of consumer information (12 CFR 40).

Objective 8: Determine whether to expand the procedures or develop a plan for corrective action. Consider whether:

- Management can adequately manage the bank's risks.
- Management can correct fundamental problems.
- To propose a strategy to address identified weaknesses and discuss strategy with the supervisory office.

Refer to asset management booklets of the *Comptroller's Handbook* for expanded procedures.

Objective 9: After completing expanded procedures, determine whether additional verification procedures should be performed.

The extent to which examiners perform verification procedures is decided case by case after consultation with the ADC. Direct confirmation with the bank's customers must have prior approval of the ADC and district deputy comptroller. The Enforcement and Compliance Division, the district counsel, and the district accountant should also be notified when direct confirmations are being considered.

Objective 10: Conclude the review of the bank's asset management activities.

1. Provide and discuss with management a list of recommendations.

2. Consult with the EIC and other examining personnel to identify and communicate to other examiners conclusions and findings from the asset management review that are relevant to other areas being reviewed.

3. Use the results of the foregoing procedures and other applicable examination findings to compose comments (e.g., asset management activities, retail brokerage, violations, MRAs) for the ROE.

4. Update, organize, and reference work papers in accordance with PPM 5400-8 (rev).

5. Update Examiner View (e.g., ratings, core knowledge, MRAs, violations).

6. In discussion with the EIC, provide preliminary conclusions about:

- Quantity of asset management risk.
- Quality of risk management.
- Aggregate level and direction of asset management risk or other applicable risk. Complete the summary conclusions in the "Risk Assessment System" section.
- Supervisory strategy recommendations.

Bank Secrecy Act/Anti-Money Laundering

Conclusion: The bank's BSA/AML compliance program is (strong, satisfactory, or weak). (Updated 9/28/2012)

Complete this section's objectives to assess the adequacy of the bank's BSA/AML compliance program and compliance with BSA/AML/OFAC regulations. BSA/AML examination findings are considered as part of the management component rating under the FFIEC CAMELS ratings and compliance risk (and other appropriate risks) under the OCC's RAS. When assessing BSA/AML/OFAC compliance, the examiner should refer to the guidance and procedures in the FFIEC *BSA/AML Examination Manual.* (Updated 9/28/2012)

Core Assessment

Minimum Objective: Assess the adequacy of the bank's BSA/AML compliance program and determine compliance with BSA/AML/OFAC regulations. (Updated 9/28/2012)

Perform the minimum core examination procedures in the FFIEC *BSA/AML Examination Manual.* Consider whether: (Updated 9/28/2012)

- The BSA/AML compliance program ensures compliance with BSA requirements and effectively controls the risks within the institution. (Updated 9/28/2012)
- Policies, procedures, and processes ensure compliance with OFAC sanctions. (Updated 9/28/2012)

Develop preliminary assessments of the quantity of risk and quality of risk management using the BSA/AML/OFAC risk indicators in appendix B. (Updated 9/28/2012)

Other Assessment Objectives: Note: Examiners should select objectives and procedures necessary to assess the bank's BSA/AML/OFAC compliance and risks. (Updated 9/28/2012)

Objective 1: Using the findings from meeting the minimum objective, determine whether the bank's risk exposure from BSA/AML/OFAC warrants performance of additional core examination procedures. (Updated 9/28/2012)

Complete selected examination procedures in the Regulatory Requirements and Related Topics section of the FFIEC *BSA/AML Examination Manual.* (Updated 9/28/2012)

Objective 2: Determine whether to expand the procedures based on the bank's specific lines of business, products, customers, or entities that may present unique challenges and exposures. (Updated 9/28/2012)

Complete appropriate expanded examination procedures in the FFIEC *BSA/AML Examination Manual.* (Updated 9/28/2012)

Objective 3: Conclude the BSA/AML/OFAC compliance review. (Updated 9/28/2012)

1. Refer to the Developing Conclusions and Finalizing the Examination section of the FFIEC *BSA/AML Examination Manual.* (Updated 9/28/2012)

2. Consult with the EIC and other examining personnel to consolidate conclusions and findings from the BSA/AML/OFAC compliance review. (Updated 9/28/2012)

3. Use results of the foregoing procedures and other examination findings to compose comments (e.g., management, MRAs) for the ROE or other supervisory communication, such as a board letter. (Updated 9/28/2012)

4. If considering a BSA/AML enforcement action, consult with the EIC and ADC to determine whether to recommend civil money penalties or an enforcement action (refer to 42 USC 4012a(f)). **Note:** There is a statutory mandate for issuing a cease-and-desist order when a violation of 12 CFR 21.21, Bank Secrecy Act Compliance Program, is cited, or if the bank fails to correct a previously reported problem with the BSA compliance program. Refer to OCC Bulletin 2007-36, Interagency Statement on Enforcement of Bank Secrecy Act/Anti-Money Laundering Requirements, for guidance. (Updated 9/28/2012)

5. Provide and discuss with management a preliminary list of deficiencies and violations. BSA/AML conclusions should not be discussed with management prior to vetting the findings though established processes. OCC Bulletin 2005-45, Process for Taking Administrative Enforcement Actions Against Banks Based on BSA Violations, sets forth the general process to be followed in enforcement cases based on BSA violations. (Updated 9/28/2012)

6. In discussion with the EIC, provide preliminary conclusions about: (Updated 9/28/2012)

   - Adequacy of the BSA/AML compliance program. (Updated 9/28/2012)
   - Compliance with BSA/AML/OFAC regulations. **Note:** OFAC violations and MRAs must be reported to the Compliance Policy division for referral to OFAC. (Updated 9/28/2012)
   - Quantity of risk. (Updated 9/28/2012)
   - Quality of risk management. (Updated 9/28/2012)
   - Aggregate level and direction of compliance, operational, reputation, and strategic risks as they relate to BSA/AML/OFAC compliance. (Updated 9/28/2012)
   - Supervisory strategy recommendations. (Updated 9/28/2012)

7. Update, organize, and reference work papers in accordance with PPM 5400-8 (rev). (Updated 9/28/2012)

8. Update Examiner View (e.g., ratings, core knowledge, MRAs, violations). (Updated 9/28/2012)

Consumer Compliance

Conclusion: Consumer compliance is rated (1, 2, 3, 4, 5).

Complete this section's objectives to assign the consumer compliance rating using the Uniform Interagency Consumer Compliance Rating System. The consumer compliance rating should reflect: (Updated 9/28/2012)

- Quantity of consumer compliance risk. (Updated 9/28/2012)
- Adequacy of the bank's risk management practices in light of the quantity of consumer compliance risk. (Updated 9/28/2012)
- Degree of reliance that can be placed on the bank's risk management systems, including the compliance review/audit function.
- Degree of supervisory concern that is posed by the bank's consumer compliance system.

When assigning the rating, the examiner should consult with the EIC, the examiners assigned to review audit and internal controls, and other examining personnel.

To determine the scope for the consumer compliance examination, examiners take into account the results of compliance risk assessments, internal screening and targeting processes that identify potential high-risk situations. For areas of low compliance risk, examiners should use procedures in the minimum objective as a starting point to scope the remaining compliance work. Even when all compliance areas are consistently identified as low risk, examiners should periodically expand supervisory activities beyond the minimum objective to include transaction testing to ensure that the bank's compliance process continues to be effective. **Note:** If a bank is identified on the final fair lending screening test, a full-scope fair lending examination must be completed using the procedures in the *Fair Lending* booklet. (Updated 9/28/2012)

Core Assessment

Minimum Objective: Determine the consumer compliance rating, quantity of compliance risk, and quality of compliance risk management.[24] Assess compliance with all appropriate consumer deposit and lending laws and regulations, including the Flood Disaster Protection Act. (Updated 9/28/2012)

Discuss with management actual or planned:

- Changes in compliance structure and key personnel responsible for compliance that weaken or strengthen the bank's compliance program.

---

[24] Guidance is provided for quantity of risk and quality of risk management for the following areas: Consumer Lending Regulations, Consumer Deposit Regulations, Fair Lending, and Other Consumer Regulations. (Updated 9/28/2012)

- Changes in the Flood Disaster Protection Act compliance procedures or in the volume of loans originated in designated flood areas to determine ongoing compliance with the statutory requirements of the National Flood Insurance Program (12 CFR 22).
- Changes in products, services, customer base, or delivery channels that affect quantity of compliance risk, including those offered through affiliated and nonaffiliated third parties.
- Significant changes in the volume of products and services offered that would affect consumer compliance.
- Significant changes in third-party relationships, contracts, and activities.
- Changes in the bank's training process for ensuring that managers and employees understand and follow new regulations or changes to existing regulations.
- Other factors that may have changed the bank's risk profile.

As requested, follow up on significant compliance-related audit or IT issues identified by the examiner reviewing the bank's audit program:

- Discuss outstanding compliance audit issues with management.
- If warranted based on the above discussions or if requested by the examiner reviewing audit, obtain and review a risk-based sample of internal compliance audit reports and management follow-up.
- Discuss with management changes in the scope, personnel, or frequency of the compliance review or audit function that could increase or decrease the function's reliability.

Contact the examiner assigned to review IT to determine whether there have been changes in vendor systems, software, and applications used to support compliance activities. If yes, determine what due diligence process the bank used to test the systems or software and whether appropriate training was provided to staff. (Updated 9/28/2012)

Obtain and review the following information:

- Compliance committee minutes to determine management and the board's ongoing commitment to compliance, including timely corrective action on noted deficiencies.
- Compliance reviews and risk assessments, including those related to the Flood Disaster Protection Act, responses, and corrective action.
- Results of the OCC's previous compliance activities and management responses.
- Results of the most recent CRA examination.
- Results of the most recent fair lending supervisory activity (fair lending screening results if not reviewed recently). Considering the high-risk factors, determine whether the bank should be added to the fair lending screening list.
- Complaint information from the OCC's Customer Assistance Group[25] and the bank.

---

[25] The OCC Customer Assistance Group maintains a database that allows for analysis of complaint activity and trends. OCC is required by the Federal Trade Commission Act of 1975 (15 USC 41, et seq.) to collect statistical data on consumer complaints involving national banks.

If the bank's activities, risk profile, or compliance process has changed significantly or if the review of the above information raises substantive issues, the examiner should expand the activity's scope to include additional objectives or procedures. If this review does not result in significant changes or issues, conclude the compliance review by completing objective 8.

Other Assessment Objectives: Note: Examiners should select objectives and procedures necessary to assess the bank's condition and risks.

Objective 1: Determine the scope of the consumer compliance review and what transaction testing, should be included. The extent of transaction testing should reflect the bank's compliance risk profile, compliance coverage and results, and time elapsed since the last examination.

1. Review the supervisory information to identify previous problems that require follow-up in this area.

2. Obtain and review the information below to determine complexity of the bank's compliance environment. Ensure that the systems management uses to supervise compliance adequately identify, measure, monitor, and control compliance risk. Obtain and review:

    - Organizational charts, job descriptions, turnover, and communication channels to determine how management communicates and manages risk through policies, procedures, compliance reviews, and internal controls.
    - Bank's training programs and criteria for compliance training for key personnel. Determine whether programs are appropriate based on functions performed and likelihood of noncompliance.
    - If applicable, documentation supporting new product development, or initiatives to determine the effectiveness of compliance and planning.
    - Complaint information from the OCC's Customer Assistance Group and the bank.

3. Discuss with the examiner responsible for completing the "Audit and Internal Controls" section of the core assessment whether significant audit findings require follow-up or whether a review of audit work papers is required. If needed, compliance worksheets[26] in the consumer compliance booklets of the *Comptroller's Handbook* can be used as a guide for the work paper review.

4. Discuss with the examiner responsible for completing the IT section of the core assessment whether significant deficiencies raise questions about integrity, confidentiality, or availability of data and require follow-up.

5. Using overall results from the "Audit and Internal Controls" section of the core assessment, determine to what extent examiners can rely on compliance reviews or audits by area to set the scope of the compliance supervisory activities. Consider:

---

[26] Compliance worksheets are also available online and in the Examiner's Library.

- Whether compliance reviews or audits cover all applicable consumer regulation requirements for all products and services and all departments of the bank, such as trust and private banking, as well as the bank's Web site and electronic banking.
- Whether compliance reviews and audits address areas with moderate and high quantities of risk and include appropriate sample sizes.
- Adequacy of documentation and frequency of reviews or audits.
- Whether the system for ensuring corrective action is effective.

6. Assess integrity, confidentiality, and availability of data used to record, analyze, and report information related to consumer compliance. Consider input, processing, storage, access, and disposal of data. Focus on measures taken to limit access to data and procedures in place to monitor system activities. Determine if these controls have been independently validated. Coordinate this review with examiners responsible for all functional areas of the examination, including internal controls, to avoid duplication of effort. Share findings with the examiner reviewing IT.

Objective 2: Determine compliance with fair lending laws and regulations.

The OCC's fair lending screening process is designed to assist supervisory offices in the annual identification of banks believed to present the highest fair lending risk. The screening process uses Home Mortgage Disclosure Act (HMDA) and complaint data to identify high-risk banks. However, assessment of fair lending risk is primarily the supervisory office's responsibility. The screening process only complements the supervisory office's fair lending risk assessment activities. Supervisory offices may request that banks be added or removed from the list that results from the screening process. In addition, supervisory offices should review bank compliance systems in all community banks to identify those with inadequate fair lending processes or systems. If activities in the core assessment are insufficient to determine whether a bank's fair lending processes and systems are adequate, or if the core assessment or other supervisory activities result in substantive concerns about fair lending, the steps that follow assist the examiner in determining whether the bank should be added to the OCC's fair lending screening list. Regardless of the outcome, the analysis should be documented in Examiner View.

If a bank is selected for a fair lending examination through the screening process or if the supervisory office determines that the bank should be added to the fair lending screening list, the supervisory office should update the bank strategy to address the areas of focus. The supervisory office may consider requesting that a compliance specialist assist or conduct the examination.

1. Review findings from objective 1 and identify higher-risk areas for fair lending. (Refer to quantity of risk indicators and quality of risk management indicators in appendix B).

2. If the bank has performed a fair lending self-evaluation, review the results. Refer to appendix H, "Streamlining the Examination" in the *Fair Lending* booklet.

3. Considering the high-risk factors present, consult with and obtain approval from the EIC and supervisory office ADC before determining whether the bank should be added to the fair lending screening list and whether a fair lending examination should be initiated. Consult with the district compliance lead expert.

4. Conduct a fair lending examination using selected procedures from the *Fair Lending* booklet.

   Note: Violations of the Fair Housing Act may require notification to the Department of Housing and Urban Development. Violations of the Equal Credit Opportunity Act or the Fair Housing Act that are the result of a pattern or practice may require referral to the Department of Justice. If these conditions are identified, refer to the supervisory office ADC and the compliance lead expert.

Objective 3: Determine the bank's compliance with lending regulations. **Note:** If the examiner, after completing these procedures, identifies other areas of high consumer compliance risk that require further review, consult with the compliance lead expert and the appropriate compliance handbooks for additional guidance.

1. Review findings from objective 1 and identify higher-risk areas in consumer lending regulations. (Refer to quantity of risk and quality of risk management indicators in appendix B).

2. If the bank actively markets to new customers by offering alternative delivery channels (e.g., Internet banking) and widespread advertising, determine whether the bank has adequate internal controls and trained staff to handle these delivery channels. Determine whether all advertisements and marketing programs are reviewed and approved by the compliance officer. (Regulation Z, including annual percentage rate and triggering terms).

3. If the bank offers complex loan products or the bank's products change frequently, determine whether the bank has adequate systems and knowledgeable personnel to accurately calculate annual percentage rates and finance charges (Regulation Z).

4. If the bank uses third-party loan originators or brokers to make or purchase loans, determine whether the bank follows the guidance outlined in OCC Advisory Letter 2003-3, "Avoiding Predatory and Abusive Lending Practices in Brokered and Purchased Loans" and OCC Bulletin 2001-47, "Third-Party Relationships: Risk Management Principles."

5. If the bank offers nontraditional or subprime mortgage products, determine whether they comply with the guidance outlined in OCC Bulletin 2007-26, "Subprime Mortgage Lending: Statement on Subprime Mortgage Lending" and OCC Bulletin 2006-41, "Nontraditional Mortgage Products: Guidance on Non-traditional Mortgage Product Risks."

6. If the bank's lending area contains a participating community and has special flood hazard areas, determine whether the bank has internal systems in place to ensure that customer notifications are made, flood insurance is obtained at loan origination, maintained throughout the life of the loan, and forced placement of insurance is done as required (Flood Disaster Protection Act).

   Select a sample of residential and commercial real estate loans in flood hazard areas for testing. The testing should include a review of the flood determination forms, borrower notification, and amount of coverage.

7. If the bank has a broker relationship and either pays or receives a high amount of fees, verify that the bank does not pay or receive a fee merely for the referral. (Real Estate Settlement Procedures Act, section 8)

Objective 4: Determine the bank's compliance with deposit regulations. **Note:** If the examiner, after completing these procedures, identifies other areas of high consumer compliance risk that require further review, consult with the compliance lead expert and the appropriate compliance handbooks for additional guidance.

1. Review findings from objective 1 and identify higher-risk areas in consumer deposit regulations. (Refer to quantity of risk and quality of risk management indicators in appendix B).

2. If the bank actively markets to new customers by offering alternative delivery channels (e.g., Internet banking) and widespread advertising, determine whether the bank has adequate internal controls and trained staff to handle these delivery channels. Determine whether all advertisements and marketing programs are reviewed and approved by the compliance officer (Regulation DD, 12 CFR 30).

3. Determine whether the bank has trained staff and adequate procedures to appropriately handle unauthorized transactions and errors reported by customers (Regulation E, 12 CFR 205.11).

4. If the bank offers complex deposit products, determine whether the bank has adequate systems and knowledgeable personnel to accurately calculate annual percentage yields (Regulation DD – APY).

5. If the bank places a large number of holds, determine whether the bank has adequate systems and knowledgeable personnel to place the holds in accordance with the exceptions cited in 12 CFR 229.13. (Regulation CC)

6. If the bank offers an overdraft protection program, determine that it complies with OCC Bulletin 2005-9, "Overdraft Protection Programs."

Objective 5: Determine the bank's compliance with other consumer regulations. **Note:** If the examiner, after completing these procedures, identifies other areas of high consumer compliance risk that require further review, consult with the compliance lead expert and the appropriate compliance handbooks for additional guidance.

1. Review findings from objective 1 and identify higher-risk areas in other consumer regulations. (Refer to quantity of risk and quality of risk management indicators in appendix B).

2. If the bank discloses information to nonaffiliated third parties (outside the statutory exceptions), determine whether the bank has adequate systems to ensure that customers are provided a clear, conspicuous opt-out notice on an annual basis (Privacy).

3. If the bank uses prescreened lists for solicitation purposes, verify that the bank uses the same criteria to evaluate the application that it used to prescreen the applicant and that record retention requirements are maintained (Fair Credit Reporting Act, permissible purpose, Regulation B).

4. If the bank receives requests from government agencies for customer's financial records, determine whether the bank has adequate procedures to ensure compliance with the Right to Financial Privacy Act.

5. If the bank operates a Web site that collects information from, or is directed to, children younger than 13, determine whether the bank has adequate procedures and trained personnel to ensure compliance with the requirements of the Children's Online Privacy Protection Act.

6. If the bank acts as a "debt collector," determine whether there is bank staff responsible for ensuring that the bank complies with the Fair Debt Collection Practices Act.

Objective 6: Using the findings from meeting the foregoing objectives, determine whether the bank's risk exposure from consumer compliance is significant.

Develop preliminary assessments of quantity of compliance risk, quality of compliance risk management, aggregate compliance risk, and direction of compliance risk. Refer to the "Risk Assessment System" section. Comment as necessary.

Objective 7: Determine whether to expand the procedures or develop a plan for corrective action. Consider whether:

- Management can adequately manage the bank's risks.
- Management can correct fundamental problems.
- To propose a strategy to address identified weaknesses and discuss strategy with the supervisory office.

Refer to booklets of the *Comptroller's Handbook* for expanded procedures.

Objective 8: Conclude the consumer compliance review.

1. Provide and discuss with management a list of deficiencies and violations.

2. Consult with the EIC and ADC to determine whether to recommend civil money penalties or an enforcement action (refer to 42 USC 4012a(f)). (Updated 9/28/2012)

3. Consult with the EIC and other examining personnel to identify and communicate to other examiners conclusions and findings from the consumer compliance review that are relevant to other areas being reviewed.

4. Use results of the foregoing procedures and other examination findings to compose comments (e.g., compliance, MRAs) for the ROE or other supervisory communication, such as a board letter.

5. Update, organize, and reference work papers in accordance with PPM 5400-8 (rev).

6. Update Examiner View (e.g., ratings, core knowledge, MRAs, violations).

7. In discussion with the EIC, provide preliminary conclusions about:

   - Quantity of risk.
   - Quality of risk management.
   - Aggregate level and direction of compliance, operational, and reputation risk, or other risk, as they relate to compliance. Complete the summary conclusions in the "Risk Assessment System" section.
   - Supervisory strategy recommendations.

Examination Conclusions and Closing

Conclusion: Bank is rated (1, 2, 3, 4, 5)
Bank's overall risk profile is (low, moderate, high)

To conclude the supervisory cycle, examiners must meet all objectives under this section, regardless of the bank's risk designation.

Objective 1: Determine and update the bank's composite rating and other regulatory ratings.

1. Consider findings from the following areas:

   - Audit and internal controls.
   - Capital adequacy.
   - Asset quality.
   - Management capability.
   - Earnings quality and quantity.
   - Liquidity adequacy.
   - Sensitivity to market risk.
   - IT.
   - Asset management.
   - Compliance with BSA/AML/OFAC laws, rules, and regulations. (Updated 9/28/2012)
   - Compliance with consumer protection laws, rules, and regulations.
   - Performance under CRA.

2. Ensure that the evaluation of all component ratings has considered the following items as outlined in UFIRS:

   - Bank's size.
   - Bank's sophistication.
   - Nature and complexity of bank activities.
   - Bank's risk profile.

Note: Although regulatory ratings are point-in-time judgments of a bank's financial, managerial, operational, and compliance performance, descriptions of each component contain explicit language emphasizing management's ability to manage risk. Therefore, the conclusions drawn in the RAS should be considered when assigning the corresponding component and the composite rating.

Objective 2: Determine the risk profile using the RAS.

Draw and record conclusions about quantity of risk, quality of risk management, aggregate risk, and the direction of aggregate risk for each of the applicable risk categories. Refer to the matrix in appendix A for additional guidance in assessing aggregate risk.

Note: Using the assessments made of the eight individual risks, the examiner can establish the bank's overall risk profile. The overall risk profile is not an average, but a combination of the assessments of the eight individual risks. In establishing the overall risk profile, examiners use judgment to weigh the eight risks by the relative importance of each risk.

Objective 3: Finalize the examination.

At a minimum, the ROE examination conclusions and comments should include:

- Summary of scope and major examination objectives, including:
  - Recap of significant supervisory activities during the examination cycle and how those activities were used to evaluate the bank's overall condition.
  - Discussions of significant expansion of the standard core assessment.
- Statements of the bank's overall condition and conclusions on ratings.
- Discussions of excessive risks or significant deficiencies in risk management and their root causes.
- Summary of actions and commitments to correct significant deficiencies and planned supervisory follow-up.
- Notice to the board if civil money penalty referrals are being made.
- Statement about applicable section 914 (12 USC 1831 and 12 CFR 5.51) requirements.

1. The EIC, or designee, should finalize required ROE comments. The comments should include significant risk-related concerns. Refer to appendix D for a detailed summary on requirements for the content of the ROE. (Updated 5/06/2013)

2. In consultation with key examining personnel, the EIC should determine whether the bank's condition and risk profile warrant including recommended MRAs in the ROE. MRAs are necessary when bank practices:

   - Deviate from sound fundamental governance, internal controls, and risk management principles which may adversely impact the bank's earnings, capital, risk profile, or reputation if not addressed.
   - Result in substantive noncompliance with laws or internal policies or processes.

3. Discuss examination conclusions and review required draft comments with the ADC or the appropriate supervisory office official.

4. Summarize examination conclusions and the bank's condition in the "Examination Conclusions and Comments" page of the report.

5. If any component area is rated 3 or worse, or if the risk profile causes sufficient concern, the EIC should contact the supervisory office before the exit meeting to develop a strategy for addressing the bank's deficiencies.

6. Hold an on-site exit meeting with management to summarize examination findings:

   • Inform management of areas of strengths as well as weaknesses.
   • Solicit management's commitment to correct material weaknesses.
   • Discuss the bank's risk profile including conclusions from the RAS.
   • Offer examples of acceptable solutions.

7. Provide bank management with an approved draft of examination conclusions, MRA comments, and violations of law to allow managers to review the comments for accuracy.

8. Perform a final technical check to make sure that the report is accurate and acceptable. The check should ensure that:

   • Report meets established guidelines.
   • Comments support all regulatory ratings, as applicable.
   • Numerical totals are accurate.
   • Numerical data in the report and other supervisory comments are consistent with the bank's records.
   • Violations of law are cited accurately.

9. If there are MRA comments in the report, they should provide specific information regarding:

   • Problems or issues resulting in the MRA.
   • Factors contributing to the problems or issues, including root causes.
   • Management's ability and commitment to corrective action.
   • Time frame and person(s) responsible for corrective action.
   • Consequences of inaction.

10. Report to the Compliance Policy division any OFAC violations or MRAs. (Updated 9/28/2012)

11. Verify that all appropriate information, including updates to core knowledge and other pertinent areas, has been entered in Examiner View and approve the examination.

12. Prepare the supervisory strategy for the next supervisory cycle. Follow specific guidance in the "Planning" section of this booklet and in the "Bank Supervision Process" booklet of the *Comptroller's Handbook*.

13. Complete and distribute assignment evaluations.

14. Schedule the board meeting.

Objective 4: Prepare for and conduct a meeting with the board of directors.

1. Before completing the supervisory cycle, prepare for the meeting by:

   - Drafting a preliminary agenda (formal or informal).
   - Preparing handouts, graphics, or audiovisual material for the meeting.
   - Reviewing the backgrounds of all board members.
   - Drafting responses to expected questions and comments.

2. Conduct the meeting after the board, or an authorized committee, has had the opportunity to review the draft report or a synopsis of examination findings. At the meeting, provide graphics and handouts to describe:

   - Objectives of OCC's supervision and how the OCC pursues those objectives.
   - Strategic issues including growth, products, and strategies.
   - Major concerns or issues, including significant risks facing the bank.
   - Bank's success or failure in correcting previously identified deficiencies.
   - Potential impact of failing to correct deficiencies.
   - What the OCC expects the bank to do and when (e.g., action plans, supervisory strategies, and commitments).
   - What the bank is doing well.
   - Industry issues affecting the bank.

   Note: During the supervisory cycle, the ADC must attend at least one board meeting or an examination exit meeting that includes board member participation.

3. Document details of the meeting in Examiner View as a significant event. Include the following information:

   - Date and location of the meeting and names of attendees.
   - Major items discussed.
   - Brief summary of the directors' reactions to the OCC briefing. (The entry documenting the meeting can refer the reader to the follow-up analysis comment for further details on commitments obtained from the board or senior management.)

Community Bank Periodic Monitoring

Conclusion: The bank's risk profile (has/has not) changed and the supervisory strategy (is/is not) valid.

Periodic monitoring activities are a key component of supervision by risk. Each bank's supervisory strategy outlines, in detail, the specific monitoring activities that will be performed and the timing of those activities. The timing of the activities is driven by the supervisory objectives rather than predetermined calendar dates. Although the timing of these activities should be risk-based, there is a presumption that some type of quarterly contact with bank management is preferred for a majority of national banks.

The objectives of periodic monitoring include but are not limited to:

- Identifying significant (actual or potential) changes in the bank's risk profile.
- Ensuring the validity of the supervisory strategy.
- Achieving efficiencies during onsite activities.

The specific objectives of periodic monitoring for a particular bank are determined by the portfolio manager in consultation with the supervisory office, and are based on knowledge of the bank's condition and risks. Depending on the circumstances and the bank's risk profile, periodic monitoring may be as limited as a brief phone call to bank management or a review of bank financial information. If circumstances warrant, periodic monitoring may also be more in-depth, and could include a comprehensive analysis of various CAMELS/ITCC components or a visit to the bank. The supervisory office's ADC and the portfolio manager are jointly responsible for determining the depth and breadth of activities needed to achieve supervisory objectives. When conducting monitoring activities at a newly chartered bank, examiners should supplement their analyses with the guidance in PPM 5400-9 (rev), "De Novo and Converted Banks."

Examiners may perform the following procedures during periodic monitoring. These procedures are provided as a guide for examiners. The portfolio manager should perform whichever procedures are appropriate, consistent with the bank's condition and risk profile.

Objective: Determine whether significant trends or events have occurred that change the bank's risk profile or require changes to the supervisory strategy using, at a minimum, available Canary system information.

1. Review quarterly financial information using the UBPR, bank-supplied information, call reports, or OCC models for significant financial trends or changes. The financial review of low-risk banks should be very brief if no anomalies are detected.

   For higher-risk banks, it may be appropriate to supplement financial information with:

- Budget and pro forma financial statements.
- Management and board reports.
- Loan review, audit, and compliance risk management reports.
- Board and committee minutes.

2. Discuss with bank management financial trends and changes in bank operations, controls, and management. Examiners may conduct this discussion by telephone or during an on-site meeting. Focus particular attention on areas of significant change or plans for significant growth. Possible discussion topics include:

- Financial performance and trends.
- Plans to raise or deployment of significant new injections of capital.
- Significant issues identified by internal and external audit and management's corrective action on those issues.
- Activities that may affect the bank's risk profile, including changes in:
  - Products, services, distribution channels, or market area.
  - Policies, underwriting standards, or risk tolerances.
  - Management, key personnel, organizational structure, or operations.
  - Technology — including operating systems, technology vendors and servicers, critical software, and Internet banking — or plans for new products and activities that involve new technology.
  - Control systems (audit, loan review, compliance review, etc.) and their schedule or scope.
  - Legal counsel and pending litigation.
- Purchase, acquisition, or merger considerations.
- Broad economic and systemic trends affecting the condition of the national banking system, as identified by OCC national or district risk committees.
- Trends in the local economy or business conditions.
- Public information disclosed since the last review:
  - Recent media coverage.
  - Market or industry information for publicly traded companies, such as 10Q and securities analyst reports.
- Changes in asset management lines of business.
- Issues regarding BSA/AML/OFAC compliance. (Updated 9/28/2012)
- Issues regarding consumer compliance or CRA.
- Other issues that may affect the risk profile.
- Management concerns about the bank or about OCC supervision.

3. Perform follow-up on previously identified weaknesses, paying particular attention to MRAs and time frames for corrective action.

4. Consult with the appropriate supervisory office official to determine whether results of the monitoring activities necessitate changes to the CAMELS/ITCC component ratings.

5. Determine whether results of the monitoring activities affect the supervisory strategy

with regard to:

- Types of supervisory activities planned.
- Scope of the reviews.
- Timing or scheduling.
- Resources (expertise, experience level, or number of examiners).

6. Update Examiner View to reflect:

- Changes to supervisory strategy and core knowledge.
- Examination conclusion and analysis comments.

Note: Documentation in Examiner View and work papers should adequately support conclusions based on the extent of findings and work performed.[27] For example, if the bank's risk profile or CAMELS/ITCC ratings have not changed, the only required Examiner View documentation is a statement that the monitoring objectives were met and that the bank's risk profile has not changed since the last review.

7. If there are significant changes that require a change to CAMELS/ITCC ratings or the RAS, open the appropriate CAMELS/ITCC component(s) in Examiner View and document additional supervisory work performed and the effect of the changes on the RAS, CAMELS/ITCC ratings, and the supervisory strategy. If significant issues are identified, send written communication or conduct a meeting with the board or management. Any significant change in an aggregate risk assessment or any CAMELS/ITCC rating must be communicated in writing to the board of directors.

---

[27] See guidelines in PPM 5400-8 (rev), "Supervision Work Papers," PPM 5000-34, "Canary Early Warning System," and the "Bank Supervision Process" booklet of the *Comptroller's Handbook.*

Appendix A: Community Bank RAS

Credit Risk

Credit risk is the risk to current or anticipated earnings or capital arising from an obligor's failure to meet the terms of any contract with the bank or otherwise perform as agreed. Credit risk is found in all activities in which settlement or repayment depends on counterparty, issuer, or borrower performance. It exists any time bank funds are extended, committed, invested, or otherwise exposed through actual or implied contractual agreements, whether reflected on or off the balance sheet. (Updated 5/06/2013)

Credit risk is the most recognizable risk associated with banking. This risk, however, encompasses more than lending. Credit risk is present in a broad range of other bank activities, such as selecting investment portfolio products, derivatives trading partners, or foreign exchange counterparties. Credit risk also arises from country or sovereign exposure as well as indirectly through guarantor performance. (Updated 5/06/2013)

Summary Conclusions

Quantity of credit risk is:

☐ Low	☐ Moderate	☐ High

Quality of credit risk management is:

☐ Strong	☐ Satisfactory	☐ Weak

Examiners should consider both the quantity of credit risk and the quality of credit risk management to derive the following conclusions:

Aggregate credit risk is:

☐ Low	☐ Moderate	☐ High

Direction is expected to be:

☐ Decreasing	☐ Stable	☐ Increasing

Quantity of Credit Risk

Quantity of credit risk is derived from the absolute amount of credit exposure and the quality of that exposure. How much credit exposure a bank has is a function of:

- Level of loans and other credit or credit-equivalent exposures relative to total assets and capital.
- Extent to which earnings are dependent on loan or other credit or credit-equivalent income sources.

All else being equal, banks that have higher loans-to-assets and loans-to-equity ratios and that depend heavily on the revenues from credit activities have a higher level of credit risk. The degree of exposure is a function of the risk of default and risk of loss in assets and exposures comprising the credit exposure. However, the risk of default and loss is not always apparent from currently identified problem assets. It also includes potential default and loss that are affected by such factors as bank risk selection and underwriting practices; portfolio composition; concentrations; portfolio performance; and global, national, and local economic and business conditions. All credit activities should be considered, including off-balance sheet, loans held for sale, and credit risk in the investment portfolio.

An assessment of low, moderate, or high credit risk should reflect the bank's standing relative to existing financial risk benchmarks or peer or historical standards and should take into consideration relevant trends in risk direction. When considering the effect of trends on quantity of risk, examiners must consider the rate of change as well as the base level of risk from which the change occurs. (For example, a modest adverse trend in a bank with a moderate quantity of credit risk should weigh more heavily on the examiner's decision to change the quantity of risk rating than a modest adverse trend in a low risk bank.) These factors represent minimum standards, and examiners should consider additional factors.

To determine the quantity of credit risk, examiners must consider an array of quantitative and qualitative risk measurements. These indicators can be leading (rapid growth), lagging (high past-due levels), static (point in time evaluation/gauge), relative (exceeds peer/historical norms), or dynamic (trend or change in portfolio mix). Many of these indicators are readily available from internal MIS as well as call report and UBPR information. Other indicators, such as a bank's risk tolerance or underwriting practices, while more subjective, should also be considered.

It is extremely important to note that banks can exhibit increasing or high levels of credit risk even though many or all traditional lagging indicators or asset quality indicators are low. Although qualitative and quantitative indicators may have opposite effects on credit risk (the one may mitigate the other's effect), the indicators may also work together (the one may add to the other's effect). Although each type of measure can provide valuable insights about risk when viewed individually, they become much more powerful for assessing the quantity of risk when viewed together.

Quantity of Credit Risk Indicators

Examiners should consider the following indicators when assessing quantity of credit risk.

Low	Moderate	High
The level of loans outstanding is low relative to total assets and equity capital.	The level of loans outstanding is moderate relative to total assets and equity capital.	The level of loans outstanding is high relative to total assets and equity capital.
Growth rates are supported by local, regional, and/or national economic and demographic trends and level of competition. Growth (including off-balance-sheet activities) has been planned for and appears consistent with management and staff expertise and/or operational capabilities.	Growth rates exceed local, regional, and/or national economic and demographic trends and level of competition. Some growth (including off-balance-sheet activities) has not been planned or exceeds planned levels and may test management and staff expertise or operational capabilities.	Growth rates significantly exceed local, regional, and/or national economic and demographic trends and level of competition. Growth (including off-balance-sheet activities) was not planned or exceeds planned levels, and stretches management and staff expertise and/or operational capabilities. Growth may be in new products or with out-of-area borrowers.
The bank has well diversified income and dependence on interest and fees from loans and leases is commensurate with asset mix. Loan yields are low and risks/returns are well balanced.	The bank is dependent on interest and fees from loans for the majority of its income, but income sources within the loan portfolio are diversified. Loan yields are moderate. Imbalances between risk and return may exist but are not significant.	The bank is highly dependent on interest and fees from loans and leases. Bank may target higher risk loan products for their earnings potential. Loan income is highly vulnerable to cyclical trends. Loan yields are high and reflect an imbalance between risk and return, and/or risk is disproportionately high relative to return.

Quantity of Credit Risk Indicators - continued

Low	Moderate	High
The bank's portfolio is well diversified with no single large concentrations and/or a few moderate concentrations. Concentrations are well within internal limits. Change in portfolio mix is neutral or reduces overall risk profile.	The bank has one or two material concentrations. Concentrations are in compliance with internal guidelines but may be approaching the limits. Change in portfolio mix may increase overall risk profile.	The bank has one or more large concentrations. Concentrations may have exceeded internal limits. Change in portfolio mix significantly increases overall risk profile.
Existing and/or new extensions of credit reflect conservative underwriting and risk-selection standards. Policies are conservative and exceptions are nominal.	Existing and/or new extensions of credit generally reflect conservative to moderate underwriting and risk-selection standards. Policies and exceptions are moderate.	Existing and/or new extensions of credit reflect liberal underwriting and risk-selection standards. Policies either allow such practices or practices have resulted in a large number of exceptions.
Underwriting policies are reasonable. Underwriting standards for loans held for sale or originated to distribute are reasonable and consistent with loans made with the intention of being held for the bank's portfolio. The bank has only occasional loans with structural weaknesses and/or underwriting exceptions. Those loans are well mitigated and do not constitute an undue risk.	Underwriting policies are satisfactory. Underwriting standards for loans held for sale or originated to distribute are reasonable but are inconsistent with loans made with the intention of being held for the bank's portfolio. The bank has an average level of loans with structural weaknesses and/or exceptions to sound underwriting standards consistent with balancing competitive pressures and reasonable growth objectives.	Underwriting policies are inadequate. Underwriting standards for loans held for sale or originated to distribute are inconsistent with loans made with the intention of being held for the bank's portfolio. The bank has a high level of loans with structural weaknesses and/or underwriting exceptions that expose the bank to heightened loss in the event of default.
Collateral requirements are conservative. Collateral valuations are timely and well supported.	Collateral requirements are acceptable. Bank practices result in moderate deviations from policy. A moderate number of collateral valuations are not well supported or reflect inadequate protection. Soft (intangible) collateral is sometimes used in lieu of hard (tangible) collateral.	Collateral requirements are liberal, or if policies incorporate conservative requirements, there are substantial deviations. Collateral valuations are not always obtained, frequently unsupported and/or reflect inadequate protection. Soft (intangible) collateral is frequently used rather than hard (tangible) collateral.
Loan documentation and/or collateral exceptions are low and have minimal impact on risk of loss.	The level of loan documentation and/or collateral exceptions is moderate, but exceptions are corrected in a timely manner and generally do not expose the bank to risk of loss.	The level of loan documentation and/or collateral exceptions is high. Exceptions are outstanding for inordinate periods and the bank may be exposed to heightened risk of loss.

Quantity of Credit Risk Indicators - continued

Low	Moderate	High
Distribution across pass categories is consistent with a conservative risk appetite. Migration trends within the pass category are balanced or favor the higher or less risky ratings. Lagging indicators, such as past dues and nonaccruals, are low and the trend is stable.	Distribution across pass categories is consistent with a moderate risk appetite. Migration trends within the pass category are starting to favor the lower or riskier pass ratings. Lagging indicators, such as past dues and nonaccruals, are moderate and the trend is stable or rising slightly.	Distribution across pass categories is heavily skewed toward the lower or riskier pass ratings. Downgrades dominate rating changes within the pass category. Lagging indicators, such as past dues and nonaccruals, are moderate or high and the trend is rising.
Classified and special-mention loans represent a low percentage of loans and capital and are not skewed to the more severe categories (doubtful or loss).	Classified and special-mention loans represent a moderate percentage of loans and capital and are not skewed to the more severe categories (doubtful or loss).	Classified and special-mention loans represent a high percentage of loans and capital or a moderate percentage of loans and capital and are growing or are skewed to the more severe categories (doubtful or loss).
Bank re-aging, extension, renewal, and refinancing practices raise little or no concern about the accuracy/transparency of reported problem loan, past due, nonperforming and loss numbers.	Bank re-aging, extension, renewal, and refinancing practices raise some concern about the accuracy/transparency of reported problem loan, past due, nonperforming and loss numbers.	Bank re-aging, extension, renewal, and refinancing practices raise substantial concern about the accuracy/transparency of reported problem loan, past due, nonperforming and loss numbers.
Loan losses to total loans are low. ALLL coverage of problem and non-current loans and loan losses is high. Provision expense is stable.	Loan losses to total loans are moderate. ALLL coverage of problem and non-current loans is moderate, but provision expense may need to be increased.	Loan losses to total loans are high. ALLL coverage of problem and non-current loans is low. Special provisions may be needed to maintain acceptable coverage.

Quality of Credit Risk Management Indicators

Examiners should use the following indicators when assessing quality of credit risk management. (For comprehensive guidelines on portfolio management, refer to the "Loan Portfolio Management" booklet of the *Comptroller's Handbook*.)

Strong	Satisfactory	Weak
There is a clear, sound credit culture. Board and management tolerance for risk is well communicated and fully understood.	The intent of the credit culture is generally understood, but the culture and risk tolerances may not be clearly communicated or uniformly implemented throughout the institution.	Credit culture is absent or is materially flawed. Risk tolerances may not be well understood.
Strategic and/or business plans are consistent with a conservative risk appetite and promote an appropriate balance between risk-taking and growth and earnings objectives. New loan products/initiatives are well researched, tested, and approved before implementation.	Strategic and/or business plans are consistent with a moderate risk appetite. Anxiety for income may lead to some higher-risk transactions. Generally, there is an appropriate balance between risk-taking and growth and earnings objectives. New loan products/initiatives may be launched without sufficient testing, but risks are usually understood.	Strategic and/or business plans encourage taking on liberal levels of risk. Anxiety for income dominates planning activities. The bank engages in new loan products/initiatives without conducting sufficient due diligence testing.
Management is effective. Loan management and personnel possess sufficient expertise to effectively administer the risk assumed. Responsibilities and accountability are clear, and appropriate remedial or corrective action is taken when they are breached.	Management is adequate to administer assumed risk, but improvements may be needed in one or more areas. Loan management and personnel generally possess the expertise required to effectively administer assumed risks, but additional expertise may be required in one or more areas. Responsibilities and accountability may require some clarification. Generally, appropriate remedial or corrective action is taken when they are breached.	Management is deficient. Loan management and personnel may not possess sufficient expertise and/or experience, or otherwise may demonstrate an unwillingness to effectively administer the risk assumed. Responsibilities and accountability may not be clear. Remedial or corrective actions are insufficient to address root causes of problems.
Diversification management is active and effective. Concentration limits are set at reasonable levels. The bank identifies and reports concentrated exposures and initiates actions to limit, reduce or otherwise mitigate their risk. Management identifies and understands correlated exposure risks.	Diversification management may need improvement but is adequate. Concentrated exposures are identified and reported, but limits or other action/exception triggers may be absent. Management may initiate actions to limit or mitigate concentrations at the individual loan level, but portfolio level actions may be inadequate. Correlated exposures may not be identified.	Diversification management is passive or otherwise deficient. The bank may not identify concentrated exposures, and/or identifies them but takes little or no actions to limit, reduce, or mitigate risk. Management does not understand exposure correlations. Concentration limits, if any, may be exceeded or are raised frequently.

Quality of Credit Risk Management Indicators - continued

Strong	Satisfactory	Weak
Loan management and personnel compensation structures provide appropriate balance between loan/revenue production, loan quality, and portfolio administration, including risk identification.	Loan management and personnel compensation structures provide reasonable balance between loan/revenue production, loan quality, and portfolio administration.	Loan management and personnel compensation structures are skewed to loan/revenue production. There is little evidence of substantive incentives and/or accountability for loan quality and portfolio administration.
Staffing levels and expertise are appropriate for the size and complexity of the loan portfolio. Staff turnover is reasonable and allows for the orderly transfer of responsibilities. Training programs facilitate ongoing staff development.	Staffing levels and expertise are generally adequate for the size and complexity of the loan portfolio. Staff turnover is moderate and may create some gaps in portfolio management. Training initiatives may be inconsistent.	Staffing levels are inadequate in numbers or skill level. Turnover is high. Bank does not provide sufficient resources for staff training.
Lending policies effectively establish and communicate portfolio objectives, risk tolerances, and loan-underwriting and risk-selection standards.	Policies are fundamentally adequate. Enhancements can be achieved in one or more areas but are generally not critical. Specificity of risk tolerance or underwriting and risk-selection standards may need improvement to fully communicate policy requirements.	Policies are deficient in one or more ways and require significant improvement in one or more areas. They may not be sufficiently clear or are too general to adequately communicate portfolio objectives, risk tolerances, and loan underwriting and risk-selection standards.
Bank effectively identifies, approves, tracks, and reports significant policy, underwriting, and risk-selection exceptions individually and in aggregate, including risk exposures associated with off-balance-sheet activities.	Bank identifies, approves, and reports significant policy, underwriting, and risk selection exceptions on a loan-by-loan basis, including risk exposures associated with off-balance-sheet activities. However, little aggregation or trend analysis is conducted to determine the affect on portfolio quality.	Bank approves significant policy exceptions but does not report them individually or in aggregate and/or does not analyze their effect on portfolio quality. Risk exposures associated with off-balance-sheet activities may not be considered. Policy exceptions may not receive appropriate approval.
Credit analysis is thorough and timely both at underwriting and periodically thereafter.	Credit analysis appropriately identifies key risks and is conducted within reasonable timeframes. Analysis after underwriting may need some strengthening.	Credit analysis is deficient. Analysis is superficial and key risks are overlooked. Credit data are not reviewed in a timely manner.

Quality of Credit Risk Management Indicators - continued

Strong	Satisfactory	Weak
Internal or outsourced risk rating and problem loan review/identification systems are accurate and timely. They effectively stratify credit risk in both problem and pass-rated credits. They serve as an effective early warning tool and support risk-based pricing, ALLL, and capital allocation processes.	Internal or outsourced risk rating and problem loan review/identification systems are adequate. Though improvement can be achieved in one or more areas, they adequately identify problem and emerging problem credits. The graduation of pass ratings may need to be expanded to facilitate early warning, risk-based pricing, or capital allocation.	Internal or outsourced risk rating and problem loan review/identification systems are deficient and require improvement. Problem credits may not be identified accurately or in a timely manner; as a result, portfolio risk is likely misstated. The graduation of pass ratings is insufficient to stratify risk in pass credits for early warning or other purposes (loan pricing, ALLL, capital allocation).
Special mention ratings do not indicate any management problems administering the loan portfolio.	Special mention ratings generally do not indicate management problems administering the loan portfolio.	Special mention ratings indicate management is not properly administering the loan portfolio.
MIS provide accurate, timely, and complete portfolio information. Management and the board receive appropriate reports to analyze and understand the bank's credit risk profile, including off-balance-sheet activities. MIS facilitates exception reporting, and MIS infrastructure can support ad hoc queries in a timely manner.	MIS may require modest improvement in one or more areas, but management and the board generally receive appropriate reports to analyze and understand the bank's credit risk profile. MIS facilitates exception reporting, and MIS infrastructure can support ad hoc queries in a timely manner.	MIS have deficiencies requiring attention. The accuracy and/or timeliness of information may be affected in a material way. Portfolio risk information may be incomplete. As a result, management and the board may not be receiving appropriate or sufficient information to analyze and understand the bank's credit risk profile. Exception reporting requires improvement, and MIS infrastructure may not support ad hoc queries in a timely manner.

Interest Rate Risk

Interest rate risk is the risk to current or anticipated earnings or capital arising from movements in interest rates. Interest rate risk results from differences between the timing of rate changes and the timing of cash flows (repricing risk); from changing rate relationships among different yield curves affecting bank activities (basis risk); from changing rate relationships across the spectrum of maturities (yield curve risk); and from interest-related options embedded in bank products (options risk). (Updated 5/06/2013)

The assessment of interest rate risk should consider risk from both an accounting perspective (i.e., the effect on the bank's accrual earnings) and an economic perspective (i.e., the effect on the market value of the bank's portfolio equity). In some banks, interest rate risk is included in the broader category of market risk. In contrast with price risk, which focuses on the mark-to-market portfolios (e.g., trading accounts), interest rate risk focuses on the value implications for accrual portfolios (e.g., held-to-maturity and available-for-sale accounts). (Updated 5/06/2013)

Summary Conclusions

Quantity of IRR is:

☐ Low	☐ Moderate	☐ High

Quality of IRR management is:

☐ Strong	☐ Satisfactory	☐ Weak

Examiners should consider both the quantity of IRR and the quality of IRR management to derive the following conclusions:

Aggregate IRR is:

☐ Low	☐ Moderate	☐ High

Direction is expected to be:

☐ Decreasing	☐ Stable	☐ Increasing

Quantity of IRR Indicators

Examiners should use the following indicators when assessing quantity of interest rate risk.

Low	Moderate	High
No significant mismatches on longer-term positions exist. Shorter- term exposures are simple and easily adjusted to control risk.	Mismatches on longer-term positions exist but are manageable and could be effectively hedged.	Re-pricing mismatches are longer-term and may be significant, complex, or difficult to hedge.
Potential exposure to earnings and capital is negligible under a +/- 200 basis point rate change over a 12-month horizon.	Potential exposure to earnings and capital is not material under a +/-200 basis point rate change over a 12-month time horizon.	Potential exposure to earnings and capital is significant under a +/-200 basis point rate change over a 12-month time horizon.
There is little or no exposure to multiple indexes that price assets and liabilities, such as prime, London Interbank Offered Rate (LIBOR), Constant Maturity Treasury (CMT), and Cost of Funds Index (COFI).	Potential exposure to multiple indexes that price assets and liabilities, such as prime, London Interbank Offered Rate (LIBOR), Constant Maturity Treasury (CMT), and Cost of Funds Index (COFI), is reasonable and manageable.	Potential exposure to multiple indexes that price assets and liabilities, such as prime, London Interbank Offered Rate (LIBOR), Constant Maturity Treasury (CMT), and Cost of Funds Index (COFI), is significant. Positions may be complex.
Potential exposure to changes in the level and shape of the yield curve is absent or negligible.	Potential exposure to changes in the level and shape of the yield curve is not material and is considered manageable.	Potential exposure to changes in the level and shape of the yield curve is significant. Positions may be complex.
Potential exposure to assets and/or liabilities with embedded options is low. Positions are neither material nor complex.	Potential exposure to assets and/or liabilities with embedded options is not material. The impact of exercising options is not projected to adversely affect earnings or capital.	Potential exposure to assets and/or liabilities with embedded options is material. Positions may be complex and the impact of exercising options may adversely affect earnings or capital.
Volume and complexity of servicing assets is either insignificant or nonexistent, presenting virtually no exposure to changes in interest rates.	Volume and complexity of servicing assets is relatively modest and does not present material exposure to earnings and capital due to changes in interest rates.	Volume and complexity of servicing assets is material and potentially exposes earnings and capital to significant exposure from changes in interest rates.
Support provided by low-cost, stable non-maturity deposits is significant and absorbs or offsets exposure arising from longer-term re-pricing mismatches or options risk.	Support provided by low-cost, stable non-maturity deposits absorbs some, but not all, of the exposure associated with longer-term re-pricing mismatches or options risk.	Support provided by low-cost, stable non-maturity deposits is not significant or sufficient to offset risk from longer-term re-pricing mismatches or options risk.

Quality of IRR Management Indicators

Examiners should use the following indicators when assessing quality of IRR management.

Strong	Satisfactory	Weak
Board-approved policies are sound and effectively communicate guidelines for management of IRR, functional responsibilities, and risk tolerance.	Board-approved policies adequately communicate guidelines for management of IRR, functional responsibilities, and risk tolerance. Minor weaknesses may be evident.	Board-approved policies are inadequate in communicating guidelines for management of IRR, functional responsibilities, and risk tolerance.
Risk-limit structures provide clear risk parameters for risk to earnings and economic value consistent with risk tolerance of the board. Limits reflect sound understanding of risk under adverse rate scenarios.	Risk-limit structures for earnings and economic value are reasonable and consistent with risk tolerance of the board.	Risk-limit structures to control risk to earnings and economic value may be absent, ineffective, unreasonable, or inconsistent with risk tolerance of the board.
Management demonstrates a thorough understanding of IRR. Management anticipates and responds appropriately to adverse conditions or changes in economic conditions. Management identifies and manages risks involved in new products, services, and systems.	Management demonstrates an adequate understanding of IRR and generally responds appropriately to adverse conditions or changes in economic conditions. Management adequately identifies and manages the risks involved in new products, services, and systems.	Management either does not demonstrate an understanding of IRR or does not anticipate or respond appropriately to adverse conditions or changes in economic conditions. Management does not identify or inadequately identifies and manages the risks involved in new products, services, and systems.
Risk measurement processes are appropriate given the size and complexity of the bank's on- and off-balance-sheet exposures. Data input processes are effective and ensure the accuracy and integrity of management information. Assumptions are reasonable and well documented. IRR is measured over a wide range of rate movements to identify vulnerabilities and stress points.	Risk measurement processes are appropriate given the size and complexity of the bank's on- and off-balance-sheet exposures. Data input processes are adequate and ensure the accuracy and integrity of management information. Assumptions are reasonable. IRR is measured over an adequate range of rate movements to identify vulnerabilities and stress points. Minor enhancements may be needed.	Risk measurement processes are deficient given the size and complexity of the bank's on- and off-balance-sheet exposures. Material weaknesses may exist in data input and interest rate scenario measurement processes. Assumptions may not be realistic or supported. Deficiencies may be material.
Earnings-at-risk is measured as well as economic value-at-risk when significant longer-term or options risk exposure exists. No weaknesses are evident.	Earnings-at-risk is measured as well as economic value-at-risk when significant longer-term or options risk exposure exists. Minor enhancements may be needed.	Earnings-at-risk may not be appropriately measured. Economic value-at-risk may not be considered despite significant exposure to longer-term or options risk.

Quality of IRR Management Indicators - continued

Strong	Satisfactory	Weak
MIS provide timely, accurate, and complete information on IRR to appropriate levels in the bank. No weaknesses are evident.	MIS are adequate, and provide complete information on IRR to appropriate levels of management. Minor weaknesses may be evident.	MIS are inadequate or incomplete. Remedial actions are necessary, as material weaknesses in MIS are evident.
A well designed, independent, and competent review function has been implemented to periodically validate and test the effectiveness of risk measurement systems. The process assesses the reasonableness and validity of scenarios and assumptions. The system is effective and no corrective actions are required.	An acceptable review function is in place. The review periodically validates and tests the effectiveness of risk measurement systems including the reasonableness and validity of scenarios and assumptions. The review is independent and competent. Minor weaknesses may exist but can be easily corrected.	A review function to periodically validate and test the effectiveness of risk measurement systems either does not exist or is inadequate in one or more material respects. The review may not be independent or completed by competent staff. Processes to evaluate the reasonableness and validity of rate scenarios and assumptions used may be absent or deficient.

Liquidity Risk

Liquidity risk is the risk to current or anticipated earnings or capital arising from an inability to meet obligations when they come due. Liquidity risk includes the inability to access funding sources or manage fluctuations in funding levels. Liquidity risk also results from a bank's failure to recognize or address changes in market conditions that affect its ability to liquidate assets quickly and with minimal loss in value. (Updated 5/06/2013)

Liquidity risk, like credit risk, is a recognizable risk associated with banking. The nature of liquidity risk, however, has changed in recent years. Increased investment alternatives for retail depositors, sophisticated off-balance-sheet products with complicated cash-flow implications, and a general increase in the credit sensitivity of bank customers are all examples of factors that complicate liquidity risk. (Updated 5/06/2013)

Summary Conclusions

Quantity of liquidity risk is:

☐ Low	☐ Moderate	☐ High

Quality of liquidity risk management is:

☐ Strong	☐ Satisfactory	☐ Weak

Examiners should consider both the quantity of liquidity risk and the quality of liquidity risk management to derive the following conclusions:

Aggregate liquidity risk is:

☐ Low	☐ Moderate	☐ High

Direction is expected to be:

☐ Decreasing	☐ Stable	☐ Increasing

Quantity of Liquidity Risk Indicators

Examiners should use the following indicators when assessing quantity of liquidity risk.

Low	Moderate	High
Funding sources are abundant and provide a competitive cost advantage.	Funding sources are sufficient and provide cost-effective liquidity.	Funding sources and liability structures suggest current or potential difficulty in maintaining long-term and cost-effective liquidity.
Funding is widely diversified. There is little or no reliance on wholesale funding sources or other credit-sensitive funds providers.	Funding is generally diversified, with a few providers that may share common objectives and economic influences but no significant concentrations. Modest reliance on wholesale funding may be evident.	Borrowing sources may be concentrated among a few providers or providers with common investment objectives or economic influences. Significant reliance on wholesale funds is evident.
Market alternatives exceed demand for liquidity with no adverse changes expected.	Market alternatives are available to meet demand for liquidity at reasonable terms, costs, and tenors. Liquidity position is not expected to deteriorate in the near term.	Liquidity needs are increasing, but sources of market alternatives at reasonable terms, costs, and tenors are declining.
Capacity to augment liquidity through asset sales and/or securitization is strong, and the bank has an established record in accessing these markets, even in distressed conditions.	Bank has the potential capacity to augment liquidity through asset sales and/or securitization but has little experience in accessing these markets. Distressed conditions could make this more problematic.	Bank exhibits little capacity or potential to augment liquidity through asset sales or securitization. Lack of experience accessing these markets or unfavorable reputation may make this option questionable, particularly in distressed conditions.
Volume of wholesale liabilities with embedded options is low.	Some wholesale funds contain embedded options, but potential impact is not significant.	Material volumes of wholesale funds contain embedded options. The potential impact is significant.
Bank is not vulnerable to funding difficulties should a material adverse change occur in market perception, even in distressed conditions.	Bank is not excessively vulnerable to funding difficulties should a material adverse change occur in market perception. Distressed conditions could make this more problematic.	Bank's liquidity profile makes it vulnerable to funding difficulties should a material adverse change occur, particularly in distressed conditions.
Support provided by the parent company is strong.	Parent company provides adequate support.	Little or unknown support provided by the parent company.

Quality of Liquidity Risk Management Indicators

Examiners should use the following indicators when assessing quality of liquidity risk management.

Strong	Satisfactory	Weak
Board-approved policies effectively communicate guidelines for liquidity risk management and designate responsibility.	Board-approved policies adequately communicate guidance for liquidity risk management and assign responsibility. Minor weaknesses may be present.	Board-approved policies are inadequate or incomplete. Policy is deficient in one or more material respects.
Liquidity risk management process is effective in identifying, measuring, monitoring, and controlling liquidity risk. The process reflects a sound culture that has proven effective over time.	Liquidity risk management process is generally effective in identifying, measuring, monitoring, and controlling liquidity. There may be minor weaknesses given the complexity of the risks undertaken, but these are easily corrected.	Liquidity risk management process is ineffective in identifying, measuring, monitoring, and controlling liquidity risk. This may hold true in one or more material respects, given the complexity of the risks undertaken.
Management fully understands all aspects of liquidity risk. Management anticipates and responds well to changing market conditions.	Management reasonably understands the key aspects of liquidity risk. Management adequately responds to changes in market conditions.	Management does not fully understand or chooses to ignore key aspects of liquidity risk. Management does not anticipate or take timely or appropriate actions in response to changes in market conditions.
Contingency funding plan (CFP) is well developed, effective, and useful. The plan incorporates reasonable assumptions, scenarios, and crisis management planning and is tailored to the bank's needs. CFP clearly establishes strategies that address liquidity shortfalls in a distressed environment. Stress testing (including bank-specific and market-wide scenarios) is performed and is effective.	Contingency funding plan (CFP) is adequate. The plan is current, reasonably addresses most relevant issues, and contains an adequate level of detail including multiple scenario analysis. The plan may require minor refinement. CFP adequately establishes strategies that address liquidity shortfalls in a distressed environment but may require some minor changes. Stress testing is adequately performed but may require some enhancement.	Contingency funding plan (CFP) is inadequate or nonexistent. Plan may exist but is not tailored to the institution, is not realistic, or is not properly implemented. The plan may not consider cost-effectiveness or availability of funds in a noninvestment grade or CAMELS "3" environment. CFP does not establish or inadequately establishes strategies that address liquidity shortfalls in a distressed environment. Stress testing is not or is inadequately performed.
MIS focus on significant issues and produce timely, accurate, complete, and meaningful information to enable effective management of liquidity, even in a distressed environment.	MIS adequately capture concentrations and rollover risk, and are timely, accurate, and complete, even in a distressed environment. Recommendations are minor and do not impact effectiveness.	MIS are deficient, particularly in a distressed environment. Material information may be missing or inaccurate, and reports are not meaningful.

Price Risk

Price risk is the risk to current or anticipated earnings or capital arising from changes in the value of either trading portfolios or other obligations that are entered into as part of distributing risk. These portfolios typically are subject to daily price movements and are accounted for primarily on a mark-to-market basis. This risk occurs most significantly from market-making, dealing, and position-taking in interest rate, foreign exchange, equity, commodities, and credit markets. (Updated 5/06/2013)

Price risk also arises from bank activities whose value changes are reflected in the income statement, such as in lending pipelines, other real estate owned, and mortgage servicing rights. The risk to earnings or capital resulting from the conversion of a bank's financial statements from foreign currency translation also should be assessed under price risk. As with interest rate risk, many banks include price risk in the broader category of market risk. (Updated 5/06/2013)

Summary Conclusions

Quantity of price risk is:

☐ Low	☐ Moderate	☐ High

Quality of price risk management is:

☐ Strong	☐ Satisfactory	☐ Weak

Examiners should consider both the quantity of price risk and the quality of price risk management to derive the following conclusions:

Aggregate price risk is:

☐ Low	☐ Moderate	☐ High

Direction is expected to be:

☐ Decreasing	☐ Stable	☐ Increasing

Quantity of Price Risk Indicators

Examiners should use the following indicators when assessing quantity of price risk.

Low	Moderate	High
Exposures are primarily confined to those arising from customer transactions and involve liquid and readily manageable products, markets, and levels of activity. Bank does trades back-to-back for customers, taking no or negligible risk positions. No proprietary trading exists. Trading personnel merely execute customer orders. Earnings and capital have no vulnerability to volatility from revaluation requirements.	Trading positions exist only to position securities for sale to customers. No proprietary trading. Open positions are small and involve liquid instruments that allow for easy hedging. Limited trading exists in option-type products. Earnings and capital have limited vulnerability to volatility from revaluation requirements.	Trading activity includes proprietary transactions, with positions unrelated to customer activity. Exposures reflect open or un-hedged positions, including illiquid instruments, options, and/or longer maturities, which subject earnings and capital to significant volatility from revaluation requirements.
Daily trading gains/losses do not occur, because bank takes no or negligible risk.	Daily trading gains/losses are small and occur infrequently. Quarterly trading losses do not occur because of limited risk appetite and emphasis on customer revenues.	Daily trading gains/losses occur periodically because the bank either does not have customer transaction revenue support, or takes positions that can create losses that eclipse customer revenues. Quarterly trading profits and losses can be large relative to budget and may occasionally result in a negative public perception.
Bank has a sales-driven culture, with sales personnel exercising greater authority than traders do.	Compensation programs reflect sales orientation, but do provide limited incentives for trading profits.	Compensation programs reward traders for generating trading profits, reflecting a trader-dominated operation.
Policy limits reflect no appetite for price risk. Customer sales activities pose no or negligible threat to earnings and capital.	Policy limits reflect limited appetite for price risk.	Policy limits permit risk-taking, with the bank willing to risk losses that can impact quarterly earnings and/or capital.
Bank has non-dollar denominated positions that are completely hedged. Assets denominated in foreign currencies equal liabilities denominated in foreign currencies. Earnings and capital are not vulnerable to changes in foreign exchange rates.	Bank may have a small volume of un-hedged, non-dollar denominated positions, but it can readily hedge at a reasonable cost. There is limited vulnerability to changes in foreign currency exchange rates.	Exposure reflects a large volume of un-hedged, non-dollar denominated positions, or a smaller volume of un-hedged positions in illiquid currencies for which hedging can be expensive. Changes in foreign currency exchange rates can adversely impact earnings and capital.

Quantity of Price Risk Indicators – continued

Low	Moderate	High
Bank has limited, or no, mortgage banking activities. The mortgage servicing asset, if any, is small relative to capital.	Bank is active in mortgage banking. The mortgage servicing asset is material relative to capital, and valuation adjustments can have a meaningful impact on earnings and capital.	Mortgage banking activities are a key business line for the bank. The mortgage servicing asset is large relative to capital, and valuation adjustments can be significant.
Bank has no current or limited exposure to other real estate (ORE).	Bank has a modest amount of or exposure to ORE, but it is in property types or areas that are not expected to realize significant value changes that could negatively impact earnings.	Bank has a large amount of or exposure to ORE, which may be concentrated in property types or areas that may realize value changes that cause significant write-downs.
Held-for-sale portfolios, if any, are small and pose minimal risk to earnings.	Bank carries a small held-for-sale loan portfolio as part of its business of distributing risk into the capital markets. However, write-downs to this portfolio would not have a significant impact on earnings.	Originating and distributing loans into the capital markets is a key business line for the bank. Write-downs occasionally have, or are anticipated to have, a significant impact on earnings.

Quality of Price Risk Management Indicators

Examiners should use the following indicators when assessing quality of price risk management.

Strong	Satisfactory	Weak
Policies reflect board's risk appetite, and provide clear authorities, conservative limits, and assigned responsibilities. Policies permit risk-taking authority consistent with the expertise of bank personnel. Policies clearly and reasonably limit the volume of translation risk and assigned responsibilities.	Policies provide generally clear authorities, reasonable limits, and assignment of responsibilities. Risk-taking authority is generally consistent with expertise of bank personnel. Policies address translation risk in a general way but may not provide specific management guidelines.	Policies reflect management's preferences for risk tolerance, rather than those of the board. Policies do not clearly assign responsibilities. Risk-taking authority does not reflect the expertise of trading personnel. The bank does not have a policy addressing translation risk or policy limits are not reasonable given management expertise, the bank's capital position, and/or volume of assets and liabilities denominated in foreign currencies. Responsibilities are not clearly assigned.
Management has broad mortgage servicing rights experience and has established strong policy controls and risk limits; policy exceptions are rare, and properly approved.	Management has sufficient mortgage servicing rights and hedging experience. Policies generally address key risk management practices; exceptions to policies occasionally occur.	Management attention to mortgage servicing is not commensurate with the risk, or management lacks sufficient experience in hedging mortgage servicing rights exposures. Policies do not address key risk management practices; exceptions frequently occur and are not properly approved.
When the bank has ORE, management obtains appraisals and takes any required write-downs on a timely basis. Management actively tries to sell ORE properties.	Appraisals for ORE are occasionally out-of-date or of lower quality. Management's actions to sell ORE properties do not always demonstrate an active interest in disposition.	The quality of appraisals for ORE properties is questionable and/or the appraisals are out-of-date. Management does not actively try to sell ORE properties (e.g., the bank may list the property for sale at an inflated price).
Policies and controls for held-for-sale assets effectively limit risk. Exceptions to policy are quickly identified and promptly raised to appropriate levels of management.	Policies and controls for held-for-sale assets are generally effective, but policy exceptions are not always identified on a timely basis and/or may not be raised to appropriate levels of management.	The bank lacks effective controls on held-for-sale assets. Policy exceptions are not identified on a timely basis and are not raised to appropriate levels of management.

Quality of Price Risk Management Indicators - continued

Strong	Satisfactory	Weak
Management effectively understands, measures, and has technical expertise in managing translation risk. Management and the board regularly review currency translation risk exposures and direct changes, if necessary, given market conditions and the size of the exposure.	Management has a reasonable understanding of translation risk and how to measure and hedge it. Management and the board regularly review translation risk exposures but generally don't direct changes even in unsettled markets.	Management does not demonstrate an understanding of translation risk, and does not have the ability to manage it effectively. Neither management nor the board is aware of the magnitude of translation risk or does not review reports outlining translation risks.
Trading and sales personnel have broad experience in the products traded, are technically competent, and are comfortable with the bank's culture. Risk management personnel have an in-depth understanding of risk and risk management principles. Policy exceptions are rare, and formal procedures exist to report how/why they occurred and how they were resolved.	Trading and sales personnel are generally experienced and technically competent. Risk management personnel, if the bank has such a unit, have a basic understanding of risk and risk management principles. Policy exceptions occur occasionally, but the bank may not have a formal process to report them and track resolution.	Trading and sales personnel may not have a broad experience in the products they trade. A risk management unit does not exist or is not independent and staffed by personnel familiar with risk management principles. Policy exceptions regularly occur and may not be reported or tracked for resolution.
New products are subject to a formal review program, with all relevant bank units participating in risk assessment and control procedures.	New products are subject to a formal review program, but relevant bank units may or may not assess their ability to properly control the activity.	Bank does not have a new product review program or has one that assesses risk in a cursory manner.
Management reports are prepared independently of the trading desk and provide a comprehensive and accurate summary of trading activities. Reports are timely, assess compliance with policy limits, and measure loss potential in both normal (e.g., value at risk) and stressed markets. Management at all levels understands and monitors price risk.	Management reports are prepared independently of the trading desk and provide a general summary of trading activities. Reports are timely but may not fully assess loss potential. Trading unit management reviews risk reports, but management at higher levels may lack the understanding to review it on a frequent basis and in depth.	Management reports are not independent of the trading desk, do not provide risk-focused information, and may not be prepared regularly. Higher-level managers do not understand price risk and do not review risk management reports.
Incompatible duties are properly segregated. Risk monitoring, valuation, and control functions are independent from the business unit.	Incompatible duties are generally segregated. Risk monitoring and control functions may not exist or do not have complete independence from the business unit.	Incompatible duties are often not segregated. Risk control functions do not exist or are not independent from the business unit. Trading positions are frequently valued on trader prices, with limited independent verification.

Operational Risk

Operational risk is the risk to current or anticipated earnings or capital arising from inadequate or failed internal processes or systems, human errors or misconduct, or adverse external events. Operational losses result from internal fraud; external fraud; inadequate or inappropriate employment practices and workplace safety; failure to meet professional obligations involving clients, products, and business practices; damage to physical assets; business disruption and systems failures; and failures in execution, delivery, and process management. Operational losses do not include opportunity costs, forgone revenue, or costs related to risk management and control enhancements implemented to prevent future operational losses. (Updated 5/06/2013)

The quantity of operational risk and the quality of operational risk management are heavily influenced by the quality and effectiveness of a bank's system of internal control. The quality of the audit function, although independent of operational risk management, also is a key assessment factor. Audit can affect the operating performance of a bank by helping to identify and ensure correction of weaknesses in risk management or controls. The quality of due diligence and business continuity planning are other key assessment factors for mitigating operational risk arising from third-party relationships and events outside a bank's direct control, such as natural disasters and damage to or loss of critical infrastructure. (Updated 5/06/2013)

Summary Conclusions

Quantity of operational risk is:

☐ Low	☐ Moderate	☐ High

Quality of operational risk management is:

☐ Strong	☐ Satisfactory	☐ Weak

Examiners should consider both the quantity of operational risk and the quality of operational risk management to derive the following conclusions:

Aggregate operational risk is:

☐ Low	☐ Moderate	☐ High

Direction is expected to be:

☐ Decreasing	☐ Stable	☐ Increasing

Quantity of Operational Risk Indicators

Examiners should use the following indicators when assessing quantity of operational risk.

Low	Moderate	High
Exposure to risk from fraud, errors, or processing disruptions is minimal given the volume of transactions, complexity of products and services, and state of internal systems. Risk to earnings and capital is negligible.	Exposure to risk from fraud, errors, or processing disruptions is modest given the volume of transactions, complexity of products and services, and state of internal systems. Deficiencies that have potential impact on earnings or capital can be addressed in the normal course of business.	Exposure to risk from fraud, errors, or processing disruptions is significant given the volume of transactions, complexity of products and services, and state of internal systems. Deficiencies exist that represent significant risk to earnings and capital.
Risks from transaction-processing failures, technology changes, outsourcing, planned conversions, merger integration, or new products and services are minimal.	Risks from transaction-processing failures, technology changes, outsourcing, planned conversions, merger integration, or new products and services are moderate.	Risks from transaction-processing failures, technology changes, outsourcing, planned conversions, merger integration, or new products and services are high.
Volume of operational losses is minimal.	Volume of operational losses is moderate.	Volume of operational losses is high.
Volume of fraud and intrusions/attacks is minimal.	Volume of fraud and intrusions/attacks is moderate.	Volume of fraud and intrusions/attacks is high.
Employee turnover is low and has not affected any mission critical areas.	Employee turnover is moderate, but effect on mission critical areas is limited.	Employee turnover is excessive and has severely affected key areas of operations.
Number of outsourced servicers is low.	Number of outsourced servicers is moderate.	Number of outsourced servicers is high.
Level of insurance bond claims is low.	Level of insurance bond claims is moderate.	Level of insurance bond claims is high.

Quality of Operational Risk Management Indicators

Examiners should use the following indicators when assessing quality of operational risk management.

Strong	Satisfactory	Weak
Governance activities are sound. Directors are qualified, appropriately compensated, ethical, and provide effective oversight. Corporate roles are clear, goals are effectively communicated, and disclosure is transparent.	Governance activities are satisfactory. Directors are qualified, appropriately compensated and ethical. Oversight provided is adequate but may have subtle weaknesses. Corporate goals and responsibilities may be clear but are not fully communicated. Disclosure is adequate.	Governance activities are deficient. Corporate structure may not be fully defined and/or communicated. Directors' qualifications, ethical standards and/or compensation are questionable. Oversight is inadequate or ineffective. Disclosure is inaccurate and process is flawed.
Management has developed a comprehensive and effective internal control environment. A commitment to internal controls is evident and well disseminated throughout the enterprise. Board oversight is strong. Integrity of control systems is tested on a regular basis.	Control environment is appropriate for the size and sophistication of the institution. Commitment to internal controls is not readily evident or well disseminated. Structure may not be fully communicated across the organization. Board oversight/control culture is considered effective, although modest weaknesses may be present. Control integrity is tested on a periodic basis.	Control environment is deficient. Findings indicate a lack of awareness, commitment and/or focus on the importance of effective and appropriate internal controls. Board oversight is ineffective. Volume and severity of control exceptions are high. Exposure to potential or realized losses from key operational areas may be present. Control integrity testing is nonexistent or is performed inconsistently.
Management anticipates and responds effectively to risks associated with operational changes, emerging/changing technologies, and external threats.	Management adequately responds to risks associated with operational changes, emerging/changing technologies, and external threats.	Management does not take timely and appropriate actions to respond to operational changes, emerging/changing technologies, and external threats.
Management fully understands operational risks and has expertise available to evaluate key technology-related issues.	Management reasonably understands operational risks and has sufficient expertise available to evaluate key technology-related issues.	Management does not understand, or has chosen to ignore, key aspects of operational risk. Expertise available to evaluate key technology-related issues is insufficient.
New/nontraditional product development and implementation is well managed with low risk exposure.	New/nontraditional product development and implementation is adequately managed, with some weaknesses and risk exposure evident.	New/nontraditional product development and implementation is inadequately managed, with significant weaknesses and high-risk exposure.

Quality of Operational Risk Management Indicators – continued

Strong	Satisfactory	Weak
Vendor management activities are sound. Risk exposure is well managed. Management comprehensively provides for continuity and reliability of services furnished by outside providers.	Vendor management activities are satisfactory but may contain modest weaknesses. Risk exposure is satisfactorily managed. Management adequately provides for continuity and reliability of services furnished by outside providers.	Vendor management activities are severely limited or nonexistent. Risk exposure is inadequately managed. Management has not provided for continuity and reliability of services furnished by outside providers.
Controls to safeguard physical assets, data, and personnel are comprehensive and effective in appropriately mitigating risks. Information security program is comprehensive, effective, and tested on a regular basis. Procedures to identify and report potential data losses are effective. Privacy practices are sound.	Controls to safeguard physical assets, data, and personnel are satisfactory but may have modest weaknesses. Information security program is acceptable overall but may require minor enhancement and/or more frequent testing to be fully comprehensive and effective. Procedures to identify and report potential data losses are satisfactory. Privacy practices are satisfactory.	Controls to safeguard physical assets, data, and personnel are deficient or nonexistent. Information security program is flawed, incomplete, and/or inadequate. Annual testing and/or reporting have not occurred and procedures to identify and report potential data losses are absent. Privacy practices are inadequate.
Processes and systems to monitor, track, and categorize operating losses are sound.	Processes and systems to monitor, track, and categorize operating losses are satisfactory but may contain modest weaknesses.	Processes and systems to monitor, track, and categorize operating losses are weak or nonexistent.
MIS provide appropriate monitoring of transaction volumes, error reporting, fraud, suspicious activity, security violations, etc. MIS is accurate, timely, complete and reliable.	MIS for transaction processing are adequate, although moderate weaknesses may exist.	MIS for transaction processing are unsatisfactory and exhibit significant weaknesses or may not exist.
Insurance coverage is sufficient and policies are current. An effective process for provider/agent selection and monitoring is present and overall coverage adequacy is reviewed at least annually.	Insurance coverage is sufficient and policies are current. Provider/agent selection process is acceptable and ongoing monitoring is limited. Coverage adequacy is reviewed on a periodic basis.	Insurance coverage is insufficient for the exposure present. Inadequate tracking procedures have allowed policies to lapse. Due diligence programs for provider/agent selection and/or ongoing monitoring are inadequate, flawed, or ineffective.

Quality of Operational Risk Management Indicators – continued

Strong	Satisfactory	Weak
Audit coverage is strong. Audit activities are frequent and ongoing and address all key areas of operations. Audit function is fully independent and competent, and scope is comprehensive. Risk assessment is effective and current. Follow-up and correction of deficiencies is proactive and effective. Repeat issues are rare or nonexistent. Board oversight is effective.	Audit coverage is satisfactory. Function is fully independent and competent, but scope may be limited. Risk assessment is acceptable overall but may be missing substance in some areas or require updating. Follow-up and correction of deficiencies is adequate but with moderate weaknesses noted therein. Repeat issues are few. Board oversight is adequate.	Audit coverage is inadequate. Independence may be impaired, competency may be questionable and scope may be inappropriate. Risk assessment is ineffective or nonexistent. Follow-up and correction of deficiencies is highly inconsistent. Repeat issues are numerous. Board oversight is limited and ability to self police is impaired.

Compliance Risk

Compliance risk is the risk to current or anticipated earnings or capital arising from violations of laws, rules, or regulations, or from nonconformance with prescribed practices, internal policies and procedures, or ethical standards. This risk exposes a bank to fines, civil money penalties, payment of damages, and the voiding of contracts. Compliance risk can result in diminished reputation, reduced franchise or enterprise value, limited business opportunities, and lessened expansion potential. (Updated 5/06/2013)

Compliance risk is not limited to risk from failure to comply with consumer protection laws; it encompasses the risk of noncompliance with *all* laws and regulations, as well as prudent ethical standards and contractual obligations. It also includes the exposure to litigation (known as legal risk) from all aspects of banking, traditional and nontraditional. (Updated 5/06/2013)

Summary Conclusions

Quantity of compliance risk is:

□ Low	□ Moderate	□ High

Quality of compliance risk management is:

□ Strong	□ Satisfactory	□ Weak

Examiners should consider both the quantity of compliance risk and the quality of compliance risk management to derive the following conclusions:

Aggregate compliance risk is:

□ Low	□ Moderate	□ High

Direction is expected to be:

□ Decreasing	□ Stable	□ Increasing

Quantity of Compliance Risk Indicators

Examiners should use the following indicators when assessing quantity of compliance risk.

Low	Moderate	High
Violations or compliance program weaknesses are insignificant in number and issues or do not exist.	Violations or compliance program weaknesses exist and represent technical issues with some reimbursement to consumers that are resolved in a timely manner.	Violations or compliance program weaknesses are significant in number, resulting in large consumer reimbursements or regulatory fines and penalties.
No e-banking or the Web site is informational or non-transactional.	Bank is beginning e-banking and offers limited products and services.	Bank offers a wide array of e-banking products and services (e.g., account transfers, e-bill payments or accounts opened via the Internet).
All loans are originated in-house with no broker or third-party relationships.	Low volume of consumer and business loans are originated by local brokers or other third parties.	High volume of consumer or business loans is originated by multiple statewide or nationwide brokers or other third parties.
Limited/no marketing or advertising of products and services.	Limited marketing or advertising practices commensurate with strategic focus.	Marketing and advertising of new products offered through multiple of channels (branch network, Internet, direct mail, solicitations, etc.).
Bank offers traditional mix of non-complex lending, investment, and deposit products.	Bank offers traditional investment and deposit products and a mix of traditional and complex lending products.	Bank offers a broad array of traditional and complex lending, investment, and deposit products.
Bank offers products and services to local market/service area.	Bank offers products and services to regional market/service area.	Bank offers products and services to national market/service area.
Financial institution competition within its marketplace is minimal.	Financial institution competition within its marketplace is considerable.	Financial institution competition within its marketplace is significant and may include large national and international companies.
Volume of products and services offered is reasonable considering its financial strength and capability, and growth is stable.	Volume of products and services offered is increasing considering its financial strength and capability, and growth is steady.	Volume of products and services offered is outpacing its financial strength and capability, and growth is unstable.
Bank has few offices, some automated teller machines and centralized operations.	Bank has statewide branching and automated teller machine network with decentralized operations.	Bank has regional or national branching and automated teller machine network with decentralized operations.
Volume of consumer complaints is minimal.	Volume of consumer complaints is moderate.	Volume of consumer complaints is high.

Quality of Compliance Risk Management Indicators

Examiners should use the following indicators when assessing the quality of compliance risk management.

Strong	Satisfactory	Weak
Board has adopted compliance risk management policies that are consistent with business strategies and risk tolerance.	Board has adopted compliance risk management policies that are generally consistent with business strategies and risk tolerance.	Board has adopted compliance risk management policies that are inconsistent with business strategies and risk tolerance.
Management fully understands all aspects of compliance risk; exhibits clear commitment to compliance. Commitment is communicated throughout the institution.	Management reasonably understands the key aspects of compliance risk. Commitment to compliance is reasonable and satisfactorily communicated throughout the institution.	Management does not understand or has chosen to ignore key aspects of compliance risk. Importance of compliance is not emphasized or communicated throughout the organization.
Authority and accountability are clearly defined and enforced.	Authority and accountability are defined, although some refinements may be needed.	Management has not established or enforced accountability.
Management anticipates and responds well to market, technological, or regulatory changes.	Management adequately responds to market, technological, or regulatory changes.	Management does not anticipate or take timely or appropriate actions in response to market, technological, or regulatory changes.
Compliance considerations are incorporated into product/system development and modification processes, including changes made by service providers or vendors.	Although compliance may not be formally considered when developing products and systems, issues are typically addressed before they are fully implemented.	Compliance considerations are not incorporated into product and system development.
Control systems effectively identify violations or compliance system weaknesses and corrective action is prompt and reasonable.	Control systems are adequate for identifying violations or compliance system weaknesses but not always in a timely manner. Management is usually responsive and corrective action is generally timely but not in all instances.	Control systems are ineffective in identifying violations and compliance system weaknesses. Management is unresponsive; corrective action is weak.
Management provides effective resources/training programs to ensure compliance.	Management provides adequate resources/training, given the complexity of products/operations.	Management has not provided adequate resources or training.

Quality of Compliance Risk Management Indicators – continued

Strong	Satisfactory	Weak
Bank has a strong record of compliance. Considering the scope and complexity of its operations and structure, compliance risk management systems are sound and minimize the likelihood of significant or frequent violations or instances of noncompliance.	Bank has a satisfactory record of compliance. Considering scope and complexity of operations and structure, compliance risk management systems are adequate to avoid significant or frequent violations or instances of noncompliance.	Bank has unsatisfactory record of compliance. Considering scope and complexity of operations and structure, compliance risk management systems are deficient, reflecting inadequate commitment to risk management.
Bank has strong record of acting on and monitoring consumer complaints.	Bank has satisfactory record of acting on and monitoring consumer complaints.	Bank has a weak record of acting on and monitoring consumer complaints.

Strategic Risk

Strategic risk is the risk to current or anticipated earnings, capital, or franchise or enterprise value arising from adverse business decisions, poor implementation of business decisions, or lack of responsiveness to changes in the banking industry and operating environment. This risk is a function of a bank's strategic goals, business strategies, resources, and quality of implementation. The resources needed to carry out business strategies are both tangible and intangible. They include communication channels, operating systems, delivery networks, and managerial capacities and capabilities. (Updated 5/06/2013)

The assessment of strategic risk includes more than an analysis of a bank's written strategic plan. It focuses on opportunity costs and how plans, systems, and implementation affect the bank's franchise or enterprise value. It also incorporates how management analyzes external factors, such as economic, technological, competitive, regulatory, and other environmental changes, that affect the bank's strategic direction. (Updated 5/06/2013)

Summary Conclusions

Aggregate strategic risk is:

☐ Low	☐ Moderate	☐ High

Direction is expected to be:

☐ Decreasing	☐ Stable	☐ Increasing

Strategic Risk Indicators

Examiners should use the following indicators when assessing aggregate level of strategic risk.

Low	Moderate	High
Board has adopted policies that are fully consistent with business strategies and risk tolerance.	Board has adopted policies that are generally consistent with business strategies and risk tolerance.	Board has adopted policies that are inconsistent with business strategies and risk tolerance.
Risk management practices are an integral part of strategic planning.	Quality of risk management is consistent with the strategic issues confronting the organization.	Risk management practices are inconsistent with strategic initiatives. A lack of strategic direction is evident.
Strategic goals, objectives, corporate culture, and behavior are effectively communicated and consistently applied throughout the organization. Strategic direction and organizational efficiency are enhanced by management's depth and technical expertise.	Management has demonstrated ability and technical expertise to implement goals and objectives. Successful implementation of strategic initiatives is likely.	Strategic initiatives are inadequately supported by operating policies and programs that direct behavior. Structure and managerial and/or technical talent of the organization do not support long-term strategies.
Management has been successful in accomplishing past goals and is appropriately disciplined.	Management has a reasonable record of decision making and controls.	Deficiencies in management decision making and risk recognition do not allow the institution to effectively evaluate new products, services, or acquisitions.
MIS effectively support strategic direction and initiatives.	MIS reasonably support the company's short-term direction and initiatives.	MIS supporting strategic initiatives are seriously flawed or do not exist.
Strategic goals are not overly aggressive and are compatible with developed business strategies.	Strategic goals are aggressive but compatible with business strategies.	Strategic goals emphasize significant growth or expansion that is likely to result in earnings volatility or capital pressures.
Strategic initiatives are well conceived and supported by appropriate communication channels, operating systems, and service delivery networks. Initiatives are well supported by capital for the foreseeable future and pose only nominal possible effects on earnings volatility.	Corporate culture has minor inconsistencies with planned strategic initiatives. Initiatives are reasonable considering the capital, communication channels, operating systems, and service delivery networks. Decisions are unlikely to have significant adverse impact on earnings or capital. If necessary, decisions or actions can be reversed without significant cost or difficulty.	Impact of strategic decisions is expected to significantly affect franchise value. Strategic initiatives may be aggressive or incompatible with developed business strategies, communication channels, operating systems, and service delivery networks. Decisions are difficult or costly to reverse.

Strategic Risk Indicators – continued

Low	Moderate	High
Strategic initiatives are supported by sound due diligence and strong risk management systems. Decisions can be reversed with little difficulty and manageable costs.	Strategic initiatives do not materially alter business direction, can be implemented efficiently and cost effectively, and are within management's abilities.	Strategic goals are unclear or inconsistent and have led to imbalance between institution's tolerance for risk and willingness to supply supporting resources.
Compensation programs achieve an appropriate balance between risk appetite and controls. Compensation strategies reflect core principle of "pay for performance." Performance goals and metrics to measure achievement are reasonably transparent.	Compensation programs are appropriately balanced between risk appetite and controls but may be informal or reflect modest weaknesses. Incentives are appropriate. Performance goals and metrics to measure achievement are reasonably transparent overall but may contain some minor obscurities.	Compensation programs unduly focus on short-term performance. Incentives may be inappropriate. Use of performance goals and metrics to measure achievement are obscure.
Board and management succession strategies are formalized, effective, and well incorporated into ongoing planning activities. Adequate expertise exists within the institution for successor management. Board vacancies are few, anticipated and replacement candidates are identified and discussed well in advance.	Board and management succession strategies are acceptable, but may be informal. Adequate expertise exists to stabilize the bank until an acceptable outside or inside candidate is identified. Board succession is discussed as needed, with candidates identified prior to vacancy.	Succession planning is not considered and no strategies are evident. Internal expertise may be questionable, with no action plans evident if management is unable to perform. Board may have several pending vacancies with limited or no discussion of suitable replacements.
Due diligence for new products and services is robust. Process considers all appropriate factors including: assessing the impact to the bank's strategic direction, assessing the associated risks, consulting with relevant functional areas, determining regulatory requirements, determining the expertise needed, researching any vendors, developing a realistic business plan, and developing viable alternatives. After introduction, appropriate risk management processes have been developed including performance monitoring and ongoing vendor management.	Due diligence for new products and services is satisfactory. Process may not fully consider all appropriate factors but provides for a general understanding of the risks associated with any new product or service. After introduction, appropriate risk management processes have been developed but may not be fully implemented.	Due diligence for new products and services is insufficient. Process does not consider the appropriate factors and the risks associated with any new product or service are not known. After introduction, appropriate risk management processes have not been developed or implemented.

Reputation Risk

Reputation risk is the risk to current or anticipated earnings, capital, or franchise or enterprise value arising from negative public opinion. This risk may impair a bank's competitiveness by affecting its ability to establish new relationships or services or continue servicing existing relationships. Reputation risk is inherent in all bank activities and requires management to exercise an abundance of caution in dealing with customers, counterparties, correspondents, investors, and the community. (Updated 5/06/2013)

A bank that actively associates its name with products and services offered through outsourced arrangements or asset management affiliates is more likely to have higher reputation risk exposure. Significant threats to a bank's reputation also may result from negative publicity regarding matters such as unethical or deceptive business practices, violations of laws or regulations, high-profile litigation, or poor financial performance. The assessment of reputation risk should take into account the bank's culture, the effectiveness of its problem-escalation processes and rapid-response plans, and its deployment of media. (Updated 5/06/2013)

Summary Conclusions

Aggregate reputation risk is:

☐ Low	☐ Moderate	☐ High

Direction is expected to be:

☐ Decreasing	☐ Stable	☐ Increasing

Reputation Risk Indicators

Examiners should use the following indicators when assessing aggregate level of reputation risk.

Low	Moderate	High
Management anticipates and responds well to changes of a market or regulatory nature that affect its reputation in the marketplace.	Management adequately responds to changes of a market or regulatory nature that affect its reputation in the marketplace.	Management does not anticipate or take timely or appropriate actions in response to changes of a market or regulatory nature.
Management fosters a sound culture that is well supported throughout the organization and has proven effective over time.	Administration procedures and processes are satisfactory. Management has a good record of correcting problems. Any deficiencies in MIS are minor.	Weaknesses may be observed in one or more critical operational, administrative, or investment activities. Management information at various levels exhibits significant weaknesses.
Bank effectively self-polices risks.	Bank adequately self-polices risks.	Bank's ability to self-police risk is suspect.
Management demonstrates outstanding performance in meeting community's credit needs. Community reinvestment is a formal part of strategic planning and daily business. Bank is routinely seen in a leadership role in community development. Lending programs targeted to low/moderate income borrowers and areas are innovative and effective. Identified lending areas are appropriate and legal.	Management demonstrates satisfactory performance in meeting community's credit needs. Bank generally participates in community development activities but not in a leadership role. Lending programs targeted to low/moderate income borrowers and areas exist but are not innovative or complex. Identified lending and service areas are appropriate and legal.	Management's performance in meeting community's credit needs requires improvement or is unsatisfactory. Participation in community development activities is rare and lending to low/moderate income borrowers or areas may be limited. Identified lending areas may arbitrarily exclude low/moderate income areas.
Franchise value is minimally exposed by reputation risk. Exposure from reputation risk is expected to remain low in foreseeable future.	Exposure of franchise value from reputation risk is controlled. Exposure is not expected to increase in foreseeable future.	Franchise value is substantially exposed by reputation risk shown in significant litigation, large dollar losses, or a high volume of customer complaints. Potential exposure is increased by number of accounts, volume of assets under management, or number of affected transactions. Exposure is expected to continue in foreseeable future.

Reputation Risk Indicators – continued

Low	Moderate	High
Losses from fiduciary activities are low relative to number of accounts, volume of assets under management, and number of affected transactions. Bank does not regularly experience litigation or customer complaints.	Bank has avoided conflicts of interest and other legal or control breaches. Level of litigation, losses, and customer complaints are manageable and commensurate with volume of business conducted.	Poor administration, conflicts of interest, and other legal or control breaches may be evident.
Management has clear awareness of privacy issues and uses customer information responsibly.	Management understands privacy issues and generally uses customer information responsibly.	Management is not aware or concerned with privacy issues and may use customer information irresponsibly.
Fair lending practices are strong and management has fostered a solid credit culture. Fair lending policies are comprehensive and well communicated to all areas of the bank. Fair lending requirements are well known, with ongoing training provided at least annually. Credit decision making is centralized. Underwriting policies are well defined and are followed with few exceptions. A formal second review process is in place and annual testing is required.	Fair lending practices are satisfactory and management's commitment is appropriate. Fair lending principles are informally understood throughout the bank but not fully integrated into all areas. Decision making may be decentralized and underwriting requirements may be general in nature, with a modest level of exceptions. A second review function exists but is informal. Testing and training are acceptable but may display subtle weaknesses.	Management has not demonstrated an effective commitment to fair lending. Fair lending practices/policies are not well communicated and concepts are not fully understood. Underwriting requirements are limited and exceptions are excessive. No second review process exists. Testing and training programs are limited, ineffective, or absent. Potential for noncompliance is high.
Internal controls and audit are fully effective.	Internal controls and audit are generally effective.	Internal controls and audit are not effective in reducing exposure. Management has not initiated or has a poor record of corrective action to address problems.

Appendix B: Other Risks

BSA/AML/OFAC Risk Indicators

Quantity of BSA/AML/OFAC Risk Indicators

Examiners should use the following indicators when assessing quantity of BSA/AML/OFAC risk.

Low	Moderate	High
Stable, known customer base.	Customer base increasing due to branching, merger, or acquisition.	Large and growing customer base in a wide and diverse geographic area.
No e-banking or Web site is informational or non-transactional.	Bank is beginning e-banking and offers limited products and services.	Bank offers a wide array of e-banking products and services (e.g., account transfers, e-bill payment, or accounts opened via the Internet).
On the basis of information received from the BSA-reporting database, there are few or no large currency or structured transactions.	On the basis of information received from the BSA-reporting database, there is a moderate volume of large currency or structured transactions.	On the basis of information received from the BSA-reporting database, there is a significant volume of large currency or structured transactions.
Identified a few high-risk customers and businesses; these may include nonresident aliens, foreign individuals (including accounts with U.S. powers of attorney), and foreign commercial customers. (Updated 9/28/2012)	Identified a moderate number of high-risk customers and businesses.	Identified a large number of high-risk customers and businesses.
No overseas branches and no foreign correspondent financial institution accounts. Bank does not engage in pouch activities, offer special-use accounts, or offer payable through accounts (PTA), or provide U.S. dollar draft services. (Updated 9/28/2012)	Bank has overseas branches or a few foreign correspondent financial institution accounts, typically with financial institutions with adequate AML policies and procedures from low-risk countries, and minimal pouch activities, special-use accounts, payable through accounts (PTA), or U.S. dollar draft services. (Updated 9/28/2012)	Bank has overseas branches or maintains a large number of foreign correspondent financial institution accounts with financial institutions with inadequate AML policies and procedures, particularly those located in high-risk jurisdictions, or offers substantial pouch activities, special-use accounts, payable through accounts (PTA), or U.S. dollar draft services. (Updated 9/28/2012)
Few international accounts or very low volume of currency activity in the accounts.	Moderate level of international accounts with unexplained currency activity.	Large number of international accounts with unexplained currency activity.

Quantity of BSA/AML/OFAC Risk Indicators – continued

Low	Moderate	High
Bank offers limited or no private banking services or trust and asset management products or services.	Bank offers limited domestic private banking services or trust and asset management products or services over which the bank has investment discretion. Strategic plan may be to increase trust business.	Bank offers significant domestic and international private banking or trust and asset management products or services. Private banking or trust and asset management services are growing. Products offered include investment management services, and trust accounts are predominantly nondiscretionary versus where the bank has full investment discretion.
Limited number of funds transfers for customers, noncustomers; limited third-party transactions, and no foreign funds transfers.	Moderate number of funds transfers. Few international funds transfers from personal or business accounts with typically low-risk countries.	Large number of noncustomer funds transfer transactions and payable upon proper identification (PUPID) transactions. Frequent funds from personal or business accounts to or from high-risk jurisdictions, and financial secrecy havens or jurisdictions.
No other types of international transactions, such as trade finance, cross border ACH, and management of sovereign debt. (Updated 9/28/2012)	Limited other types of international transactions. (Updated 9/28/2012)	A high number of other types of international transactions. (Updated 9/28/2012)
No history of OFAC actions. No evidence of apparent violation or circumstances that might lead to a violation. (Updated 9/28/2012)	A small number of recent actions (e.g., actions within the last five years) by OFAC, including notice letters, or civil money penalties, with evidence that the bank addressed the issues and is not at risk of similar violations in the future. (Updated 9/28/2012)	Multiple recent actions by OFAC, where the bank has not addressed the issues, thus leading to an increased risk of the bank undertaking similar violations in the future. (Updated 9/28/2012)
Bank is not in a High Intensity Drug Trafficking Area (HIDTA) or High Intensity Financial Crime Area (HIFCA). No fund transfers or account relationships involve HIDTAs or HIFCAs.	Bank is in a High Intensity Drug Trafficking Area (HIDTA) or High Intensity Financial Crime Area (NIFCA). Bank has some fund transfers or account relationships that involve HIDTAs or HIFCAs.	Bank is in a High Intensity Drug Trafficking Area (HIDTA) and an HIFCA. Large number of fund transfers or account relationships involve HIDTAs or HIFCAs.
No transactions with high-risk geographic locations.	Minimal transactions with high-risk geographic locations.	Significant volume of transactions with high-risk geographic locations.
Low turnover of key personnel or frontline personnel (e.g., customer service representatives, tellers, or other branch personnel).	Low turnover of key personnel, but frontline personnel in branches may have changed.	High turnover, especially in key personnel positions.

Quality of BSA/AML/OFAC Risk Management Indicators

Examiners should use the following indicators when assessing quality of BSA/AML/OFAC risk management.

Strong	Satisfactory	Weak
Management fully understands the aspects of compliance risk and exhibits strong commitment to compliance.	Management reasonably understands key aspects of compliance and commitment is generally clear and satisfactorily communicated.	Management does not understand or has chosen to ignore key aspects of compliance risk. Importance of compliance is not emphasized or communicated throughout the organization.
Compliance considerations are incorporated into all products and areas of the organization.	Compliance considerations are overlooked or are weak in one or two areas.	Compliance considerations are not incorporated into numerous areas of the organization.
When deficiencies are identified, management promptly implements meaningful corrective action.	Problems can be corrected in the normal course of business without significant investment of money or management attention. Management is responsive when deficiencies are identified.	Errors and weaknesses are not self-identified. Management may only respond when violations are cited.
Authority and accountability for compliance are clearly defined and enforced, including designation of qualified BSA officer.	Authority and accountability are defined, but some refinements are needed. Qualified BSA officer has been designated.	Authority and accountability for compliance has not been clearly established. No qualified BSA officer or an unqualified one may have been appointed. Role of BSA officer is unclear.
Independent testing is in place and is effective.	Overall, independent testing is in place and effective. However, some weaknesses are noted.	Independent testing is not in place and/or is ineffective.
Board has approved a BSA compliance program that includes adequate policies, procedures, controls, and information systems.	Board has approved a BSA compliance program that addresses most policies, procedures, controls, and information systems but some weaknesses are noted.	Board may not have approved a BSA compliance program. Policies, procedures, controls, and information systems are significantly deficient. For example, there are substantial failures to file currency transaction reports and/or suspicious activity reports.
Training is appropriate, effective, covers applicable personnel, and necessary resources have been provided to ensure compliance.	Training is conducted and management provides adequate resources given the risk profile of the organization; however, some areas are not covered within the training program.	Training is not consistent and does not cover important regulatory and risk areas.

Quality of BSA/AML/OFAC Risk Management Indicators – continued

Strong	Satisfactory	Weak
Effective customer identification processes and account-opening procedures are in place.	Customer identification processes and account-opening procedures are generally in place but not well applied to all high-risk areas.	Customer identification processes and account-opening procedures are absent or ineffective.
Management has identified and developed controls that are applied appropriately to high-risk areas, products, services, and customers of the bank.	Management is aware of high-risk areas, products, services, and customers, but controls are not always appropriately applied to manage this risk.	Management is not fully aware of high-risk areas of the bank. Inadequate policies, procedures, and controls have resulted in instances of unreported suspicious activity, unreported large currency transactions, structured transactions, and/or substantive violations of law.
Compliance systems and controls quickly adapt to changes in various government lists (e.g., OFAC, Financial Crimes Enforcement Center [FinCEN], and Other Government Provided List).	Compliance systems and controls are generally adequate and adapt to changes in various government lists (e.g., OFAC, Financial Crimes Enforcement Center [FinCEN], and Other Government Provided List).	Compliance systems and controls are inadequate to comply with and adapt to changes in various government lists (e.g., OFAC, Financial Crimes Enforcement Center [FinCEN], and Other Government Provided List).
Compliance systems and controls effectively identify and appropriately report suspicious activity. Systems are commensurate with risk.	Compliance systems and controls generally identify suspicious activity. However, monitoring systems are not comprehensive or have some weaknesses.	Compliance systems and controls are ineffective in identifying and reporting suspicious activity.
Low volume of correspondence from IRS indicates that CTRs are accurate.	Volume of correspondence from IRS indicates some errors in CTR reporting.	Volume of correspondence from IRS indicates a substantive volume of CTR reporting errors.
Appropriate compliance controls and systems are implemented to identify compliance problems and assess performance.	No shortcomings of significance are evident in compliance controls or systems. Probability of serious future violations or noncompliance is within acceptable tolerance.	Likelihood of continued compliance violations or noncompliance is high because a corrective action program does not exist or extended time is needed to implement such a program.

Fair Lending Risk Indicators

Quantity of Fair Lending (F/L) Risk Indicators

Examiners should use the following indicators when assessing quantity of fair lending risk.

Low	Moderate	High
Significant and explainable volume of consumer lending.	Lower volume of consumer lending, but explainable.	Low and unexplainable volume of consumer lending. (Bank could be discouraging applicants).
Generic, non-complex products offered.	Limited number of complex products offered.	Several complex products offered (e.g., subprime high-cost mortgages, etc.).
Low number of policy exceptions/overrides.	Modest number of policy exceptions/overrides and may exceed guidelines.	High number of policy exceptions/overrides.
Lending policies allow little or no lender discretion in the loan decision process.	Lending policies allow some lender discretion in the loan decision process.	Lending policies allow high level of lender discretion in the loan decision process.
Little or no disparities among approval/denial rates or pricing by prohibited basis groups.	Some disparities among approval/denial rates or pricing by prohibited basis groups.	Substantive disparities among approval/denial rates or pricing by prohibited basis groups.
Low proportion of withdrawn/incomplete applications for prohibited basis groups.	Moderate proportion of withdrawn/incomplete applications for prohibited basis groups.	Higher proportion of withdrawn/incomplete applications for prohibited basis groups.
No conspicuous gaps in lending patterns.	Explainable conspicuous gaps in lending patterns.	Unexplainable conspicuous gaps in lending.
Centralized underwriting and makes own loans.	Local brokers originate a low volume of loans.	Decentralized underwriting and high volume of loans originated by multiple statewide or nationwide brokers.
No marketing practices or products that are targeted to any specific group or location.	Limited marketing practices or products that are targeted to specific groups. Activity is commensurate with strategic focus.	Marketing practices or products are targeted to specific groups or locations, (e.g., advertising sub-prime or higher cost consumer loans in a language other than English).
No F/L complaints or complaints to Departments of Justice (DOJ) or Housing and Urban Development (HUD) regarding discrimination or discouraged applications.	Limited number of F/L related complaints.	Numerous F/L related complaints.

Quantity of Fair Lending (F/L) Risk Indicators – continued

Low	Moderate	High
No F/L lawsuits or claims regarding discrimination or discouraged applicants.	Community groups have raised F/L issues. Some potential lawsuits (e.g., allegations of predatory lending).	Actual F/L lawsuits or claims. Investigations of fair lending complaints by DOJ or HUD.
No special compensation incentives for lenders	Lenders do receive incentives for number of loans made, but activity is closely monitored.	Lenders receive incentives for number of loans made without review.

Quality of Fair Lending Risk Management Indicators

Examiners should use the following indicators when assessing quality of fair lending risk management.

Strong	Satisfactory	Weak
Bank conducts an effective F/L risk assessment. Results are discussed with the board.	Bank conducts a F/L risk assessment but system is flawed.	Little or no monitoring of F/L compliance.
Centralized decision making with ongoing monitoring for consistency. Bank adheres to well-defined underwriting standards and override procedures.	Centralized decision making but with limited monitoring. Staff generally adheres to underwriting standards and override procedures.	Decentralized decision making without monitoring of discretionary pricing, overrides, or policy exceptions.
Bank has an effective second review process in place.	Bank has implemented an informal second review process (e.g., inconsistent consideration of denied applications, exceptions, and/or overrides.	No second review process.
F/L considerations are incorporated into all areas of the bank, (e.g., rollout of new products, advertising, changes in forms, disclosures, etc.)	F/L considerations sometimes overlooked and not incorporated into all areas of the bank. Management effects corrective action when identified.	F/L considerations are not incorporated in numerous areas of the bank. Management does not effect corrective action.
Policies and procedures are adequate.	Policies and procedures are generally adequate but certain weaknesses are noted.	Policies and procedures are significantly flawed and do not provide sufficient guidance as to why business reasons or other factors are not discriminatory.
When deficiencies are identified, management promptly implements meaningful corrective action.	Management is responsive when deficiencies are identified in the normal course of business or second review process.	Errors and deficiencies are not self-identified. Management may only respond when violations are cited.
Training to ensure consistent treatment is appropriate and effective. Necessary resources have been provided to ensure compliance. Experienced, well-trained, and knowledgeable staff.	Training is conducted but is conducted infrequently or is not timely. Management might not provide adequate resources and employee turnover may be high.	Training is sporadic and ineffective (as evidenced by inconsistent application of underwriting standards); high volume of withdrawn/incomplete applications may indicate bank is discouraging applicants.
Bank is responsive and resolves complaints promptly when received.	In general, complaints are promptly and adequately addressed.	Management does not monitor or adequately and promptly address complaints.

Quality of Fair Lending Risk Management Indicators - continued

Strong	Satisfactory	Weak
Appropriate fair lending compliance controls and systems (e.g., quality control functions, compliance audits, and self-assessments) are implemented to identify compliance problems and assess performance.	No significant shortcomings are evident in fair lending compliance controls or systems (e.g., compliance reviews, compliance audits, and self-assessments). Probability of serious future violation or noncompliance is within acceptable tolerance.	Significant shortcomings are evident in fair lending compliance controls or systems (e.g., quality control functions, compliance reviews, compliance audits, and self-assessments). The probability of serious future violation or noncompliance is not within acceptable risk tolerances.
Clear and objective standards for referring applicants to subsidiaries or affiliates; classifying applicants as "prime" or "subprime" or deciding what alternative loan products should be offered.	Objective standards for referring applicants to subsidiaries or affiliates; classifying applicants as "prime" or "subprime" or deciding what alternative loan products should be offered.	Missing clear and objective standards for referring applicants to subsidiaries or affiliates; classifying applicants as "prime" or "subprime" or deciding what kinds of alternative loan products should be offered.

Consumer Lending Regulations Risk Indicators

Quantity of Consumer Lending Regulations (FDPA/RESPA/TILA/HPA/HMDA) Risk Indicators

Examiners should use the following indicators when assessing quantity of consumer lending regulations risk.

Low	Moderate	High
Noncomplex and stable types of products offered (e.g., fixed-rate long-term mortgages, simple consumer loans).	Limited number of complex loan products offered. Products change occasionally.	Complex loan products offered (e.g., ARMS, HELOC, construction loans). Products change frequently.
Consistent, high volume of loan originations with no recently identified violations of law/regulation indicating bank is accustomed to dealing with technical regulations.	Consistent high volume of loan originations with occasional technical violations noted.	Low level or infrequent loan originations and/or frequent violations noted.
Experienced, knowledgeable staff in key lending control positions. May be indicated by low staff turnover or frequency of training.	Experienced, knowledgeable staff in moderately critical lending control positions.	Inexperienced or untrained staff in key or high volume critical lending control positions. High turnover or infrequent training may be an indicator.
Stable software and processes with low errors in technical requirements (disclosures, notices, APRs, changes in indices, etc.).	Implementation of new software, or software conversions with some errors in technical requirements.	System conversions or software changes due to vendor changes or merger activity. Problems indicated by high level of errors in technical requirements.
Electronic banking is not offered or is limited to account inquiries.	Electronic banking is limited to non-transactional functions, and is informational only. Information includes triggering terms. No on-line loan applications permitted.	Loan application and transactions accepted via the Internet increasing the difficulty of delivering disclosures and makes bank more susceptible to fraud.
Marketing activities are limited to local area, stable environment, centralized.	Marketing activities are limited to standard products, decentralized channels (branches), and wider geographical area.	Active marketing of new products offered through multiple channels (Internet, direct mail, solicitations, etc.).
Interest rate environment is stable.	Interest rate environment is changing but loan volume is manageable.	Interest rates environment is unstable causing unmanageable loan volume.
Few competitors.	Multiple competitors. May result in bank offering some loan products they are not experienced in	High level of competition causing increased loan volume, particularly in complex loan products they are

| handling. | not experienced in handling. |

Quantity of Consumer Lending Regulations (FDPA/RESPA/TILA/HPA/HMDA) Risk Indicators - continued

Low	Moderate	High
Few or no consumer complaints are received. There is no obvious pattern as to regulation type when complaints are reviewed.	Some consumer complaints are received. There is no obvious pattern as to regulation type.	Several consumer complaints are received and may represent a pattern.
No special flood hazard areas in lending area. (FDPA)	Lending area has few special flood hazard areas.	Lending area has numerous special flood hazard areas.
No broker relationship or limited broker relationships with low amount of unearned fees either paid or received. (RESPA)	Moderate use of broker and moderate amount of unearned fees either paid or received.	Broker relationship coupled with high amount of unearned fee income either paid or received.
Bank does not offer products or services that require expanded, detailed regulatory compliance such as: • Credit cards (TILA) • Home equity loans/lines (TILA) • Consumer leases (Leasing) • Escrow (RESPA, HPA) • Private mortgage insurance (TILA, HPA) • Required service providers (RESPA) • Controlled business arrangements	Bank may offer some products or services that require expanded, detailed regulatory compliance such as: • Credit cards (TILA) • Home equity loans/lines (TILA) • Consumer leases (Leasing) • Escrow (RESPA, HPA) • Private mortgage insurance (TILA, HPA) • Required service providers (RESPA) • Controlled business arrangements	Bank offers numerous products or services that require expanded, detailed regulatory compliance such as: • Credit cards (TILA) • Home equity loans/lines (TILA) • Consumer leases (Leasing) • Escrow (RESPA, HPA) • Private mortgage insurance (TILA, HPA) • Required service providers (RESPA) • Controlled business arrangements
Low number of consumer complaints received. No pattern as to type of complaint. Few or no substantive issues.	Moderate number of consumer complaints received without a pattern as to compliance type. Moderate number of substantive issues.	Several consumer complaints are received and may represent a pattern. Significant number of substantive issues. OCC Customer Assistance Group has notified the supervisory office.
Bank does not provide disclosures electronically.	Bank provides electronic and paper disclosures. Staff is knowledgeable of E-Sign Act and there is effective consumer opt-in as required by the act.	Bank only provides disclosures electronically. Staff has some knowledge of E-Sign Act. Effective consumer opt-in, as required by the act, is inconsistent.
No loans subject to the Servicemembers Civil Relief Act and the Talent Amendment.	Some loans subject to the Servicemembers Civil Relief Act and the Talent Amendment.	Significant number of loans subject to the Servicemembers Civil Relief Act and the Talent Amendment.

Quality of Consumer Lending Regulations (FDPA/RESPA/TILA/HPA/HMDA) Risk Management Indicators

Examiners should use the following indicators when assessing quality of consumer lending regulations risk management.

Strong	Satisfactory	Weak
Management fully understands all aspects of lending compliance risk and exhibits clear commitment to compliance. Commitment is communicated throughout affected areas of the institution.	Management reasonably understands the key aspects of lending compliance risk. Commitment to lending compliance is reasonable and satisfactorily communicated throughout affected areas of the institution.	Management does not understand or has chosen to ignore key aspects of lending compliance risk. Importance of lending compliance is not emphasized or communicated throughout affected areas of the institution.
Authority and accountability for lending compliance are clearly defined and enforced.	Authority and accountability for lending compliance are defined, although some refinements may be needed.	Management has not established or enforced accountability for lending compliance performance.
Management anticipates and responds well to changes of a market, technological or regulatory nature that affect lending regulations compliance.	Management adequately responds to changes of a market, technological or regulatory nature that affect lending regulations compliance.	Management does not anticipate or take timely or appropriate actions in response to changes of a market, technological or regulatory nature that affect lending regulations compliance.
Lending compliance considerations are incorporated into products and system development processes, including changes made by outside service providers or vendors or affiliates.	Lending compliance may not be formally considered when developing products and systems, and issues are typically addressed before they are fully implemented.	Lending compliance considerations are not incorporated into product and systems development.
When lending compliance deficiencies are identified, management promptly implements meaningful corrective action.	Lending compliance problems can be corrected in the normal course of business without a significant investment of money or management attention. Management is responsive when lending deficiencies are identified.	Lending compliance errors are often not detected internally, corrective action is often ineffective, or management is unresponsive.
Appropriate lending compliance controls and systems (e.g., quality control functions, compliance audits, and self-assessments) are implemented to identify compliance problems and assess performance.	No shortcomings of significance are evident in lending compliance controls or systems (e.g., quality control functions, compliance reviews, compliance audits, and self-assessments). Probability of serious future violations or noncompliance is within acceptable tolerance.	Likelihood of continued lending compliance violations or noncompliance is high because a corrective action program does not exist, or extended time is needed to implement such a program.

Quality of Consumer Lending Regulations (FDPA/RESPA/TILA/HPA/HMDA) Risk Management Indicators – continued

Strong	Satisfactory	Weak
Lending compliance training programs are effective, and the necessary resources have been provided to ensure compliance.	Management provides adequate resources and training for compliance.	Management has not provided adequate resources or training for compliance with lending regulations.
Compliance risk management processes and information systems are sound, and the bank has a strong control culture that has proven effective for lending compliance.	Compliance risk management processes and information systems are adequate to avoid significant or frequent violations or noncompliance with lending regulations.	Compliance risk management processes and information systems are deficient in the lending regulations.
Effective control systems are in place to assure maintenance of flood insurance throughout the loan term. This includes mechanism to force place flood insurance if necessary. (FDPA)	Control systems are in place to detect the expiration of insurance but there is not a mechanism to provide for the timely force placement of insurance (gaps in insurance can occur).	Bank does not have effective system to maintain flood insurance.
Control systems are effective to collect and accurately report all HMDA and CRA loans.	Control systems do not capture all loans or there are errors. Bank's internal control systems found data errors and corrected them.	Control systems are not capturing all loans. Bank does not have a quality control system to detect errors.
HMDA or FHHLD System data are evaluated quarterly for trends and accuracy.	HMDA or FHHLD System data are not evaluated for trends but accuracy is assessed quarterly.	HMDA or FHHLD System data are not evaluated for trends nor reviewed for accuracy until prepared for submission to the FFIEC.

Consumer Deposit Regulations Risk Indicators

Quantity of Consumer Deposit Regulations (Reg. D, Reg. DD, Reg. CC, Reg. E) Risk Indicators

Examiners should use the following indicators when assessing quantity of consumer deposit regulations risk.

Low	Moderate	High
Staff is experienced and knowledgeable regarding regulatory requirements that apply to their functions. Staff turnover is generally low.	Staff is generally experienced and knowledgeable regarding regulatory requirements that apply to their functions. Some turnover is identified.	Staff is inexperienced or is not knowledgeable regarding regulatory requirements that apply to their functions. Turnover may be high.
Noncomplex products are offered. Product types are stable. (Reg. D, Reg. DD, Reg. CC, Reg. E)	Limited number of complex products is offered. Product types change occasionally. (Reg. D, Reg. DD, Reg. CC, Reg. E)	Several complex deposit products offered (e.g.. index-powered CDs, tiered rate, stepped-rate). Product types change frequently. (Reg. D, Reg. DD, Reg. CC, Reg. E)
Electronic banking is not offered or is limited to account inquiries. (Reg. D, Reg. DD)	Electronic banking is limited to non-transactional functions and is informational only (which may trigger Reg. DD advertising requirements). No account opening permitted. (Reg. D, Reg. DD)	Accounts can be opened via the Internet and transactions conducted (account-to-account transfers, electronic bill payment, etc.). (Reg. D, Reg. DD, Reg. CC, Reg. E)
Marketing activities are limited to local area, stable environment, centralized. (Reg. DD)	Marketing activities are limited to standard products, decentralized channels (individual branches or lines of business) (Reg. DD)	Active marketing of new products offered through multiple channels (Internet, direct mail, etc.). (Reg. DD)
Interest rate environment is stable. (Reg. DD)	Interest rate environment is unstable but volume is manageable. (Reg. DD)	Interest rates are unstable. May result in rapid shift in demand for certain products (Reg. DD). May indicate a need for further disclosures to the consumer.
Few competitors. (Reg. DD)	Multiple competitors. May result in the bank developing more complex products. (Reg. DD)	High level of competition. May result in the bank offering premiums or bonuses for deposit products. (Reg. DD)
Tested and proven software and processes are in use. Few if any errors regarding technical requirements (disclosures, notices, APYs, etc) are noted. (Regs. DD, CC, D, E)	New software has been implemented, or software conversions have taken place. Some errors regarding technical requirements are noted. (Regs. DD, CC, D, E)	System conversions or software changes have been implemented due to vendor changes, or merger activity. Numerous errors regarding technical requirements are noted. (Regs. DD, CC, D, E).

Quantity of Consumer Deposit Regulations (Reg. D, Reg. DD, Reg. CC, Reg. E) Risk Indicators – continued

Low	Moderate	High
Next day availability of deposits across the board. Few exception holds. (Reg. CC)	Case-by-case, new account and large deposit exceptions occur occasionally. Deposit holds are done infrequently. (Reg. CC)	Holds are placed frequently. (Reg. CC)
Low number of consumer complaints received. No pattern as to type of complaint. Few or no substantive issues.	Moderate number of consumer complaints received without a pattern as to compliance type. Moderate number of substantive issues.	Several consumer complaints are received and may represent a pattern. Significant number of substantive issues.
Access devices are not offered or are limited to ATM cards. (Reg. E)	Access devices such as ATM and debit cards are offered. Multiple channels may be available. (Reg. E)	Bank's ATM network may be extensive. Access devices such as ATM and debit cards are offered. Multiple channels may be available. (Reg. E)
Bank does not offer MMDA or NOW accounts. (Reg. D)	MMDA and/or NOW accounts may be offered as permitted by regulation. (Reg. D)	MMDA and/or NOW accounts are offered. NOW accounts may not be limited to consumers only. (Reg. D)
Bank does not provide disclosures electronically.	Bank provides both electronic and paper disclosures. Staff is knowledgeable of E-Sign Act and there is effective consumer opt-in as required by the act.	Bank provides disclosures electronically only. Staff has some knowledge of the E-Sign Act. Effective consumer opt-in, as required by the act, is inconsistent.

Quality of Consumer Deposit Regulations (Reg. D, Reg. DD, Reg. CC, Reg. E) Risk Management Indicators

Examiners should use the following indicators when assessing quality of consumer deposit regulations risk management.

Strong	Satisfactory	Weak
Management fully understands all aspects of deposit compliance risk and exhibits clear commitment to compliance. Importance of deposit compliance is emphasized and communicated throughout the organization.	Management reasonably understands key aspects of deposit compliance risk. Commitment to deposit compliance is reasonable and satisfactorily communicated.	Management does not understand key aspects of deposit compliance risk. Commitment to deposit compliance is not reasonable or satisfactorily communicated.
Authority and accountability for deposit compliance is clearly defined and enforced.	Authority and accountability for deposit compliance is defined, although some refinements are needed.	Management has not established or enforced accountability for deposit compliance performance.
Management anticipates and responds well to changes of a market, technological, or regulatory nature that affect deposit regulations compliance.	Management adequately responds to changes of a market, technological, or regulatory nature that affect deposit regulations compliance.	Management does not anticipate or take timely or appropriate actions in response to changes of a market, technological, or regulatory nature that affect deposit regulations compliance.
Deposit compliance considerations (APYs, periodic statements, deposit holds, MMDA withdrawals/transfers, etc.) are incorporated into products and system development and modification processes, including changes made by outside service providers or vendors. (Regs. DD, E, CC, D)	Although deposit compliance may not be formally considered when developing products and systems, issues are typically addressed before they are fully implemented.	Deposit compliance considerations are not incorporated into product and systems development.
When deposit compliance deficiencies are identified, management promptly implements meaningful corrective action. These include responding to customer complaints and resolving EFT errors.	Deposit compliance problems can be corrected in the normal course of business without a significant investment of money or management attention. Management is responsive when deposit deficiencies are identified.	Deposit compliance errors are often not detected internally, corrective action is often ineffective, or management is unresponsive.

Quality of Consumer Deposit Regulations (Reg. D, Reg. DD, Reg. CC, Reg. E) Risk Management Indicators – continued

Strong	Satisfactory	Weak
Appropriate deposit compliance controls and systems (e.g., quality control functions, compliance audits, self-assessments) are implemented to identify compliance problems and assess performance.	No shortcomings of significance are evident in deposit compliance controls or systems (e.g., quality control functions, compliance reviews, compliance audits, and self-assessments). The probability of serious future violations or noncompliance is within acceptable tolerance.	Likelihood of continued deposit compliance violations or noncompliance is high because a corrective action program does not exist, or extended time is needed to implement such a program.
Deposit compliance training programs are effective, and the necessary resources have been provided to ensure compliance.	Management provides adequate resources and training given the complexity of products and operations for compliance with deposit regulations.	Management has not provided adequate resources or training for compliance with deposit regulations.
Compliance risk management processes and information systems are sound and the bank has a strong control culture that has proven effective for deposit compliance.	Compliance risk management processes and information systems are adequate to avoid significant or frequent violations or noncompliance with deposit regulations.	Compliance risk management processes and information systems are deficient in the deposit regulations.

Other Consumer Regulations Risk Indicators

Quantity of Other Consumer Regulations Risk Indicators
(Privacy of Consumer Financial Information, Fair Credit Reporting Act, Right to Financial Privacy Act, Fair Debt Collection Practices Act, Children's On-Line Privacy Protection Act, Controlling the Assault of Non-Solicited Pornography and Marketing Act, Telephone Consumer Protection Act)

Examiners should use the following indicators when assessing quantity of other consumer regulations risk.

Low	Moderate	High
Bank does not share customer information with affiliates and non-affiliates outside of the regulatory exceptions contained in 12 CFR 40.13, .14, and .15 (Privacy)	Bank shares limited customer information with affiliates and non-affiliates.	Bank actively shares customer information with affiliates and non-affiliates.
Bank does not disclose information to nonaffiliated third parties outside the statutory exceptions, and an opt-out election is therefore not necessary. (Privacy)	Bank discloses information to nonaffiliated third parties outside the statutory exceptions. Consumers are provided a reasonably clear and conspicuous opt-out notice and a generally reasonable means to do so. Bank has devised a generally effective means to record, maintain, and effectuate opt-out election by consumers.	Bank discloses information to nonaffiliated third parties outside the statutory exceptions. Consumers are either not provided with an opt-out notice, or it is not clear and conspicuous. It is difficult for consumers to submit the notice. Bank either has not devised a means to record, maintain, and effectuate opt-out election by consumers, or it is not effective.
Bank has no relationships with nonaffiliated entities. (Privacy)	Bank has relationships with a limited number of nonaffiliated entities.	Bank has relationships with a large number of nonaffiliated entities.
Bank does not report credit information on its customers other than to a consumer-reporting agency. (Fair Credit Reporting Act)	Bank provides credit information on its customers to their holding companies or affiliates as permitted by the law.	Bank routinely provides credit information on its customers to other creditors or correspondents to market new products.
Bank has not received requests from government agencies for information related to customers' financial records. (Right to Financial Privacy Act)	Bank has received limited requests from government agencies for customers' financial records.	Bank has received a significant number of requests from government agencies for customers' financial records.

Quantity of Other Consumer Regulations Risk Indicators – continued

Low	Moderate	High
Bank does not operate a Web site or online service directed to children younger than 13 or does not have actual knowledge that it is collecting or maintaining personal information from a child online. (COPPA).	Bank's Web site may collect information from children younger than 13 but does not have an FTC-approved program.	Bank's Web site collects information from children younger than 13. Bank participates in an FTC-approved, self-regulatory program and independent review/audit has verified bank's compliance with the program.
Bank does not market products or services via e-mail or telephone (CAN-SPAM, TCPA).	Bank may market products or services via e-mail or telephone, but its program does not meet all requirements of CAN-SPAM or TCPA.	Bank markets products or services via e-mail or telephone. It does not have a process to review or ensure compliance with requirements of CAN-SPAM or TCPA.
Bank does not regularly collect consumer debts for another person or institution or use any name other than its own when collecting consumer debts and is therefore not a "debt collector." (Fair Debt Collection Practices Act)	Bank occasionally acts as a "debt collector."	Bank frequently acts as a "debt collector.

Quality of Other Consumer Regulations Risk Management Indicators

(Privacy of Consumer Financial Information, Fair Credit Reporting Act, Right to Financial Privacy Act, Fair Debt Collection Practices Act, Children's On-Line Privacy Protection Act, Controlling the Assault of Non-Solicited Pornography and Marketing Act, Telephone Consumer Protection Act)

Examiners should use the following indicators when assessing quality of other consumer regulations risk management.

Strong	Satisfactory	Weak
Management has effective privacy and marketing policies that accurately reflect the operations of the bank. (Privacy, CAN-SPAM, TCPA)	Management has privacy and marketing policies that adequately reflect the operations of the bank.	Management does not understand or has chosen to ignore key aspects of risk within the privacy regulation. Privacy and marketing policies are ineffective and do not accurately reflect the operations of the bank.
Bank has implemented a comprehensive, board-approved written information security program that complies with section 501(b) of GLBA. (Privacy)	Bank has implemented an adequate, board-approved written information security program that generally complies with section 501(b) of GLBA but has some weaknesses.	Bank has not implemented a written information security program or does not adequately comply with section 501(b) of GLBA.
Compliance actively monitors to ensure that the bank does not report credit information on its customers other than to a consumer-reporting agency. (Fair Credit Reporting Act)	Compliance adequately monitors to ensure that the bank does not report credit information on its customers other than to a consumer-reporting agency.	Compliance does not monitor to ensure that the bank does not report credit information on its customers other than to a consumer-reporting agency.
Bank has an effective system to ensure that requests for information related to customer's financial records from government agencies are responded to appropriately. (Right to Financial Privacy Act)	An adequate control system may not be fully implemented to ensure that requests for information from government agencies are responded to appropriately.	Bank does not have a control system in place to ensure that requests for information related to customer's financial records from government agencies are responded to appropriately.
Training related to privacy and marketing laws and regulations is effective, and resources have been provided to ensure compliance.	Management provides adequate resources and training given the complexity of products and operations for compliance with privacy and marketing laws and regulations.	Management has not provided adequate resources or training for compliance with privacy and marketing laws and regulations.
Authority and accountability for privacy and marketing compliance is clearly defined and enforced.	Authority and accountability for privacy and marketing compliance are defined, although some refinements may be needed.	Management has not established or enforced accountability for privacy and marketing compliance performance.

Quality of Other Consumer Regulations Risk Management Indicators – continued

Strong	Satisfactory	Weak
Turnover of bank staff responsible for privacy-related compliance is minimal.	Bank has experienced some turnover of bank staff responsible for privacy-related compliance, but management has quickly and effectively replaced them.	Turnover of bank staff responsible for privacy-related compliance has occurred. Replacement staff has not been found.
Bank either has not received any consumer complaints or, if it has, the complaint resolution process is timely and complete.	Bank responds to consumer complaints in a generally timely and complete manner.	Bank either does not respond to consumer complaints, or does so after an extended period of time. Responses are generally inadequate.
Appropriate compliance controls and systems (e.g., quality control functions, compliance audits, and self-assessments) are implemented to identify compliance problems and assess performance.	No shortcomings of significance are evident in compliance controls or systems (e.g., quality control functions, compliance reviews, compliance audits, and self-assessments). Probability of serious future violations or noncompliance is within acceptable tolerance.	Likelihood of continued compliance violations or noncompliance is high because a corrective action program does not exist, or extended time is needed to implement such a program.

Asset Management Risk Indicators

Quantity of Asset Management Risk Indicators

Examiners should use the following indicators when assessing quantity of asset management risk.

Low	Moderate	High
Amount of capital allocated to asset management is low and insignificant in relation to total capital.	Substantial amount of capital is allocated to asset management but still not high in relation to total capital.	Amount of capital allocated to asset management is substantial and significant in relation to total capital.
Asset management revenue or operating profit is insignificant in relation to the bank's overall revenue or operating profit.	Asset management revenue or operating profit is an important contributor to the bank's total revenue or operating profit.	Asset management revenue or operating profit is a substantial contributor to the bank's total revenue or operating profit.
Asset management accounts administered and/or managed are mostly noncomplex and small in size.	Asset management accounts administered and/or managed may be complex and large in size.	Significant number of asset management accounts administered and/or managed are complex and large in size.
Asset management products and services are provided in a limited number of locations or branches in one state.	Asset management products and services are provided in locations or branches in more than one state.	Asset management products and services are provided in multiple locations or branches in multiple states.
Asset management account growth is low and stable, and usually below management expectations. New product volume is low.	Asset management account growth is significant and generally meets or exceeds management expectations. New product volume is high.	Asset management account growth is significantly above management expectations. New product volume is significant and complex.
Transaction volume of asset management accounts is not significant, and the probability of significant loss from errors, disruptions, or fraud is minimal.	Transaction volume of asset management accounts is substantial, but the probability of significant loss from errors, disruptions, or fraud is acceptable.	Transaction volume of asset management accounts is substantial, and the probability of significant loss from errors, disruptions, or fraud is high.
Compliance with applicable law is good and the potential for noncompliance is minimal. Identified violations are quickly and effectively corrected.	Compliance with applicable law is satisfactory, but compliance can be improved. Identified violations are normally corrected in a satisfactory manner.	Compliance with applicable law is unsatisfactory and the potential for additional noncompliance is high. Identified violations are not corrected in a timely and effective manner.

Quantity of Asset Management Risk Indicators – continued

Low	Moderate	High
Financial losses from asset management are low relative to allocated capital.	Financial losses from asset management are moderate relative to allocated capital.	Financial losses from asset management are high relative to allocated capital.
Volume and significance of litigation related to asset management is minimal.	Volume and significance of litigation related to asset management is satisfactory, but increasing.	Volume and significance of litigation related to asset management is high and increasing.
Volume and significance of complaints by clients is minimal.	Volume and significance of complaints by clients is satisfactory but increasing.	Volume and significance of complaints by clients is high and increasing.
Compliance with asset management related policies and procedures is good and the potential for significant noncompliance is minimal.	Compliance with asset management related policies and procedures is satisfactory, but unauthorized policy exceptions exist and policy compliance can be improved.	Compliance with asset management related policies and procedures is unsatisfactory and potential for additional noncompliance is high.
Asset management related audit findings are usually good. The type and volume of audit exceptions are minor. Audit deficiencies are quickly and effectively corrected.	Asset management related audit typically identifies a moderate level of exceptions that require a higher level of management involvement. Audit deficiencies are normally corrected in a satisfactory manner.	Asset management related audit typically identifies a high level of exceptions that require a significant senior management involvement. Audit deficiencies are not corrected in a timely and effective manner.

Quality of Risk Management for Asset Management Indicators

Examiners should use the following indicators when assessing quality of risk management for asset management activities.

Strong	Satisfactory	Weak
Strategic planning processes fully incorporate asset management. Asset management strategic planning and financial budgeting processes are sound.	Strategic planning processes include asset management. Asset management strategic planning and financial budgeting processes are adequate with some deficiencies.	Strategic planning processes do not include asset management. Asset management strategic planning and financial budgeting processes are inadequate and ineffective.
Board has adopted asset management policies that are fully consistent with business strategies and risk tolerance.	Board has adopted asset management policies that are generally consistent with business strategies and risk tolerance.	Board has adopted asset management policies that are inconsistent with business strategies and risk tolerance.
Asset management is well-organized with clear lines of authority and responsibility for monitoring adherence to policies, procedures, and controls.	Asset management is adequately organized. Lines of authority and responsibility have been established, but improvement can be made.	Asset management is poorly organized. Clear lines of authority and responsibility have not been established.
Board has employed a strong asset management team. Management is competent, experienced, and knowledgeable of business strategies, policies, procedures, and control systems.	Board has employed an adequate asset management team. Management is competent, experienced, and knowledgeable in most areas.	Board has employed an inadequate asset management team. Management is inexperienced and may not be competent. Inadequate knowledge of business.
Processes effectively identify, approve, track, report, and correct significant asset management related policy and control exceptions.	Processes generally identify, approve, track, report, and correct significant asset management related policy and control exceptions. Processes can be improved.	Processes do not identify, approve, track, report, and correct significant asset management related policy and control exceptions in an acceptable manner.
Staffing levels and expertise are appropriate for the size and complexity of the asset management business.	Staffing levels and expertise are adequate for the size and complexity of the asset management business.	Staffing levels and expertise are inadequate for the size and complexity of the asset management business.
Personnel policies, practices, and training programs related to asset management are reasonable and sound.	Personnel policies, practices, and training programs related to asset management are satisfactory, but can be improved.	Personnel policies, practices, and training programs related to asset management are deficient and ineffective.

Quality of Risk Management for Asset Management Indicators – continued

Strong	Satisfactory	Weak
Policies and controls to prevent and detect inappropriate conflicts of interest and self-dealing are comprehensive and effective.	Policies and controls to prevent and detect inappropriate conflicts of interest and self-dealing are adequate and generally effective.	Policies and controls to prevent and detect inappropriate conflicts of interest and self-dealing are inadequate and ineffective.
Management and the board receive comprehensive information reports to manage asset management risk.	Management and the board receive adequate information reports. Content and/or timeliness could be improved.	Management and the board do not receive adequate and/or timely information reports to manage asset management risk.
Management uses legal counsel appropriately and effectively.	Management uses legal counsel in an adequate and generally effective manner.	Management does not use legal counsel appropriately and effectively.
Risks from new asset management products and services, strategic initiatives, or acquisitions are well controlled and understood. Products and services are thoroughly researched, tested, and approved before implementation.	Risks from new asset management products and services, strategic initiatives, or acquisitions are adequately controlled and understood. Products and services are researched, tested, and approved before implementation, but processes could be improved.	Risks from new asset management products and services, strategic initiatives, or acquisitions are not adequately controlled and understood. Products and services are not adequately researched, tested, and approved before implementation.
Asset management compliance program is comprehensive and effective.	Asset management compliance program is adequate and generally effective.	Asset management compliance program is deficient and ineffective.
Account acceptance and administration processes are strong and effective.	Account acceptance and administration processes are adequate and generally effective.	Account acceptance and administration processes are deficient and ineffective.
Processes to develop, approve, implement, and monitor client investment policies, including performance measurement, are comprehensive and effective.	Processes to develop, approve, implement, and monitor client investment policies, including performance measurement, are adequate and generally effective.	Processes to develop, approve, implement, and monitor client investment policies, including performance measurement, have significant deficiencies and are ineffective.
Processes to analyze, acquire, manage, and dispose of client portfolio assets are comprehensive and effective. Policies and procedures for the selection and monitoring of third-party vendors, including investment managers and advisors, are comprehensive and effective.	Processes to analyze, acquire, manage, and dispose of client portfolio assets are adequate and generally effective. Policies and procedures for the selection and monitoring of third-party vendors, including investment managers and advisors, are adequate and generally effective.	Processes to analyze, acquire, manage, and dispose of client portfolio assets have significant deficiencies and are ineffective. Policies and procedures for the selection and monitoring of third-party vendors, including investment managers and advisors, have significant deficiencies and are ineffective.

Quality of Risk Management for Asset Management Indicators – continued

Strong	Satisfactory	Weak
Management fully understands technology risks and has readily available expertise to evaluate technology-related issues.	Management generally understands technology risks and has reasonable access to expertise on technology-related issues.	Management does not understand technology risks and does not have or use available expertise on technology-related issues.
Management effectively anticipates and responds to risks associated with operational changes, systems development, and emerging technologies.	Management adequately anticipates and responds to risks associated with operational changes, systems development, and emerging technologies.	Management does not adequately anticipate and respond to risks associated with operational changes, systems development, and emerging technologies.
Management provides continuous and reliable operating systems, including financial and operational services provided by third-party vendors. Contingency planning is comprehensive and frequently tested.	Management provides continuous and reliable operating systems, including financial and operational services provided by third-party vendors, but occasional disruptions occur. Contingency planning is adequate but could be improved.	Management does not provide continuous and reliable operating systems, including financial and operational services provided by third-party vendors. Significant disruptions occur and contingency planning is poor.
Asset management audit program is suitable and effective. Oversight by the board and management is strong.	Asset management audit program is satisfactory but can be improved. Oversight by the board and management is adequate.	Asset management audit program is significantly deficient. Oversight by the board and management is weak and ineffective.

Appendix C: Standard Request Letter

Note: This appendix is provided as a guide and should be modified as needed depending on the scope of the supervisory activity and the risk profile of the bank. The EIC should indicate which items need to be provided before the start of the supervisory activity and which will be reviewed during the on-site portion of the supervisory activity. If activities are being conducted throughout the supervisory cycle, examiners should only request the information they need to complete the current activity. The EIC is responsible for getting the general information and maintaining it in Examiner View to avoid duplicate requests to the bank.

During examination planning, the EIC should discuss with bank management the feasibility of obtaining the request letter information in a digital format. If the bank can facilitate providing a digital format, the following paragraph should be included in the request letter:

In order for us to prepare effectively for this supervisory activity, please provide the information listed in the attachment to this request letter in digital format and send to the designated EIC via OCC secure mail, which can be accessed by going to www.banknet.gov. When this is not possible, we request the data be faxed to a designated number at our office. For larger pieces of hard copy information and for security purposes, we request that you provide the information by mail using a "tracking" service. Please indicate whether hard copy information needs to be returned.

In addition, the request letter should include the following statement with regard to the consumer compliance portion of the examination:

The consumer compliance examination is being conducted under the authority of 12 USC 481. However, it also constitutes an investigation within the meaning of section 3413(h)(1)(A) of the Right to Financial Privacy Act. Therefore, in accordance with section 3403(b) of the Act, the undersigned hereby certifies that the OCC has complied with the Right to Financial Privacy Act, 12 USC 3401, et seq. Section 3417(c) of the Act provides that good faith reliance upon this certification relieves your institution and its employees and agents of possible liability to the consumer in connection with the disclosure of the requested information.

Management and Supervision

1. The most recent board packet. Information included in the packet and requested below need not be duplicated.

2. Current organizational chart.

3. If changes have occurred since the last examination, a list of directors and executive management, and their backgrounds, including work experience, length of service with the bank, etc. Also, a list of committees, including current membership.

4. If changes have occurred since the last examination, a list of related organizations (e.g., parent holding company, affiliates, and operating subsidiaries).

5. Changes in use of third-party loan originators and relationship to the bank.

6. Most recent external audit and consultant reports, management letters, engagement letters, and management's responses to findings (including audits of outside service providers, if applicable).

7. Internal audit schedule, including compliance and other separate audits, for the current year. Please note those audits that have been completed and their summary ratings, as well as those that are in process.

8. Most recent internal audit reports including compliance and other separate audits, as well as management's responses. Include (prior year) audit reports covering loan administration, funds management and investment activities, risk-based capital computations, Bank Secrecy Act, information processing and audit areas that were assigned a less than satisfactory rating.

9. A copy of risk assessments performed by management or an outside party.

10. Brief description of new products, services, lines of business, delivery channels, or changes in the bank's market area.

11. List of data processors and other servicers (e.g., loan, investment). The detail of the list should include:

   - Name of servicer.
   - Address of servicer.
   - Contact name and phone number.
   - Brief explanation of the product(s) or service(s) provided.
   - Note of affiliate relationships with the bank.

   For example, services provided may include the servicing of loans sold in whole or in part to other entities, including the service provider. OCC examiners use this list to request trial balances or other pertinent information not otherwise requested in this letter.

12. Minutes of board and major committee meetings (e.g., Audit, Risk, Loan, Asset/Liability Management, Compliance, Fiduciary, Technology Steering Committee) since our last examination.

13. A brief summary of corrective action taken to address MRA identified in the last examination report.

Asset Quality

14. List of watch list loans, problem loans, past-due credits, and nonaccrual loans.

15. List of the 10 largest credits, including commitments, made since the last examination and the new loan report for the most recent quarter.

16. Most recent concentrations of credit reports.

17. Most recent policy, underwriting, collateral, and documentation exception reports.

18. List of insider credits (to directors, executive officers, and principal shareholders) and their related interests. The list should include terms (rates, collateral, structure, etc.) and be cross-referenced with exception reports.

19. List of loan participations purchased and sold, whole loans purchased and sold, and securitization activity since the last examination.

20. List of overdrafts.

21. Most recent analysis of ALLL including risk rating changes from the most recent quarter.

22. List of other real estate, repossessed assets, classified investments, and cash items.

23. List of small business and farm loans "exempt" from documentation requirements.

24. Latest loan review report, including responses from the senior lending officer, account officers, etc.

25. List of board-approved changes to the loan policy and underwriting standards since the last examination.

26. Most recent loan trial balance.

27. Bank's loan policy including a description of the bank's risk rating system.

Financial Performance

28. Most recent ALCO package.

29. Most recent reports used to monitor and manage IRR (e.g., gap planning, simulation models, and duration analysis).

30. Most recent liquidity reports (e.g., sources and uses).

31. List of investment securities purchased and sold for (current year) and (prior year). Please include amount, seller/buyer, and date of each transaction.

32. Most current balance sheet and income statement.

33. Most recent strategic plan, budget, variance reports, etc.

34. Current risk-based capital calculation.

35. Securities acquired based upon "reliable estimates" authority in 12 CFR 1.3(i).

36. Securities acquired using the bank's lending authority.

37. Prepurchase analysis for all securities purchased since the last examination.

38. Summary of the primary assumptions used in the IRR measurement process and the source.

39. Current CFP.

40. Investment portfolio summary trial, including credit ratings.

41. List of board-approved securities dealers.

42. List of shareholders and ownership.

43. Most recent annual and quarterly shareholders' reports.

44. Most recent Report of Condition and Income (call report).

45. List of pending litigation, including a description of circumstances behind the litigation.

46. Details regarding the bank's blanket bond and other major insurance policies (including data processing-related coverage). Provide name of insurer, amount of coverage and deductible, and maturity. Also, please indicate the date of last board review and whether the bank intends to maintain the same coverage upon maturity.

47. Summary of payments to the holding company and affiliates.

48. Bank work papers for the most recent call report submitted.

IT Systems

49. List of in-house computer systems and networks. Include equipment vendor, type/version of system, operating system, number of terminals, and major applications

accessed/processed. Provide schematics for networks (including local or wide area networks).

50. List of major software applications used by the bank. Include developer (in-house or vendor), individual/company responsible for maintenance, and computer system(s) where application is used. Include PC-based applications or spreadsheets that support the bank's risk-management processes (for example, internally developed gap report).

51. As applicable, contracts, financial analyses, and performance monitoring reports for servicers/vendors.

52. Meeting minutes from IT steering committee (or similar group) since the last examination.

53. Bank and servicer plans for disaster recovery and corporate-wide business recovery including report from most recent disaster recovery test.

54. Reports used to monitor computer activity, network performance, system capacity, security violations, and network intrusion attempts.

55. Bank policies and procedures relating to information processing or information security.

Asset Management

56. Asset management organizational chart and resumes of senior asset Management officers hired since the last examination.

57. Bank policies and procedures relating to asset management activities.

58. Most recent management reports, including those used to monitor new and closed accounts, account investment reviews, overdrafts, financial results, etc.; exceptions; and compliance/risk information related to asset management.

59. Information on investment activities, including most recent analysis of investment performance, approved securities lists, arrangements with mutual funds, and approved brokers/dealers.

60. Information on asset management operations, including a user access report for the trust accounting system. Please make available the most recent reconcilements of general ledger, cash/DDA and suspense/house accounts, and securities held at depositories.

61. Asset master list reflecting CUSIP (if applicable), description, number of units, book value, and market value for each asset. Asset master list should include unique assets such as real estate, closely held securities, and other non-marketable assets.

62. Most recent asset management trial balance. Please include account name, account number, account type, the bank's investment authority, and market value for each account. Also identify accounts opened within the past 12 months.

Retail Sales of Non-Deposit Investment Products

63. Information on retail sales activities including the bank's program management statement, agreements with vendors providing retail sales services, MIS used to monitor activities, employee referral programs, and complaints.

Insurance Activities

64. Description of the bank's insurance activities, planned changes, and client complaint information.

Consumer Compliance

65. List of approved changes to the bank's compliance policies, procedures, and compliance review process since the last examination.

66. Changes to the bank's CRA assessment area(s).

67. Changes in third-party relationships, contracts, or activities.

68. List of real estate secured loans originated in special flood hazard areas since the last examination.

69. List of consumer complaints received since the last examination with brief descriptions.

70. Copies of (1) fair lending self-assessments; (2) written analyses of the bank's home mortgage lending; and (3) information regarding credit scoring model validations and compliance with Regulation B.

71. Description of the bank's training programs and criteria for ensuring that employees receive job-appropriate compliance training.

BSA/AML Compliance

72. Board-approved BSA/AML compliance program, including compliance with 12 CFR 21.21. (Updated 9/28/2012)

73. List of products, services, customers, and geographies with a high risk for money laundering. In addition, if you have not already done so for the current calendar year, please complete the attached "Quantity of Risk Summary Form."

74. Provide an overview of your key internal controls and management information reports to detect suspicious cash activity, wire transfer activity, monetary instrument sales, and transactions involving high-risk jurisdictions.

75. List of non-resident alien accounts.

Appendix D: Community Bank Report of Examination

Since 1993, examiners have written examination reports consistent with the interagency uniform common core ROE format. More recently, the federal banking agencies agreed to a more flexible approach in writing reports of examination. Specifically, a streamlined ROE generally is used for all community banks. For community banks supervised by the Large Bank division, examiners should follow guidance on communications in the "Large Bank Supervision" booklet of the *Comptroller's Handbook*.

Examination reports for community banks with composite ratings of 1 or 2 need only address the mandatory items below. Individual ROE pages are available for each of these items. Based on the bank's condition and risk profile, examiners have the discretion to use these individual ROE pages or address the mandatory items under the "Examination Conclusions and Comments" page. Examiners should include additional supplemental pages, based on the risk profile of the bank and the results of the supervisory activities. If any component rating is 3 or worse, the examiner must use the appropriate narrative page. Other schedules related to that component rating should also be used, as needed. In addition, examiners use the applicable narrative page to communicate significant supervisory concerns, such as the bank's unwarranted risk taking. A narrative page can also be used to explain when supervisory activities have been expanded due to the bank's high overall risk profile.

As specified in Examining Bulletin 93-9, the examiner is still required either to complete a separate ROE for targeted examinations of areas such as compliance or asset management or to include the information on the appropriate optional page in the ROE at the end of the supervisory cycle.

The uniform common core ROE is still required for:

- Community banks rated composite 3 or worse, or
- Community banks that have been in operation less than 3 years.

Mandatory ROE Items

- **Examination Conclusions and Comments**

  Examiners detail the conclusions and recommendations identified during the examination. This page should also include composite and component CAMELS/ITCC ratings, and other regulatory ratings. A brief comment should be included to support each rating. As appropriate, a statement that no MRA was noted should also be included on this page.

- **Management/Administration**

  Examiners assess the board's and management's supervision, including audit and internal controls.

- **Summary of Items Subject to Adverse Classification/Items Listed as Special Mention**

  Examiners list a summary of assets subject to adverse classification/special mention.

- **Risk Assessment Summary**

  Examiners assess quantity of risk, quality of risk management, aggregate level of risk, and direction of risk for each risk category using the RAS matrix. A brief narrative comment of each risk category may be included to communicate concerns that are not addressed elsewhere in the ROE. The RAS page in the ROE can be used to articulate future problems and potential vulnerabilities. When used effectively, the page can provide a valuable platform for an examiner to discuss prospective issues.

- **Signature of Directors**

  Examiners include the "Signature of Directors" page from the standard ROE shell.

The following pages become mandatory under the circumstances described below:

MRAs must be completed when bank practices deviate from sound fundamental governance, internal controls, and risk management principles which may adversely impact the bank's earnings, capital, risk profile, or reputation if not addressed. MRAs are also necessary when bank practices result in substantive noncompliance with laws or internal policies and procedures.

Concentrations must be completed when concentration levels that pose a challenge to management are identified, or present unusual or significant risk to the bank. The concentration data must also be entered into Examiner View.

Compliance with Enforcement Actions must be completed whenever the bank is under a formal or informal enforcement action.

Violations of Laws and Regulations is required whenever substantive legal and regulatory violations are identified.

Supplemental Pages

Examiners include supplemental pages if they are relevant to the supervisory activity and justified by the bank's condition and risk profile. If a component rating is 3 or worse, the examiner must use the applicable narrative page. Other schedules relating to the component rating are not necessarily required but should be used as needed.

Supplemental pages:

- Capital Adequacy
- Asset Quality
- Earnings
- Liquidity — Asset/Liability Management
- Sensitivity to Market Risk
- Comparative Statements of Financial Condition
- Capital Calculations
- Analysis of Earnings
- IT Systems
- Consumer Compliance
- Fair Lending
- Asset Management
- CRA
- Loans With Structural Weaknesses
- Items Subject to Adverse Classification
- Items Listed for Special Mention
- Credit or Collateral Exceptions
- Loans and Lease Financing Receivables/Past Due and Nonaccural Loans and Leases
- Other Matters
- Additional Information
- Report Abbreviations

References

Note: This section lists some of the references frequently used by examiners to supervise community banks.

Capital

12 USC 56 and 60, Dividends
12 USC 1817(j), 12 CFR 5.50, "Control of the Bank
12 CFR 3, "Minimum Capital Ratios"
OCC Banking Circular 268, "Prompt Corrective Action"

Asset Quality

12 USC 84, 12 CFR 32, "Lending Limits"
12 CFR 34, Real Estate Lending and Appraisals
OCC Advisory Letter 2000-9, "Third-Party Risk"
OCC Banking Bulletin 93-18, "Interagency Policy on Small Business Loan Documentation"
OCC Banking Circular 181, "Purchases of Loans in Whole or in Part — Participations"
OCC Bulletin 99-10, "Interagency Guidance on Subprime Lending"
OCC Bulletin 2000-20, "Uniform Retail Credit Classification and Account Management Policy"
OCC Bulletin 2001-37, "Policy Statement on Allowance for Loan and Lease Losses Methodologies and Documentation for Banks and Savings Institutions"
OCC Bulletin 2005-22, "Home Equity Lending: Credit Risk Management Guidance"
OCC Bulletin 2006-41, "Nontraditional Mortgage Products: Guidance on Nontraditional Mortgage Product Risks"
OCC Bulletin 2006-46, "Concentrations in Commercial Real Estate Lending, Sound Risk Management Practices: Interagency Guidance on CRE Concentration Risk Management"
OCC Bulletin 2006-47, "Allowance for Loan and Lease Losses: Guidance and Frequently Asked Questions on the ALLL"
OCC Bulletin 2007-26, "Subprime Mortgage Lending"
OCC Bulletin 2007-14, "Working with Mortgage Borrowers — Interagency Statement"
SFAS 66, "Accounting for Sales of Real Estate"
SFAS 114, "Accounting for Creditors for Impairment of a Loan"

Management

12 USC 371c and 371c-1, Banking Affiliates and Restrictions on Transactions with Affiliates
12 USC 375a & b, 12 CFR 31, 12 CFR 215, Loans to Executive Officers, Directors and Principal Shareholders
12 CFR 30, Safety and Soundness Standards
OCC Bulletin 99-37, "Interagency Policy Statement on External Auditing Programs"

OCC Bulletin 2003-12, "Interagency Policy Statement on Internal Audit and Internal Audit Outsourcing"

Earnings

Federal Financial Institutions Examination Council, "Consolidated Reports of Condition and Income — Instructions"

Liquidity and Sensitivity to Market Risk

12 CFR 1, Investment Securities
OCC Banking Circular 277, "Risk Management of Financial Derivatives"
OCC Bulletin 98-20, "Investment Securities — Policy Statement"
OCC Bulletin 99-2, "Risk Management of Financial Derivatives — Supplemental Guidance"
OCC Bulletin 99-46, "Interagency Guidance on Asset Securitization Activities"
OCC Bulletin 2000-16, "Risk Modeling — Model Validation"
OCC Bulletin 2002-19, "Unsafe and Unsound Investment Portfolio Practices: Supplemental Guidance"
OCC Bulletin 2004-25, "Classification of Securities: Uniform Agreement on the Classification of Securities"
OCC Bulletin 2004-29, "Embedded Options and Long Term Interest Rate Risk"
OCC Bulletin 2004-56, "Bank-Owned Life Insurance: Interagency Statement on the Purchase and Risk Management of Life Insurance"
FAS 52, "Foreign Currency Translation"
FAS 115, "Accounting for Certain Investments in Debt and Equity Securities"

IT

Federal Financial Institutions Examination Council Information Technology Examination Handbook (Updated 9/28/2012)
OCC Bulletin 98-3, "Technology Risk Management — Guide for Bankers and Examiners"
OCC Bulletin 2001-8, "Guidelines Establishing Standards for Safeguarding Customer Information"
OCC Bulletin 2005-13, "Response Programs for Unauthorized Access to Customer Information and Customer Notice: Final Guidance"
OCC Bulletin 2005-35, "Authentication in an Internet Banking Environment"

Asset Management

12 CFR 9, Fiduciary Activities of National Banks, Rules of Practice and Procedure
12 CFR 12, Record Keeping and Confirmation Requirements for Securities Transactions
OCC Banking Circular 275, "Free Riding in Custody Accounts"
OCC Bulletin 96-25, "Fiduciary Risk Management of Derivatives and Mortgage-backed Securities"
OCC Bulletin 97-22, "Fiduciary Activities of National Banks – Q&As 12 CFR 9"
OCC Bulletin 2001-33, "Loans Held for Sale"

OCC Bulletin 2001-47, "Third-Party Relationships: Risk Management Principles"
OCC Bulletin 2004-2, "Banks/Thrifts Providing Financial Support to Funds Advised by the Banking Organization or its Affiliates: Interagency Guidance"
OCC Bulletin 2006-24, "Interagency Agreement on ERISA Referrals"
OCC Bulletin 2007-6, "Registered Transfer Agents: Transfer Agent Registration, Annual Reporting, and Withdrawal from Registration"
OCC Bulletin 2007-7, "Soft Dollar Guidance: Use of Commission Payments by Fiduciaries"
OCC Bulletin 2007-21, "Supervision of National Trust Banks: Revised Guidance on Capital and Liquidity"
OCC Bulletin 2007-42, "Bank Securities Activities: SEC's and Federal Reserve's Final Regulation R"

Bank Secrecy Act/Anti-Money Laundering

12 CFR 21.21, Bank Secrecy Act Compliance (Updated 9/28/2012)
Federal Financial Institutions Examination Council Bank Secrecy Act/Anti-Money Laundering Examination Manual (Updated 9/28/2012)

Consumer Compliance

12 USC 3401, Right to Financial Privacy Act
12 USC 4901, Homeowners Protection Act
15 USC 1681, Fair Credit Reporting Act
15 USC 1692, Fair Debt Collection Practices Act
15 USC 6501, Children's Online Privacy Protection Act
15 USC 7701, Controlling the Assault of Non-Solicited Pornography and Marketing Act (CAN-SPAM)
50 USC 501, Service members Civil Relief Act
12 CFR 22, Loans in Areas Having Special Flood Hazards
12 CFR 27, Fair Housing Home Loan Data System
12 CFR 202, Equal Credit Opportunity (Regulation B)
12 CFR 203, Home Mortgage Disclosure Act (Regulation C)
12 CFR 205, Electronic Funds Transfers (Regulation E)
12 CFR 226, Truth in Lending (Regulation Z)
12 CFR 229, Availability of Funds (Regulation CC)
12 CFR 230, Truth in Savings (Regulation DD)
24 CFR 3500, Real Estate Settlement Procedures Act
47 CFR 64.1200, Telephone Consumer Protection Act (TCPA)
OCC Bulletin 2000-25, "Privacy Laws and Regulations"
OCC Bulletin 2007-30, "Telephone Consumer Protection Act and Junk Fax Prevention Act: Revised Examination Procedures"
OCC Bulletin 2007-41, "Truth in Savings Act: Revised Examination Procedures"

Other

OCC Bulletin 2001-47, "Third-Party Relationships: Risk Management Principles"

OCC Bulletin 2002-9, "National Bank Appeals Process"
OCC Bulletin 2003-12, "Interagency Policy Statement on Internal Audit and Internal Audit Outsourcing"
OCC Bulletin 2004-20, "Risk Management of New, Expanded, or Modified Bank Services: Risk Management Process"
PPM 5000-34, "Canary Early Warning System"
PPM 5400-8 (rev), "Supervision Work Papers"
PPM 5400-9, "De Novo and Converted Banks"

Comptroller's Handbook

Safety & Soundness

"Accounts Receivable and Inventory Financing"
"Agricultural Lending"
"Allowance for Loan and Lease Losses"
"Asset Securitization"
"Bankers' Acceptances"
"Bank Supervision Process"
"Commercial Real Estate and Construction Lending"
"Consigned Items and Other Customer Services"
"Country Risk Management"
"Credit Card Lending"
"Emerging Market Country Products and Trading Activities"
"Examination Planning and Control"
"Federal Branches and Agencies Supervision"
"Internet Banking"
"Insider Activities"
"Insurance Activities"
"Interest Rate Risk"
"Internal and External Audits"
"Internal Control"
"Large Bank Supervision"
"Lease Financing"
"Liquidity"
"Litigation and Other Legal Matters"
"Loan Portfolio Management"
"Management Information Systems"
"Merchant Processing"
"Mortgage Banking"
"Rating Credit Risk"
"Related Organizations"
"Retail Lending"
"Risk Management of Financial Derivatives"
"Sampling Methodologies"
"Trade Finance"

Asset Management

"Asset Management"
"Collective Investment Funds"
"Conflicts of Interest"
"Custody Services"
"Investment Management Services"
"Personal Fiduciary Services"

Consumer Compliance

"Community Reinvestment Act Examination Procedures"
"Compliance Management System"
"Depository Services"
"Fair Credit Reporting"
"Fair Lending"
"Flood Disaster Protection"
"Home Mortgage Disclosure"
"Other Consumer Protection Laws and Regulations"
"Overview"
"Real Estate Settlement Procedures"
"Truth in Lending"

For examination areas that are not covered by booklets from the *Comptroller's Handbook*, examiners should continue to refer to appropriate sections in the *Comptroller's Handbook for National Bank Examiners.*